Acclaim for
Your Guide to Earth's

"The world needs more books like this one during these uncertain and chaotic times. *Your Guide to Earth's Pivotal Years* is a clear and comprehensive treasure chest that helps us to remember who we really are and how to access the divine within. You won't be able to read this without experiencing a consciousness shift."

—**Susan G. Shumsky**,
author of *Divine Revelation*

"This is a wonderful introduction to what's ahead. As an anthropologist I can confirm that many of the insights shared with you in this book are based on sound logic and research."

—**William Gladstone**,
author of *The Twelve*

"Must reading for anyone who wants to understand why living right now is so extraordinary. The more of us who receive and act on Selacia's timely message, the more quickly our world will become loving and peaceful."

—**Gregory Hoag**,
noted expert in sacred geometry and
contributing author of *Transforming through 2012*

"*Earth's Pivotal Years* presents a new way to view the momentous shifts occurring in our world and shows you how to move into your 'divine changemaker' role to help not only yourself but others navigate these tumultuous times."

—**Edwin Harkness Spina**,
author of *Mystic Warrior*

YOUR GUIDE TO EARTH'S PIVOTAL YEARS

A Direct Path to Enlightened Living

SELACIA

iUniverse, Inc.
Bloomington

Your Guide to Earth's Pivotal Years
A Direct Path to Enlightened Living

Copyright © 2011 Selacia

All rights reserved. No part of this book may be used or reproduced by any means, graphic, electronic, or mechanical, including photocopying, recording, taping or by any information storage retrieval system without the written permission of the publisher except in the case of brief quotations embodied in critical articles and reviews.

iUniverse books may be ordered through booksellers or by contacting:

iUniverse
1663 Liberty Drive
Bloomington, IN 47403
www.iuniverse.com
1-800-Authors (1-800-288-4677)

Because of the dynamic nature of the Internet, any Web addresses or links contained in this book may have changed since publication and may no longer be valid. The views expressed in this work are solely those of the author and do not necessarily reflect the views of the publisher, and the publisher hereby disclaims any responsibility for them.

Any people depicted in stock imagery provided by Thinkstock are models, and such images are being used for illustrative purposes only.

Certain stock imagery © Thinkstock.

ISBN: 978-1-4502-9706-6 (pbk)
ISBN: 978-1-4502-9707-3 (cloth)
ISBN: 978-1-4502-9708-0 (ebk)

Library of Congress Control Number: 2011904632

Printed in the United States of America

iUniverse rev. date: 4/6/2011

Contents

Preface	**xiii**
A Sense of Wonder	xiii
My Early Questions	xiv
What People Want to Know Now	xvi
Acknowledgments	**xix**
Introduction	**xxi**
Answering the Call	xxi
This Book Is for You	xxiii
1. Preparing for the Revolutionary Paradigm Shift	**1**
The Great Reconfiguration—What It Is and Why We Care	2
Out with the Old, in with the New	3
What Earth Changes Mean for You	3
A Revolution in Consciousness	4
Progress Creating the New Paradigm	5
A New Type of Revolution	6
Stress Triggers	7
Feeling the Effects of Change	8
Your Access to Great Opportunities	9
Unfinished Business	9
Higher-Frequency Energy—What This Means	10
Banish Your Fears with Understanding	12
2. Understanding the Future—Prophecies and Realities	**15**
You Have Options	16
People You Can Help	16
2012 and Beyond—Pivotal Crossroads	17
Preoccupation with the Future	18
It's Wired into Your DNA	19
Your Own Inner Prophecy Station	20
Why the Boom in Prophecies?	21
Mayan Predictions	21
The Challenge of Interpreting Prophecies	22
What Is Prophecy?	23
Process: Your Questions about the End of the World	25
Calling upon Your Higher Wisdom	26

Your Higher Wisdom through a Dream	27
Intuitive Skills Come of Age	28
2012 Phenomena	28
Solstice of December 21, 2012	29
2012 Leap Year	29
Cycles—Truth, Fiction, and the Unknowable	30
Our Spiritual Journey over Time	31
Humanity's Future Is Not Predestined	32
Meet the Divine Changemakers	33
Process: Honing Your Questioning Skills	34
New Approaches to Time	36
Shifting from a Linear View	36
Tips: Working with Time	36
Personal Needs to Consider	38
Interactions with Others	39
Being Where You Are	40
The Media—Blessing or Curse?	41
Questions: What to Ask Now	42
Role of a Divine Changemaker	44

3. Times of Great Change — 45

Seeing What Was There All Along	46
Personal Awakening	46
Self-Love Is the Key	47
Unique Opportunities of This Life	49
Timing of the Shift	49
Energetic Shifts and Physical Symptoms	51
Tips: Tuning into Your Body	52
Understanding DNA Changes	53
Living with Ongoing Uncertainty	54
Making Sense of the Shift in Your Own Life	55
Creating the Life You Want	56
Tapping into Your Divine Power	57
Finding the Sacred During Turmoil	58
Tips: Staying Sane in Chaos	60
Process: Imagining a Brand-New World	62
Coming Back to What You Know	64

4. Choosing a Light-Filled Path During Crisis — 65

Shift in Global Power	66
The Tipping Point—Economic Crisis	67

Opportunity of This Unique Window	68
Choose Your Cushion	69
Process: Checking in with Your Heart's Wisdom	70
Your Personal Response to Financial Crisis	71
How DNA Patterns Affect You	71
Humanity's Relationship with Money	72
People Everywhere Have a Role to Play	73
What You Can Do	74
Your Role as a Divine Changemaker	74
Educate Yourself about the Big Picture	74
Let the Past Be the Past	75
Avoid Fantasy Thinking	75
Take Better Care of You	75
Put Spirit First	76
Benefit from Understanding the Success of Others	77
Identify Your Patterns of Self-Sabotage	77
Tips: Moving from Fear to Abundance	78
Focus on Conscious Creation	79
Give Your Gifts	79
Remember the Time Frame	80
Today's Unprecedented Challenges	80
Punish the Wealthy?	81
A New Model for Success	82
Changing Your Dream of Success	83
Tips: Remap Your Path to Success	83
When You Question Your Progress	85
A Quantum Shift for You and Humanity	86

5. The Art of Making Choices — **89**

Demystifying the Process of Choice	90
New Times, New Choices	91
Choice and the Divine Changemakers	92
Beliefs about Choice in Your DNA	92
Feeling Frozen and Powerless	95
Tips: Checking in with Your Heart	95
Decide What You Want	96
Process: Seeing the Gifts in Relationships	97
The Child You Birthed	97
A Life Partner	98
A Work Colleague	98
A Parent or Guardian	99

    An Acquaintance   99
    Questions: Learning from Pivotal Relationships   100
    How to Make Better Decisions   104
    New Approaches to Choice   105
    Remedy for the Toughest Choices   106
    Tips: Making Choices without Pain   109
    Checklist: Integrating Spirit into Choices   113
    Choice and Ascension   117

6. In Pursuit of Truth   119

    Knowing Who to Trust   121
    A Time of Truths Revealed   121
    Empowerment through Questioning   123
    Government   123
    Religion   124
    Teachers   125
    Tips: Recognizing Truth—Telling Fact from Fiction   127
    When Truth Is Elusive   129
    You Alone Can Determine Your Truth   129
    Humanity's Deeper Questioning   130
    The New Path of Heart   130
    Your Deeper Questions   131
    The Shift on a Global Scale   131
    Restoring Atrophied Talents   133
    The Media during Earth's Pivotal Years   134
    Steady Parade of Information   135
    The Legacy of Earth's Great Sages   135
    Your Pivotal Choice Point   136
    Connecting the Past with the Present   137
    Humanity Seeing Itself   137
    Tips: Gathering Information Sensibly   138
    Different Skills for Different Times   142
    Your Intentions and Actions Count   143
    Checklist: Accelerating Your Personal Transformation   144

7. Heart-Centered Living   149

    Moving from "What's in It for Me?" to "How Can I Help?"   149
    Understanding Fear   150
    The Real Threat of Violence   151
    Reversing the Cycle of Violence   152
    Balancing Feminine and Masculine—A New Paradigm   152

Choosing Love and Kindness 154
Why Relationships Matter 154
Questions: Discovering Remedies for a Difficult Relationship ... 156
Blocks to Openheartedness 158
Process: Shifting into Openheartedness 159
What to Do When You Feel Wronged 160
Recognizing Your Progress 161
How to Move into Your Heart 162
Checklist: Connecting to Your Heart 163
Creating More Joy—Having More Love 165
Tips: Finding Inner Peace 166
Checklist: Sabotaging Belief Systems in Your DNA 168

8. Shifting into a Lightness of Being   171

Spiritual Awakening—From Darkness into Light 171
Why Are These Times Different? 172
What People Are Asking Now 173
The Practice of Patience 174
Tips: Moving into Your Power 176
Rethinking Your View 180
The Poison of Self-Doubt 181
Your Spiritual Transformation 182
Help for Your Journey 183
Reaching Out to Others 184
Reclaiming Your Light 185
Process: Setting Intention to Reclaim Your Light 185
Accelerate Your Enlightenment with a Light Journal 186
Process: Connecting with Your Light 187

9. Creating within the New Energies   189

What Are the New Energies? 190
Accelerated Momentum of Cause and Effect 191
How to Create Powerfully 192
Checklist: Managing Your Energy 193
   Body 193
   Thoughts 194
   Emotions 195
Tips: Relating to Others 195
Spirit Connection and Energy Mastery 196
Switching Out of Worry Mode 197
Your Catalyzing Life Event 198

Understanding Wake-up Calls 199
Process: Imagining a New Start 202
   Your Biggest Obstacle 202
   Your Biggest Choice 203
   Your Greatest Allies 203
   Your Greatest Opportunities 203

10. Living Your Mission of Light   205

Understanding Your Role in These Times 205
Consider What Will Matter in Three Hundred Years 206
You and Your Relationships 207
Considering Your Perfect Work 207
Discovering What Matters 208
Knowing How You Fit In 209
Unique Opportunities Available Now 209
Connecting More of the Dots 210
Finding More Like-Minded People 211
Realizing You Cannot Do It Alone 211
Sparking Beneficial Changes in Others 212
The Challenge of Seeing Yourself Clearly 212
Transcending Your Conditioning 214
Moving from Willfulness into Willingness 215
Identifying Arrogance 215
Discovering Your Unique Contribution 216
Making Your Life Count 217
Your Place in the World 218
Young Adult 218
Midlife 219
Retired or Elderly 219
Tips: Connecting with Your Mission of Light 220

11. Rethinking Where and How You Live   227

You Are the Architect of Your New Home 227
Understanding Humanity's History on the Earth 228
Know That Everything Can Change—Trusting You Can Change 230
A Restructuring of Your DNA Is Under Way 231
The Great Migration—Rethinking Where You Live 232
Tips: Relocating to a New Home 233
Reconsidering How You Live 235
Tips: Staying Centered When the Road Gets Rocky 237
Preparing to Reside in Your New Home 239

Process: Imagining Your New-Paradigm Earth 239
   What It Looks Like 240
   What It Feels Like 240
   Who Is There 241
   How You Express Your Life's Purpose 242
   Consider Your Gifts 243
   A New State of Consciousness 245

12. Humanity's New Chapter — 247

Everyone Is Impacted 248
Deciding to Care 249
A Time of Transparency 249
Understanding Others 250
Honing Your Discernment 251
You as a Divine Changemaker 251
Putting What You Know into Action 252
An Unprecedented Demystifying of Life 253
The Blinders Are Gone 254
Questions: Knowing What to Ask Now 255
Power to Change the World 256
Your Life Has a Purpose 257
The Heart of Humanity Speaks 258
Recognize You Are the Light of the World 258
New Levels of Energy Are Available 259
Physical Symptoms 259
Your DNA Is Changing 260
Opportunities to Remember 261
Checklist: Tapping into Today's Unique Opportunities 261
Seeing the Big Picture 264
Contemplating the Big Picture 265
Creating a Life worth Remembering 265
Tips: Taking Charge of Your Life 265
Your One Choice about Change 267
A Brand-New Start—For You and Humanity 268

Afterword — 271
Awakening Process for Divine Changemakers 271

Glossary — 273

Recommended Reading — 287

About the Author — 293

Preface

In the Tibetan Buddhist culture that is part of my training, all writing is sacred. This is because a written instruction can open your mind and help reveal your true self. Such an instruction, within a book like this or in another form, can help you to rediscover your divine nature. You then begin to remember who you truly are and the larger purpose of your earthly life.

Right now there is an added component. This involves the auspicious opportunity of being alive during the greatest revolutionary shift of all time.

It is very difficult to grasp how enormous this opportunity is. Similarly, you cannot imagine the consequences for you and the Earth if you allow this occasion to pass unnoticed and without acting to your fullest capability. If you could understand the pivotal nature of this time frame, you would be in awe of the unique prospects available.

A Sense of Wonder

From an early age, I had a sense of wonder about life. I loved learning new things and being able to spend time in nature. On some evenings when I gazed at the stars, seeing the vastness and unbounded beauty, I felt an unexplainable sense of connection to the universe.

Like many children, I was very observant; little escaped my attention. I was also very curious and often asked questions about what I saw in the world. I truly wanted to understand why people were the way they were and why the world was the way it was. I had an innate knack for being able to see both the big picture and the details. I was also naturally intuitive, often sensing when people were being dishonest and regularly knowing in advance what was going to happen.

My Early Questions

Here are some examples of the questions that I asked myself as a child.

- "Why do people say that they love me one minute, and the next minute they are mean to me?"
- "When people want me to do something, why do they mention how I did it wrong last time and speak harshly about how this time I must get it right?"
- "Why do my parents tell me that it's bad to do something when they continue to do that same thing?"
- "When it's obvious to me that someone is angry, why does he or she pretend that everything is okay?"

I didn't realize until later in life that many of the things I experienced as a young person were common. As I matured and grew spiritually, I discovered that men and women from all walks of life share similar disappointments, puzzlements, joys, dreams, and desires. I learned that everyone has the same basic wish: to be loved.

Ever since I can remember, I've been interested in the deeper meanings of life. In hindsight, I realize that it was my deep connection to spirit that fueled my questioning from the time that I could form sentences. I now know that one way my inner wisdom guided me was through the vehicle of questions. As an example, a topic of inquiry would come into my mind. Quite often, as I consciously asked the question inside myself, the answer would also come.

Sometimes before taking an action, I inquired whether it was the best time to do it. If it was optimal to wait, I delayed the action. On countless occasions, a delay led to success that was born when I combined right action with divine timing.

This tool of inquiry was—and still is—like being guided by a wise elder, someone who had insight and knew how to best proceed.

The ability to question, combined with my love of words and writing, helped me to succeed in journalism. A skill with inquiry has been helpful in many other areas of my life too. The path of spiritual transformation, for example, requires an ability to look beyond surface appearances and question reality. Success on that path is directly related to knowing what questions to ask, how to ask them, and when to ask them.

In my career as an international journalist, I had many opportunities to interview world leaders, public figures, and ordinary citizens. The stories that interested me most were those involving people and social change. Researching and writing a page-one article about Europe's homeless for *The Wall Street Journal* in the 1980s before the issue was a hot topic worldwide was one of my most fulfilling assignments.

Covering global politics was enjoyable, too, but not for the doom-and-gloom factor. My interest in politics and macroeconomics came from a deep longing to understand the human condition and the many imbalances I observed throughout the world. I developed a keen insider's view of finance during my years reporting on the White House, US Federal Reserve, US Congress, global trade talks, and international economic summits. Those experiences have helped me to understand the recent economic meltdown and the urgent need to reconfigure key elements of our world's society.

Like most people, I've had a life filled with ups and downs. There have been enormous joys and achievements as well as great losses and sad times.

The catalysts for my spiritual awakening were multiple, yet they had one thing in common. Each of them involved a crossroads or crisis of some kind. Something in my life was not working, and I had to choose something different. The shift that was required in every case involved a change in view. No matter how hard I tried to keep the status quo, in order to progress and get beyond my turning point, I needed to awaken to a higher view than my lower, small self provided.

The catalyst appeared differently depending upon what was happening in my life. Examples include the ending of close intimate relationships, health challenges, career disappointments, and financial reversals. I consciously initiated some of the catalysts, such as relocating to foreign countries and leaving corporate work to pursue my heart's dream of establishing my own company.

People often first seek healing when they are facing a life-defining moment. The catalyst for each person is different; sometimes the crisis is described as a wake-up call because it is as though the person's consciousness needs to wake up to some truth about his or her reality.

Spiritual growth occurs as a person responds to a wake-up call and moves into greater awareness and wholeness.

In today's times of great change, increasing numbers of people are facing crossroads. Humanity at large faces a multitude of crossroads, too, during the greatest ever reconfiguration of how life is lived and viewed. Because of this, a stirring of deeper questioning is taking place. In the pages of this book, you will be given a guide to what the reconfiguration means, and you will have answers to key questions about these times.

What People Want to Know Now

This book was written to answer questions being asked by people all over the world. Some are universal in nature, having been asked by countless generations before. Today there is often more urgency underlying the inquiry. People are feeling more uncertain about the future. There is more awareness that this is indeed an unusual time with much at stake. It's not uncommon to feel a sense of urgency about the world and one's place in it. Here's a sampling of what people have asked in recent times.

1. How do I manage time when it's going faster and faster and I'm always behind?
2. What can I do to find real love?
3. How can I succeed and thrive when everything is so uncertain?
4. What can I do to discover my life's purpose?
5. How do I understand the prophecies about these times?
6. Where can I live and be safe?
7. How can I stop worrying?
8. Is there a place for someone like me in this mixed-up world?
9. How do I connect with my own truth and intuitive knowing?
10. What can I do to find inner peace?

Any one of these questions could lead to some sleepless nights. If you are like most of us, you have pondered the answer to more than one question on this list.

The stream-of-consciousness writing in this book will allow you to tap into what you need to know during Earth's pivotal years and beyond. You will be impacted not so much by the words themselves, but more by the way the words act as catalysts for your mind. Like a flower closed for the night, your mind will naturally open and reveal its contents to you when exposed to the light.

To read this book, then, is more of a process of discovery than a gathering of facts or inspirations. You will receive these, too, but that is not why you will benefit. The real gift you will receive is a series of signposts that point you in the direction of your own truth. As you follow these signposts, your inner divine self is revealed.

You will receive the most from this type of writing when you approach it with a willingness to be touched in a new way. You will benefit when you take time to contemplate the ideas and to allow the energy on the pages to stir a deeper questioning than you allowed before. This means that you may prefer to read a few paragraphs or a chapter and then sit still, allowing a germination process to unfold.

Sometimes you will put the book down and come back to it days later. Books such as this one are meant to be read more than once. They are alive and are designed to be digested in small nuggets, with each one building upon the next to help you grow spiritually. Sometimes you will read a chapter over again and come away with a brand-new set of insights.

You don't have to believe that there is anything special about these important years to benefit from this book. The words are timeless and can be ongoing, helpful catalysts for your growth. This book is rooted in ideas that are both ancient and futuristic. They can serve as your big-picture guide to the massive changes happening now, providing you with a direct path to enlightened living. You can come back to them again and again, each time receiving practical and inspirational reminders of your purpose for this life. As you begin to act on what you receive, something amazing will begin to occur.

Thank you for allowing me to share this wonderful journey with you!

Acknowledgments

It is with deep gratitude that I acknowledge some of those who have helped to make this book possible. Each of them has made a great contribution, helping me to bring this book to the world.

I first thank the force of spirit in my life. It is my connection with spirit that is my rock, my inner strength, and the source of my passion for writing and sharing with others. My inner world teachers, The Council of 12, have lovingly guided me throughout my life. These evolved, nonphysical guides—my spiritual family— have inspired me and showed me how to travel a path of balance and inner peace. Our integral connection, honed over decades, became so strong a number of years ago that their wisdom and healing energies come through me spontaneously, even in ordinary conversation. I am most grateful for their loving presence.

I am also especially grateful to the divine spark that shows up in my life through other people and through the diverse beauty and forms in nature. I have a special affinity with animals and my longtime companion cat, Chelsea, now in spirit form on the other side. My life is inspired by the simple things, such as the pleasure of seeing a rainbow or walking along the ocean on a sunny day.

I thank my dear friends who have graciously helped with the production of this book: Alicia White, Amos Alexander, Deborah Thompson, Francis Bischetti, Joel Grossman, Lareena Alitheeana Besse, Margo Berman, Patrice Hall, Patrick Wall, and Rosalie Kahn.

I truly appreciate the masterful editing by Mindi White. To find the optimal editor is such a joy! During my years in professional communications, I've worked as both writer and editor. Experience has taught me how important the editor is to the process, even if the writer is a skilled editor. As in life, we can be so close to our own material that we simply do not see an error. Fortunately, there are talented editors like Mindi who can catch these things.

David Andor, my book cover designer, is a delight to work with. I am very thankful for his sense of style and color, his professionalism, and his skill in creating a beautiful book cover.

I express my gratitude to all of the readers worldwide who have followed my earlier writings and presentations. I value your trust and your enthusiasm for what I write and offer in the world. The community we have created together is an inspiration. Thank you so much for sharing my writings with your friends and loved ones, and for being a part of our growing community.

I send my love to all of you!

Introduction

The Earth now sits at a precipice. You have a front-row seat. You sit where you do because of a long history of human evolution. Humanity is coming out of a very dark time. There is an awakening under way. People like you all across this planet are becoming aware of the state of dysfunction that exists in every aspect of life.

An energetic call has sounded, reverberating within humanity's collective psyche. Not everyone hears it yet, but you do. The sound invites you to awaken fully to your divine nature. It led you to this book.

Answering the Call

As you answer the call and read what is written on these pages, you will discover a new source of inspiration and courage for taking the next steps. You will have a new respect for yourself, others, and the home that we call Earth. You will have a big-picture view of how we got here and where we are headed. You will have validations of many things that you have long suspected to be true.

This book explains the nonsense of these times. A brief history of prophecies is included so that you can find your own truth and move into the future in a more empowered way.

Dates like 2012 are addressed too, but not in the fatalistic way seen in countless other books. This is not a book about 2012 or the end of the world. The Mayan predictions are mentioned without agenda, simply to provide context and clarity. There are no scare tactics here;

the purpose of including prophecies about the 2012 window is to provide a neutral reference point.

When you read this book—whether before 2012 or long afterward—you will benefit from knowing what fueled the pre-2012 plethora of books, movies, and Internet postings. End-times predictions are not really new. They are cyclic, and they typically have a fear-based message.

For society to move forward fearlessly, people need to understand how previous generations have perpetuated fear-based responses with nonsensical views like doomsday prophecies.

No one knows the future. It is not a rigid construct; the future is fluid and is being created right now, as you read these words. You create your future, and collectively you join with others to create the future of the world.

As you read this book, your inner wisdom will speak to you about what is real. The future will take on a new, more light-filled meaning. The past will be seen in a brand-new way too. With past and future in a fresh context, your present can become lighter.

Allow this book to become a fruitful resource as you navigate the uncertain path ahead. Let the words within these pages open your heart and your mind to a more loving way to be. Discover a new, more heart-centered way to live your life. Find out how to move into your joy and purpose during humanity's revolutionary paradigm shift.

Although any single chapter can be digested on its own, the chapters build upon each other for a larger message.

As you read, you will receive useful personal understandings, practical tools, and a more global way to look at the multitude of crises that appear in your backyard. What you receive will have a beneficial application for many decades to come.

Examples of what you will receive:
- Know what the paradigm shift really means for you and everyone on Earth.

- Understand why this is the most important time that you could be alive.
- Have a new appreciation of Earth's pivotal years, with your own take-action guide.
- Know beyond a doubt that a new, more heart-centered world is in the making.
- Have an introduction to the divine changemakers.

If you don't yet see yourself as one of the divine changemakers, you *will* by the end of this book! You also will be certain that you have an integral role to play—and that this role begins right now. You will realize that you are not too young or too old to embrace and fully live your life mission. Regardless of your age or other worldly status, you will find a new confidence for moving forward.

This Book Is for You

You may be new to the path of awakening, or you may simply want to expand your awareness to progress spiritually. Either way, this book will give you the understanding needed to change your life during Earth's pivotal years.

The specific transformational tools given in this book will help you to catalyze personal changes that you have long yearned to make. As you put in motion beneficial changes, you will advance spiritually.

The words on these pages will help you to awaken more fully to your light within. You will discover how to powerfully create the more light-filled world that you seek to inhabit.

You are invited to reflect on what you read here. Take the ideas into your dream state and into your meditations. Allow the concepts to speak to your heart. This will give you validation about who you really are and about your long journey to arrive at this pivotal juncture. You will know deep within your bones that you will succeed!

Feelings of joy and gratitude will come from realizing that you have a direct path for enlightened living. As you walk that path, you can find peace. As you discover peace, you become a potent peacemaker in the world. In that role, you *are* the change that you want to see everywhere you go.

Chapter 1

Preparing for the Revolutionary Paradigm Shift

Right now, as you are reading these words, is the most important time you could live on Earth.

This is true regardless of how you see yourself through the lens of worldly markers of success, progress, prosperity, and happiness. The significance of your living now, during these unique moments, transcends these markers. You may feel that you are awakened and that you are on the road to enlightenment, or you may just now be waking up—but you are impacted all the same.

You live during a grand reconfiguration process that is both personal and planetary. The shifting that is occurring, though it has been under way for a very long time, will lead to a radical reshaping of life on Earth. Many worn-out structures and ways of being will be disappearing.

You and society are being remade, and when the cycle is finally complete, you will not recognize your way of life or how you feel about living on the Earth.

The Great Reconfiguration—What It Is and Why We Care

In future years, when you look back on these times, you will be amazed at the magnitude of changes. You will marvel at how profoundly different human existence has become during your lifetime.

You now live in a construction zone. The new Earth is not yet created. Society is dismantling the outmoded one, piece by piece. The foundation for your new-paradigm existence is not yet assembled.[1] This won't be like any other foundation that you have seen before, for it will have global connections and linkups with every element of society. The new foundation will reflect an understanding of interconnectedness. It will recognize wholeness and a cooperative spirit.

On a grand scale, the new foundation now being created relates to human society rearranging itself. Humanity has not seen such a rapid rearranging of this magnitude in any earlier time frame. There is no template for it, because the way it is being carried out is brand new.

With no road map to follow and with so many uncertain variables, the unfolding of the reconfiguration is quite fluid. Likewise, the challenges being faced are too complex and wide reaching to be resolved with yesterday's methods. This is true for both individuals and society as a whole.

Those at the leading edge of change are now in the process of

---

[1] A paradigm is a pattern or model that is the accepted norm of operation. People often say, "Let's think outside the box." This means shifting your habit of reasoning to include a broader perspective. We humans are habitual, and we can get stuck in a box with our old habitual reasoning. In our society, the paradigm we operate within is a very powerful indicator of consciousness. This is because the paradigm relates to our values and what we decide is acceptable to do or not do. As human beings, we tend to filter our experiences through the paradigm operable in our world. For example, centuries ago people believed that the Earth was at the center of the universe. The paradigm of thinking then shifted to the idea that the sun was the center of the universe. Our worldview changed dramatically with the new perspective. In general, we learn to see our world through the prevailing paradigm model. The generations of people alive today are witnessing and participating in the most revolutionary paradigm shift of all time.

discovering new, more enlightened approaches and ways of viewing the growing list of dilemmas.

Where is this movement headed, and what will it look like?

Out with the Old, in with the New

Institutions based on old-paradigm approaches will either fade away or be reconfigured to match the new energies. Outmoded codes of human behavior, elite power bases, and allocation of resources will be challenged and changed by those who carry an awakening consciousness.

Every aspect of life and living as you now know it will be impacted. The changes will reconfigure your outer world. More important, they will reshape your inner world and how you experience the human condition. It is happening, and will happen, in phases—each one building upon the last and setting the stage for future ones. The process will continue for many years.

What Earth Changes Mean for You

Earth changes will be felt in some of the familiar places; some examples are earthquakes in California and hurricanes in Florida. Changes in climate will also be experienced in some new locations that have not been touched by erratic weather patterns. Over the coming years, this means that many people who moved to other locations to escape the effects of weather changes will find that their new locations are also beset with unusual climate-related alterations.

Increasing numbers of people will feel the effects of climate change. Media attention and a concerned public will keep the issue in the spotlight. As more people awaken, new approaches can be found. Fear and competitiveness can be transformed into compassion, connectedness, and helpfulness.[2]

---

2   When you have compassion for someone, you care about his or her welfare.

Solutions for many of the world's imbalances can come from these more enlightened viewpoints, to be seeded during some of humanity's darkest times. The new thought forms or ideas will become a part of humanity's mass consciousness, helping to shift long-established views that involve fear, competition, and dominance.

A Revolution in Consciousness

The trailblazers of new-paradigm thought will fuel a revolution in how life is lived. They will model this new way of being, showing other people and the world the fruits of an awakened life.

You are one of those trailblazers, and this is your time to shine! You are alive now to help catalyze the greatest revolution in consciousness ever seen.

The revolution occurring now is chaotic, feeling messy at times. You don't have an accurate picture of how it will turn out, because it's still a work in progress. It's a bit like the run-down house that is being remodeled before being put back on the market. Prospective buyers may be shown design plans, but they usually don't see the finished house until the renovation is complete and the house has a fresh coat of paint.

A key difference here is that you, as the residing Earth tenant, cannot move elsewhere while reconstruction takes place. In fact, because you play a key role in creating the changes, you will need to

---

This caring is selfless and without agenda. You have empathy for the person out of genuine concern for his or her happiness. This can be someone you know or a stranger. It is easier to develop compassion for others when you have first learned to be compassionate with yourself. This means you have an active desire to help yourself. This compassion in action allows you to accelerate your spiritual transformational process. For many people, it is easier to generate compassion for a pet. As this feeling is developed, it can then be applied to oneself and other people. When you truly care about the welfare of yourself or another being, you are more likely to connect with inspired solutions for challenges. Compassion helps you to deepen your connection to others, thereby enriching your life experience.

be fully present and to actively participate. Things won't always look pretty, and you won't always feel comfortable.

On many days you may seriously wonder whether the reconstruction you are helping to shepherd will yield positive results. You may even have moments during which you question whether anything of merit will be created. You may fear that you will simply be stuck with a world in reconstruction. A wiser part of you knows that these fears are unfounded.

Progress Creating the New Paradigm

Despite appearances to the contrary, a brand-new paradigm of enlightened consciousness is in the process of being born! Much progress has been made, including during recent years when the playing out of opposites was amplified in every corner of the planet.[3]

Oppositional thinking, power mongering, and lies of many stripes showed up in political campaigns, country power plays, and international trade talks. On a personal scale, increased stress levels took many people to the edge, fueling ego-based responses to a host of situations. Sometimes, even those usually able to respond to life sanely and kindly became reactionary.

---

[3] The playing out of opposites relates to viewpoints. During times of great change, there are often extremes between viewpoints. Many people want change, but there is often disagreement about what needs to change and how to create the change. Humans are conditioned to resist change, so there are many who will fight new-paradigm concepts. Oppositional thinking is seen in every sector of society during our paradigm shift. To oppose something means to actively disapprove of that thing. You can oppose violence, for example. Similarly, you can oppose methods others use or systems now in place. Oppositional thinking can be accompanied by energies of competition, conflict, judgment, resistance, and combativeness. To oppose something with these energies adds a harsh tone. Anger often dominates. Compromises and creative solutions are more difficult when people are oppositional. Light-filled approaches can be found when people discover how to let go of their personal agendas and resistance and move into a cooperative spirit.

With the volume of stress and uncertainty turned up significantly, people from all walks of life increasingly found that they had a lower boiling point than before. To be sure, hot buttons for many were the economy, personal finances, and the what-if fears generated with each exposure to the news.

Some of the changes being made now—considered separately and measured against utopian goals—may seem minor or insufficient. However, when you look at the big picture and the overall reconfiguration process, each of these seemingly miniscule shifts is quite potent and vital to the big picture of where humanity is headed.

Consciousness is changing not due to legislation or other forceful means, but within the hearts of people on every continent.

A New Type of Revolution

There have been countless earlier revolutions on the planet, but none quite like this one. Our current ground-breaking shift touches every aspect of life and reaches into every corner of the world. No matter where you live, no matter what your circumstances, you will feel the effects of the leap to the next stage of human evolution. It is a paradigm shift on a grand scale!

The old paradigm involves a species so driven by technology and greed that it could destroy itself. In the new paradigm, humans are being challenged to find a new, more enlightened way to relate to one another and to the planet. This new paradigm holds the promise of humans evolving more consciously, choosing to cooperate with one another, and coexisting without violence.

Humans are now feeling the pressure to remedy a diverse set of potentially dire consequences set in motion by previous human choices. Dilemmas such as weather changes and resource imbalances are of global concern.

You are personally impacted in countless ways. If you wore a stress meter with an alarm to warn of overload, it probably would beep frequently! An endless variety of things can trigger your stress.

Stress Triggers

- Worry—focusing on something in the present, past, or future.
- World concerns—contemplating issues like weather changes, the economy, and basic resources of food and shelter.
- Time pressures—feeling squeezed on all fronts and noticing that there is more to do, more to read, and more to process on all levels.
- Money—wondering about having enough to meet basic necessities.
- Relationships—feeling drained or conflicted rather than nurtured and supported.
- Health—feeling anxious about how to address ill health; if well, being concerned about what happens if sickness occurs.
- Uncertainty—feeling uncomfortable with not knowing; sometimes worse than this is the realization that there is no answer.

It is challenging to be suffering from a stomachache or emotional turmoil at the same time that a flood threatens to wash away your house. Personal dilemmas sit alongside planetary ones, each demanding your attention. The stress on some days may feel as if it's too much to take.

Whether you live in Miami, Montreal, or Munich, there is a feeling of urgency in the air as more people awaken and begin to discern the true state of the world. There is mounting pressure to come up with solutions.

The pressure that you and others feel isn't likely to dissipate anytime soon. The current cycle is one of the most crucial in all of our history. These are times of magnification, with light shining on disparities and outmoded ways of being. The growing gap between the rich and the poor is becoming more obvious. Unstable climatic conditions are impacting more places in the world while attracting increasing amounts of attention from concerned citizens of diverse backgrounds.

The current playing out of opposites will gain even more momentum, with the duality of love and hate being expressed on personal and global levels. It's not really a battle, yet it can seem like one at times.

Similarly, people on a path of conscious awakening are finding that they have less and less in common with the average, unaware person. Why? As you advance spiritually, you discover how to look deeper than surface appearances. You have a much wider perspective, which usually means that your interests change.

For example, in the past your conversations with friends may have been dominated by petty concerns or gossip about other people. As you grow, you have more desire to be authentic and to explore the deeper aspects of life. You also realize the importance of surrounding yourself with people who can mirror your more positive and light-filled approaches. It is much less appealing to spend an afternoon with friends who are interested only in complaining or attacking others.

Feeling the Effects of Change

The more awake you are, the more you will feel the effects of change. This is because to be awake means to be aware. When you are aware of more, you will feel more. Your sensitivity will increase. You will see more of the truth of the world. You will recognize more about yourself too. That means being able to see your good qualities as well as your challenges.

One misconception about spiritual growth is the false notion that a person's path becomes free of rocks as he or she advances. The advanced person continues to have rocks in the road. Sometimes, in fact, it can feel like there are *more* rocks—or more troublesome rocks—because you have gone deeper in your process. With a deepening, you are able to face issues that would have been unthinkable to look at before. It can feel like the universe is delivering your biggest challenge. The key here is that this challenge could not be delivered until you were spiritually ready to face it. Trust that.

Your Access to Great Opportunities

As you grow spiritually, you also have access to great opportunities. When you evolve and learn from relationships, your subsequent ones can be more harmonious. Your past actions involving loving kindness can bring you a sequence of fortunate circumstances in the present.

As an example, perhaps you have long dreamed of establishing a healing center. In recent years, nothing happened to fulfill the dream. However, you held the vision of the dream inside of you, and you courageously responded to the rocks showing up on your path.

One of the rocks represented an old wound involving someone from your past. A decade earlier, you had shelved the issue in your mind, thinking that it was complete. The rock that appeared ten years later was enormous. To pick it up and examine it involved one of your biggest crossroads. You did it, though, and over time you healed the old wound. When you were fully complete with the issue, and not a moment before, the rock disappeared from your path. It was then that the beneficial connections for your healing center began to come together. As you responded to them and took action, your dream became a reality.

Unfinished Business

During today's pivotal juncture, life issues not yet addressed are coming into inescapable view. There is a need to clear up unresolved concerns. Whatever unfinished business is lurking in the corner will come into the spotlight.

In tandem with this, people are feeling a kind of pressure from within to do, be, or become something that they have not yet manifested in the world. Relationships are being reevaluated. If someone is in an old-paradigm type of relationship, involving control or domination or fear, imbalances must be addressed, or else a substantial amount of negative, life-depleting energy force is generated. People are seeing more clearly the need to change how they communicate and relate to one another, to themselves, to their world, and to spirit.[4]

Oftentimes the more highly evolved a person is, the more he or she may be feeling the effects of the current transformational shifting. There is a heightened knowingness of the truth that comes from being more aware. That commonly means intensified feelings and processing of energies.

What does this mean on a practical level?

As your outer world is getting an overhaul, you find yourself reexamining your values, your aspirations, your relationships, and more. With that assessment, you may feel a whole range of emotions—from anxiety and uncertainty to gratitude and joy.

Higher-Frequency Energy—What This Means

You may begin to tap into the expanded energy that comes from raising your consciousness to hold a higher frequency.[5] You then

---

4   Sometimes used as a synonym for soul, the spirit of a person is the spiritual self. Spirit is a mystical and living energy connected to all forms of life. A person's spiritual nature is often thought of as divine—meaning that it is sacred and emanates basic goodness or wholeness. In this book, I refer to spirit and related terms in generic ways. The purpose is to allow the reader his or her own view of what the terms mean.

5   Frequency relates to energy. It is now understood that everything in the universe has a frequency. Even humans have an energy field that can be measured. During recent decades, with instruments like the SQUID

move outside of the limitations of society's third-dimensional norm.[6] You access a multidimensional state that allows for great spiritual openings. This means an expanded view of what you normally see, an enhanced perception of feelings, and an increased ability to connect with your higher wisdom.

This higher-frequency energy helps you to join with your multidimensional self.[7] As part of that, you more easily access the wisdom of your heart, your intuition, your courage, and your ability to forgive and let go.

---

    magnetometer, scientists have been able to detect minute energy fields around the human body. SQUID is an acronym for Superconducting Quantum Interference Device. In scientific terms, frequency is the measurable rate of electrical energy flow. It is believed that there is a connection between a person's frequency and his or her health. Researchers have found that when the frequency of a human body drops below 62 MHz, illness can occur. In some clinical research, it was discovered that negative thoughts can lower a person's frequency. Likewise, researchers found that meditation and prayer can raise frequency. More information on these topics can be found in this book's glossary and recommended reading list.

6   Dimensions have a frequency. Humanity has existed within the lower frequency of the third dimension for thousands of years. It is not about a specific location; it relates to a level of consciousness. During Earth's pivotal years, humanity is experiencing a gigantic dimensional shift. As people begin to reside more fully in the higher frequencies, they can more easily access the wisdom of their hearts and move out of their fear-based agendas. A shift like the one occurring now is revolutionary and unprecedented. No previous generations have lived through, or have completed, such a radical change in consciousness.

7   A multidimensional being has the capacity for expanded levels of thinking and being. New-paradigm thinking is often associated with multidimensional approaches. This means a wider spectrum of ideas and options. As humanity evolves, people become increasingly aware of the universe's larger reality. This is because people learn to perceive things they could not perceive before. Sometimes this happens when an instrument like a microscope reveals a structure not seen before. There is a learned tendency to define reality by what we can see or prove through physical means. As people grow spiritually, they increase their ability to perceive reality through more subtle means. A person learns to broaden his or her perception of reality to include both the physical and spiritual worlds. Intuitive abilities, honed with training and practice, can help a person to expand his or her range of perception. The more that a person uses these abilities, the more tangible the spiritual dimensions become.

What is occurring here is a dimensional shift. Humanity at large is in this process, and so are you. It is an integral part of the shift into a higher consciousness. Your frequency increases as you drop the density of your limited thinking, feeling, and being.

Banish Your Fears with Understanding

You and the rest of humanity are in a spiritual transformational process, discovering how to embody a higher consciousness. As you progress in this process, fear becomes less of a driving force in your life.

As you grow spiritually, the energy that you broadcast to the world is more loving. This love energy carries a frequency, also thought of as a measurement of vibration. The love frequency is higher than that of fear. The more that you can embody and broadcast the love frequency, the more love you will experience in the world.

You are in the process right now of making this shift. It is big and will change everything in your life. This change happens over time. It involves energy and awareness. You will do better on some days than others. After all, the fear-based way of being that you have learned must be unlearned. It is very ingrained in you and in everyone that you meet.

You cannot effectively hold the higher-frequency energies if you are out of balance on any level—physical, emotional, mental, or spiritual. Even the most experienced person will be challenged to stay in balance, so don't judge yourself or others. Discover how to become more mindful of what you are thinking, feeling, and doing. Investigate and put into action the transformational tools that will help you to find and stay in your center.

Banish your fears by learning about what is really going on during these unique times. Ask deeper questions. Investigate unconventional approaches that feel grounded and light-filled. Gain clarity to discover your own truth about humanity's future. Become clearer about the bigger picture, and about what others around you are hearing, so that you can better help people who need your assistance now.

In the following pages of this book, you will receive an understanding of the bigger picture and of your role during Earth's pivotal years. You will also receive useful, easy-to-apply methods that can help you to begin changing your life experience. These tools will assist you in getting and staying on track in realizing your higher purpose. You don't need to wait for any calendar marker to initiate this shift; claim it for yourself today!

Chapter 2

Understanding the Future
—Prophecies and Realities

The year 2012 is a date, but its true meaning cannot be found on a calendar. Similarly, the authentic meaning of 2012 cannot be found through a literal interpretation of ancient prophecies. And certainly the truth about 2012 cannot be found in the plethora of today's doom-and-gloom reports about the end of the world.

One purpose of this chapter is to provide an understanding of the 2012 window.[8] On these pages you will find an overview of the 2012 phenomena. Included is some of the history behind the doomsday

---

[8] The 2012 window refers more to a cycle of time than a specific date. We are already in this cycle. The 2012 window of time is a period during which humanity is facing its greatest tipping point, having the opportunity to choose a dramatically different path. Humanity is, indeed, at a crossroads during this auspicious time. People can individually and collectively choose to create a new type of existence that is based on love. The energies leading up to this juncture have been building for decades. In the future, people will look back on this time in an effort to understand humankind's evolutionary cycles. The changes put into motion during the 2012 window, individually and collectively, will help determine humanity's future. Because this book is being published during the 2012 window, it is timely to refer to it here. More information on this and other terms is provided in the book's glossary.

prophecies associated with these times. As you read, you will discover a new way to look at time, dates, and the future. As you work with the self-help processes given in this and subsequent chapters, you will have a framework for empowered questioning. Each time you work with a process, you will hone your intuition. This will accelerate your spiritual growth by leaps and bounds.

You will find answers to the many questions being asked during these historic moments. Your inner wisdom—the part of you guiding you to read this book—wants you to have a higher spiritual view. It wants you to understand the deeper meaning of this great shift of ages and to become fearless about the changes now unfolding.

You Have Options

When you have a larger picture of reality, you can find your own truth. You will discover that you *do* have options.

Knowing you have options puts you in a position of empowerment. Confident that you have choices, you will be less fearful. Understanding the human condition—including the background of how we arrived at this pivotal juncture—helps you to have compassion for yourself and others.

When you express empathy, you contribute to a more loving world. Another bonus: when you are compassionate, you shift your energy into a higher state. From that expanded state, being more secure in your own truth, the fears of others have less negative impact on you.

As you expand your view of these times, you become more of a resource for yourself and others. People will be naturally drawn to you, instinctively knowing that you can help.

People You Can Help

Who are these people who you can help? They could be coworkers, friends, neighbors, or family members. They could be strangers who come into your life because of shared activities.

As an example, you wait in line at the grocery store and overhear two women expressing fearful concern about a doomsday scenario portrayed in a movie. They are half laughing and half anxious, not quite knowing how to process what they saw on the big screen.

They shake their heads, shrug their shoulders, and turn to you. One woman asks you if you believe that it's safe to stay in town.

She says, "In the movie we just saw, no one who stays here lives through the disaster. I know it's just a movie, but there's plenty of talk now about end times and who will survive. Crazy, isn't it?"

In a scenario like this, you don't necessarily need to have a profound comment. Some ideas, expressed casually to a stranger, are not really meant to be answered. Perhaps you will nod and give a knowing smile, reassuring the women that you have heard their concern and that you understand the craziness of these times. If it feels appropriate, you could tell them about books like this one and share a bit of what you have learned.

When you develop a personal language to describe what is real about these pivotal years, you can more easily share your truth with others.

2012 and Beyond—Pivotal Crossroads

Today, as humanity stands within the 2012 window, increasing numbers of people are realizing that these aren't ordinary times. There is plenty of media focus on 2012, but it is more than that. You don't have to be a psychic or historian to feel the magnitude of changes occurring today. You can feel the undercurrent of change even if you don't regularly watch the news.

Most likely, you feel more uncertain about your future than you did a few years ago. As you observe the world's fragile state, you no doubt wonder how humanity can come together with the needed solutions for the growing list of concerns. You don't need to understand politics or economics to know that the planet is at a tipping point. You can see it all around you.

Similarly, you don't need to be on the path of conscious awakening to feel the acceleration in time. Everyone feels it; all of the people around you are working with the same twenty-four hours that you are. Time pressures are felt by anyone connected with the pulse of modern society. It is more than simply growing older and feeling that you have less time to live before you die.

What is the bigger picture here? How do you make sense of the linear yardstick we call time?[9] How can you intelligently approach the topics of time, the 2012 date, and the massive shifting occurring? What is important to understand at this moment? How about the future—why is that getting so much more attention right now?

As you read, you will understand how to answer questions such as these.

Preoccupation with the Future

You are conditioned from the time you are born to wonder, worry, and wish about the future. It is always there staring back at you. You know it is coming just like you know summer follows spring. You know you can't stop it anymore than you can stop the advance of your chronological age. You have learned to have a fixation on the future and to spend lots of your time focused on what will happen next.

Looking at the future takes on a whole new meaning during the 2012 window. These are historic moments during which you and humanity have vital decisions to make. Individually and collectively,

---

[9] The word "linear" relates to old-paradigm views that are limited and without in-depth understanding. These approaches can be rigid and fixed. When someone is thinking in linear terms, he or she often views things in black and white. This means without the variations that contribute to a fuller view. On the other hand, new-paradigm thinking has multidimensional approaches. This means a wider spectrum of ideas and options.

you are setting in motion a powerful wave of changes on the Earth. With so much at stake, it is normal that you would feel pressured to get it right.

The future you are moving toward will feel fluid. That means you will be accessing future energies in the now, and time will lose its linear feel. The linear approach to time is rigid and limited. Your future involves a connection with your eternal and unlimited potential; it involves moving into your true multidimensional state.

Shifting into that state of being is a journey, and the process evolves over time. It is a path you have long traveled. You embarked on that journey long before you learned that there are realities beyond the third-dimensional realm.

It's Wired into Your DNA

It's wired into your DNA to be multidimensional.[10] This more expanded state is your natural way of being. You and humanity are shifting into a higher consciousness that will allow you to reside in this fuller life experience beyond the third dimension.

Here is an example of what is happening. As you advance into

---

10   DNA, also known as deoxyribonucleic acid, is found in almost all living things. DNA resides within the cells of our bodies. DNA governs things like cell growth and inheritance. In nearly all human cells, DNA is contained in chromosomes, located in the cell's nucleus. Shaped like a double helix or spiral, the DNA is constantly communicating instructions about life processes. It is like a library of information about who a person is on every level—physical, mental, emotional, and spiritual. This library is a living blueprint of a person's life experiences. The record includes the person's ancestry and the imprint of the person's spiritual lineage. Belief systems—both positive and negative—are recorded there. At a DNA level, each person is encoded as a divine being, with a blueprint for awakening to that divine nature at some point along the journey. The basis for all forms of healing is this awakening. The purpose of healing is to release discordant energies so that the person realizes his or her divine nature. For further information on this topic, see this book's glossary and recommended reading list. Additional background, along with practical life examples, is provided on the author's website.

higher consciousness, you will be able to access energies—including knowledge, healing, and an understanding of timeless wisdom—through telepathic thought and intuitive knowing. When this happens, your concept of the future will be much less mundane and much more cosmic. That means less worry about the what-ifs of tomorrow and a more empowered conscious creation that puts you in the driver's seat of prophecy.

Your Own Inner Prophecy Station

Having your own inner prophecy station will help you to navigate today's chaos with less fear.[11] You will become wiser about your past, present, and future. You will discover how to crosscheck prophecies of others with your own and to find your own truth in each moment. You can then make wiser choices and take actions that you will not regret.

To be sure, even well after 2012 the prophecies about humanity's future will continue to make headlines. Remember that it is human nature to want predictions of the future. These forecasts will continue to be made. Many years after 2012, you will hear your wisdom keepers speaking about the great shift of the 2012 window.[12] They will be

---

11 An inner prophecy station is a person's developed ability to go within and get his or her own answers. This is a form of intuitive knowing that anyone can develop.

12 Wisdom keepers are those who hold timeless and universal knowledge about humanity's past and ancient traditions. Today's living wisdom keepers include those who teach this knowledge and those who have studied ancient teachings. During humanity's early history, much of the universal knowledge was transmitted orally and passed from generation to generation. In some of the very early Tibetan Buddhist traditions, a teacher would share this wisdom with only one student during a lifetime. To be the recipient of such a sacred teaching was considered a unique honor. In many ancient spiritual traditions, the teachings were considered so sacred that no written record was permitted. The wisdom was transmitted orally, and students memorized spiritual practices. For more information about these ancient traditions, see this book's recommended reading list.

putting in context what began happening during that window of time, providing predictions of what you can expect next.

Why the Boom in Prophecies?

Why do we seem to have more prophecies these days? We passed the heralded 2000 mark without the predicted Y2K technology meltdown. Why is the 2012 window getting so much attention? Is it just one date, or are there lots of dates to consider?

You will find answers to these and related questions in the next several pages. As you take in this information, it is recommended that you set your intention to be as open-minded as possible and to turn on your discernment filter. Only you can determine what is real and what your future will hold.

Mayan Predictions

The 2012 date has been popularized by a plethora of media attention showcasing ancient prophecies from diverse cultures. Dominant among these are the Mayan predictions based on their distinctive calendar of galactic cycles. Other forecasts come from ancient religious texts like the Bible and the Koran, or from famous prophets like Nostradamus and Moses.

The Maya were very advanced in their use of mathematics to calculate planetary changes.[13] From their vantage point in ancient times, the Maya predicted a great shift upon the Earth. Their forecasts came from sophisticated calendars that allowed them to chart time and events. Modern researchers have proposed varied interpretations of these forecasts.

---

13 The Mayan civilization, which reached its heights in Central America and Mexico between AD 300 and 900, is known today for its calendars and advanced mathematics involving time and astronomy. Archaeologists and other researchers have studied numerous Mayan hieroglyphs, colorful painted walls, and ancient temples. For further information about the Maya, see this book's glossary and recommended reading list.

Many of the Mayan prophecies were misinterpreted by well-meaning and sometimes self-serving researchers. These mistaken translations are not surprising because the sophisticated Mayan calculations and symbols can be accurately understood only with a trained eye and a discerning wisdom.

When looking at any ancient calendar, keep in mind that humanity has changed calendars many times. Religion and politics were chief reasons behind the changes. Most calendars used in the past several thousand years were based on a conventional, third-dimensional view of reality that sees separation rather than unity. These calendars include the Julian calendar introduced by Julius Caesar in 46 BC, the Gregorian calendar first adopted in the 1500s, and the current standard international civil calendar.[14]

The Mayan calendars were not based on dualistic thinking but on oneness with the world. When you understand how different the Mayan approach to time was and how many different types of calendars humans have used over the ages, you can see how tricky it is to accurately interpret an exact date in an ancient prophecy.

The Challenge of Interpreting Prophecies

Keep in mind that quite often, the essence of prophecies was not written down anywhere, but rather passed down orally from generation to generation. Unless you hear a prophecy with your own ears, from a source that you can validate has an unbroken oral tradition with the original culture, you don't know the whole picture.

With symbols especially, much is left open to interpretation that will depend upon one's consciousness and on what one wants to see. Fear-based agendas will produce fear-based interpretations. Discernment is required. One can develop discernment skills through training and lots of practice.

---

14 The Gregorian calendar is among the conventional calendars society used in the past. More information on calendars is in this book's glossary.

What Is Prophecy?

Having a big-picture view will help you to stand back from the craziness that tends to accompany interpretation of prophecies. Predictions and prophecies have been a part of the human landscape for thousands of years.

Prophecy is a kind of advance divine knowing of a future event. Throughout time, prophecy has been offered by oracles and seers of many cultures. These include the Maya, Hebrews, Tibetans, Christians, and North American Indians. Some of the current prophecies about the end of time were first made a very long time ago and have been repeated many times since. You will find a number of them in sacred religious texts; others have been passed down through the generations in oral form.

The future is not a rigidly set construct. It is a potential only. The future is fluid in nature and comes with no guarantee. It is formed by what happens in the now. Because of this, a prophecy or prediction can only provide a potential future outcome. If it's true, it can only be a relative truth, based upon what is happening during the moment in time when it is received.

The future that is predicted, therefore, can radically change by the time it arrives.

Another thing to keep in mind is that if the prediction indeed is coming from a high-level consciousness, it will not be fear-based or create negativity of any kind. Instead the prediction will be something that focuses on positive change, helping others, and creating love.

Consider the source of any prediction. This includes ancient prophecies. You will want to know whether the person referencing the prophecy is giving an accurate and full recitation of its original message.

It can be difficult or often impossible to confirm such accuracies. One reason is that prophecies contained within ancient texts such as the Bible's Book of Revelation have been translated and interpreted many times over the centuries. Each time a prophecy is translated, there is the potential for new interpretations that reflect the language and beliefs of that period.

Some examples are the terms "apocalypse" and "Armageddon."[15] Apocalypse is often associated with Armageddon, commonly described as the end of the world. The doomsday Armageddon story has been around for so long that it is part of our mass consciousness.

Dire accounts of a final judgment and global catastrophe are in the Bible's Book of Revelation. Originally, however, the word "apocalypse" meant unveiling, or bringing to light things that were hidden from view.

We live during moments when secrets of all sorts are coming to light. It is a time when we are remembering our real heritage. It is a period when we are evolving out of constriction and into a lightness of being. In that process, countless veils are being lifted.

Human beings have always wanted to know what will happen and when. For the typical person, the veils of ignorance are so great that there is little appreciation of the larger purpose of existence. There is a tendency to ask surface-oriented questions. The future is approached with a mixture of fear, fantasy, and denial. Few people can predict what will happen ten years from now, or even tomorrow.

Sometimes the purpose of a disaster-oriented prophecy is to awaken people and birth a series of transformational changes that will nullify the dire predictions. Even with some of Hollywood's blockbuster disaster films, the filmmakers may intentionally be seeking to awaken people.

Keep in mind that nothing is as it appears!

---

15   The terms "apocalypse" and "Armageddon" are highly charged. In some religious texts, words like these are linked with prophecies about the end of the world. This view is based on the idea that humanity's destiny is set in stone. In fact, humanity has a choice of how to respond to Earth's pivotal years. It might be more appropriate to view Armageddon as a pivotal choice point. Humanity is at a tipping point; its choices will determine the future of generations to come, and Armageddon is symbolic of these momentous options. The cumulative effect of these choices will determine our future. More information on both of these terms is in this book's glossary.

Process: Your Questions about the End of the World

Realize that a prophecy is simply a prophecy. Human suffering comes not from something that is said or that happens, but from what people have made the thing *mean*. In other words, an event in current time or predicted time will impact you based upon your view of it. What does the end of the world mean to you?

Invite your intuitively guided reason to speak to you about the following possible meanings of a predicted end of the world.

1. Does it mean that this would be the end of all life, including your own?

2. Does it mean the end of the old-paradigm world, falling away to make room for a more enlightened way to coexist?

3. Does it mean having your freedoms and way of life taken away?

4. Does it mean redefining freedom and opening to a more heart-centered and intuitive way to live?

5. Does it mean that people with higher consciousness lost the battle, and the negative forces of greed and hate won?

6. Does it mean that those people ready for the shift into higher consciousness can discover a new type of Earth to call home?

7. Does it mean that the world will be destroyed on a specific day at a specific time?

8. Does it mean that there is nothing you can do to prevent certain disaster?

9. Does it mean that everything you have worked for is wasted effort?

10. Does it mean that a brand-new, more light-filled Earth will take the place of the old one?

11. Does it mean that humans have an opportunity to benefit from the past at the eleventh hour?

12. Does it mean that humanity and the Earth can finally coexist in peace and harmony?

Calling upon Your Higher Wisdom

When you ponder questions such as these—with conscious intent to have your own answers—you evoke the movement of your own higher wisdom. You take yourself out of the victim role and move past your fears.

Humans have been conditioned to accept what they are told. From one generation to the next, your ancestors learned to look to outside authorities for answers. They forgot that they could access their own truth. They were not taught that everyone has a natural ability to connect with his or her divine knowing.

The people alive today represent the first generations that are breaking these habits. You are here now to help break the mold.

Changing old habits is not easy. It becomes easier, though, when you understand that you have a habit and know that it is not serving you. When you realize the source of your habit and discover that it obscures your light, you have positive motivation for change.

Be mindful of your role, then, and take every opportunity to question. If an answer does not come immediately to your inquiry, ask again later. Perhaps phrase the question another way.

When you have no immediate response, invite your higher wisdom to give you understanding through the happenstance of your life. This could be a dream, a billboard or license plate, words you overhear, a tingling in your body, a knowing, or a train of thought in your head. The possibilities for input are unlimited. Pay attention to what shows up.

Your Higher Wisdom through a Dream

As an example, perhaps you ask whether it's really possible to create a new type of light-filled Earth.

Two nights later, you have a vivid dream about a meeting of world leaders. You see the heads of state sitting around a large table and having a meaningful and interactive dialogue. They agree on a novel plan to balance the world's key resources. The plan addresses hunger, financial inequalities, and Earth changes. The agreement they reach incorporates technologies and resources that had been under wraps.

You see in the dream that, indeed, it is possible for the world to come together. You have your validation. The dream is your symbolic answer to the question; it helps you to connect with your truth—what you believe inside your heart.

This is just one way that your higher wisdom will naturally communicate to your consciousness when you invite the input. Remember to keep asking. Trust that in the very process of asking, you are already receiving your answer. Allow the answer to come in its own time, in its own way—helping you to feel confident and fearless.

Dreams like this one are not meant to be interpreted literally. They are symbolic and a vehicle for your consciousness to speak to you. Paying attention to your dreams—and using them as a tool for your spiritual growth—is one way to expand your intuitive abilities.

Intuitive Skills Come of Age

Intuitive skills have come of age. The notion of asking questions of your intuition—and getting an answer—has moved out of the esoteric and into the mainstream. This development is part of the paradigm shift. It is also a necessary catalyst for that shift.

Intuition is not a magical tool possessed by a select few. There is really nothing magical about it; every man, woman, and child has a natural ability to connect with inner knowing. It is a skill that can be developed by anyone with sincere desire, training, and practice.

Hone your intuition; you then will have an indispensable tool for navigating the paradigm shift. Develop trust in your own answers so that you can be more discerning about today's phenomena and crises.

2012 Phenomena

It may sometimes seem like the 2012 phenomena came out of nowhere. Most people had no idea that this date meant anything before the extensive media exposure of recent years. Even now you may question what it will mean after 2012.

Keep in mind that the 2012 window is not one moment in time but a cycle of energy in which we exist. It is here now.

Elders of diverse traditions, including the Maya and the Tibetans, spoke of massive changes during this period of time. They documented great cycles of change, providing us with clues about previous climatic shifts and humanity's repetitive remembering and forgetting of universal truths. They reminded us of our eternal nature.

Solstice of December 21, 2012

The Maya are known for speaking about the December 21, 2012, date within the context of planetary cycles. That date, which is the solstice, has been described by some modern researchers as the endpoint of the Mayan calendar.[16]

Today it is not yet clear what this endpoint signifies. However, there is one message heard repeatedly by those who study the wisdom of our elders. They tell us about a time at the end of a grand cycle when we could take a great leap forward and create a light-filled existence.

We now live in one of those grand cycles, and if our elder timekeepers have been correctly understood, the 2012 window could be interesting indeed.

2012 Leap Year

One fascinating coincidence is that 2012 is a leap year. Consider the possibility that the 2012 leap year is more than an artificial altering of the calendar to adjust for the seasons. It just may be the spark needed to catapult our great leap!

---

16 The solstice occurs twice annually, when the sun is at its greatest distance from the celestial equator. In the northern hemisphere, the winter solstice date is typically December 21 or 22 and marks the beginning of winter. For the southern hemisphere, with its reversed seasons, that same date is the start of summer. Likewise, the solstice date of June 20 or 21 in the northern hemisphere marks the start of summer, while it is the beginning of winter in the southern hemisphere. The December 21, 2012, solstice date has been referenced by some Maya and other wisdom keepers as a kind of marker that shows the end of a very long evolutionary cycle. A date on a calendar, however, is a linear reference point and outer-world marker only. For those interested in enlightenment and creating a new type of light-filled world, the element to focus on is consciousness. When enough people are awakened and focus their lives positively, the higher consciousness created will result in the desired shift. That will occur in a process over time, not on one day.

Cycles—Truth, Fiction, and the Unknowable

The Maya talked about the end of time. Elders of numerous traditions spoke about endings of cycles. It's now common knowledge that there have been numerous Earth changes, as well as beginnings and endings of life forms on this planet. These things are known to happen in cycles, which by their very nature repeat themselves.

Ice core research in recent decades has revealed cyclic patterns involving Earth changes, introduction of new species, and extinctions.[17]

Keep in mind that there are often numerous interpretations of ancient writings and teachings. Be mindful as you take in the world's messages that say the end of time means the end of the world. This is false.

The end of time means the end of a way of being and the start of something brand new. It is about cycles of change and movement. It refers to our radical changes. We face a multitude of crises.

The thing that makes now different from some earlier shifts is that we are moving into a higher consciousness. When there is a tipping point—involving anything from an abrupt weather change

---

[17] Ice core research involves scientific studies from samples of accumulated snow and ice found at the polar ice caps of Antarctica, Greenland, and other high mountain glaciers. The ice cores contain helpful climate information and other data that help scientists to confirm the history of Earth. Ice core science became a new research field in the 1950s when Willi Dansgaard of Denmark discovered that the ice caps could reveal past climatic conditions. Ice core research, continuing today, shows patterns in time. It reveals the historical periods that had conditions most suitable for life. By studying the ice cores, scientists are also able to confirm periods when there were massive extinctions. More on cycles and the latest thinking about Earth changes can be found in general and scientific media. Television science programs, print and online publications, and a growing number of books are available on these topics. For a few suggested resources, see this book's recommended reading list.

to the crash of a devastating comet—a civilization with a higher consciousness will be better equipped to adapt and cooperate.

Humans have been evolving over time, and today's humans have much greater awareness than those who faced earlier crises. It will be consciousness that determines our fate. We have an unprecedented opportunity during these pivotal times to catapult ourselves and our planet into an enlightened consciousness.

Having the opportunity is not the same thing as a guarantee. There are no guarantees of what will happen. There is no magic carpet arriving to whisk us out of harm's way. It is up to us to fully use this unique opportunity while we have it.

Our Spiritual Journey over Time

Our historians, cosmologists, and spiritual teachers of diverse paths have taught us about the very slow and repetitive cycles of human existence. They have used numerous words and symbols to describe this natural unfolding. For example, the Hindus call our time in darkness the Kali Yuga.[18]

History has shown us that the 26,000-year cycle is comprised of smaller cycles of approximately 5,000 years. Humanity has lived through other great shifts at these 5,000-year junctures.

Within your DNA is a record of your entire spiritual journey, including all of your past experiences and conditioning. There is a mass-consciousness level of energy within your DNA too. That means you are subconsciously connected with the memories and experiences of the whole of humanity. The mass-consciousness energy field is not something outside of you. You and others have created it over time and continue to add to it by responding to life's circumstances.

You will sometimes feel anxiety that comes from the mass consciousness. When you get fearful, it's helpful to remember this

---

18 The Kali Yuga is an ancient Indian term. It refers to the last of the four stages of human evolutionary cycles. For more information, see this book's glossary.

and to open your eyes to the source of your fear. It could be your own fear, and it could also be fear triggered within the masses. Remember that everything and everyone is connected.

It is vital that you approach today's pivotal times with new eyes and without the baggage of your past. This current shift is unlike the previous ones. It is a much more potent catalyst for shifting the planet into light. You are experiencing your own cycle within the cycle of the whole. You are the determiner of your own future. This is the lifetime during which you can be an integral part of humanity's conscious evolution. To be conscious is to be awake.

Within your awareness—either conscious or unconscious—you are connected to a collective memory of past shift cycles involving great cataclysm and loss of life. Be mindful of that. Stay present, focused, and awake and remember that this time is different. You don't need to repeat mistakes of the past. The 2012 window is unique, and you have never been within these energies before.

In fact, what you and the Earth are doing is brand new! The opportunities that you have for revolutionary shifting are profound. Trust this and focus on the present and the light-filled future you want to create with the rest of humanity. Do not wait for any special date to do this; the time to act is now. Move into your power and see the fear-based reports about certain disaster for what they are—misinformed scare tactics.

Humanity's Future Is Not Predestined

Some people believe that humanity's future is predestined. According to this view, the human race and the planet are certain to ascend into higher consciousness in a predetermined way. The process of creation, however, is not one of predetermination. Humanity's future is not rigidly laid out.

So what is happening? Humans are evolving and shifting at an unprecedented pace. People in every corner of the planet are being impacted. Other life forms, and even the Earth itself, are in the process of a massive reconstruction. A dramatic leap into higher consciousness is under way.

Outmoded societal structures are collapsing, sometimes quickly and at other times over a span of years or decades. The institutions and systems most impacted and controlled by greed and power mongering are oftentimes the places most resistant to new, more enlightened approaches. The people with the power want to keep the power.

Never before on Earth have there been so many changes so fast. Young people born today will need to become skilled in adapting to change, not only the types of change typical in a lifetime, but countless other shifts in circumstances that their ancestors did not face. Because it is all so new, the previous generations have not created a road map for how to navigate these tumultuous times.

During these unique years, you are being impacted even if you know nothing about cycles or humanity's past. It is helpful to become acquainted with these things and to investigate how you are personally affected. When you have that understanding, you can make wiser choices and feel more connected to the bigger picture. You can become skilled in creating within the new energies. You can discover how to be skillful in navigating the cycle of change.

Meet the Divine Changemakers

If you are feeling like something important is about to happen, you are correct! Change is in the air, but you must work with it in your own way and make your energies count. That is our role as divine changemakers.[19]

---

19 A divine changemaker is someone who is on Earth now to make the changes needed for a more light-filled world. Those changes start inside oneself as the person progresses on his or her spiritual path. A divine changemaker is also someone who makes sense of the changes for others, helping people to understand what is occurring and how to optimally respond. This is a person

We live during that unique window of time our ancient ones foresaw. Exactly how things play out is up to us, of course. We are the ones who will decide our own fate. As divine changemakers, we can create a brand-new start for ourselves and our planet. That is why we are here right now—we and more than six billion other people who came to participate.

Chances are you haven't thought of yourself as a divine changemaker. However, you and others on the path of awakened consciousness *are* divine changemakers. You fulfill that role as you make the needed changes—first within yourself, and then in the world—so that our planet can move into enlightened consciousness. As part of that, it is your birthright to remember that you are divine, and to express that divine nature on Earth.

※

Process: Honing Your Questioning Skills

You are discovering how to question. This is a natural ability, yet it is often underdeveloped and even discouraged in modern culture. In order to move into your authentic power, become more practiced with inquiry. Begin monitoring your mind to discover the types of questions you ask.

For example, any inquiry that is future oriented and fear-based will keep you feeling small. Avoid questions such as these.

- Will I be successful at some future time?
- When will I have success?
- What if I get a disease such as cancer?
- What will happen if I lose my home, my husband, or my job?

---

who regularly redefines oneself as a human being too. This means ongoing reviews of one's life and regular letting go of outmoded energies. Rather than trying to force changes on others, a divine changemaker discovers how to help others appropriately and offers help without an agenda.

- How long will this situation last?
- When will the world become peaceful?
- What if someone or something sabotages my success?
- Will I be okay when big changes happen?

Rather than questioning in this future-oriented way, consider inquiry that is present oriented. Ask what you can do to change your current situation. Because we can't always change our situation, inquire about how you can shift your view of what is occurring. Keep your perspective in the now, and you will feel more confident about what's coming next.

To change your experience of the future, you must change your experience of the present. You can do this by asking questions like these.

- What is preventing me from having the success I want?
- What can I shift in my view, or do differently, to have my desired results sooner?
- Is the delay I'm experiencing related to something I can change?
- How can I live differently to prevent disease?
- What can I do now to establish friendships that will support me in a health crisis?
- What are my options if I lose my home, my husband, or my job?
- How can I move through this crisis with more ease?
- What am I not seeing about my situation?
- How can I be more peaceful?
- What specific things can I do to influence my own happiness, success, and peacefulness?
- What tools and wisdom do I already have for coping with big changes?

- What additional training, healing, or spiritual development would help me become more stable, healthy, and happy?
- Where do I go to find these resources?

New Approaches to Time

As a divine changemaker, you are in the process of discovering new approaches to time. You and others like you are now in the midst of a revolutionary shift in how time is viewed and worked with. This shift is happening in stages, for the gap between the old and new is too great to simply jump to the new overnight.

Shifting from a Linear View

The linear view of time is now outmoded and too limited for where humanity is headed. A rigid linear approach keeps people thinking in a narrow way. Concepts of timelessness, natural time, cyclic existence, and the eternal cannot be explained in a linear way. These ideas are vast and run counter to an unbending notion of time.

When you shift from a linear view, you still have clock time, of course, and calendars. These are tools humans have devised to synchronize activities and plan for the future. Although they are still useful in our modern-day world, consider these seven new approaches for using clocks and calendars.

✷

Tips: Working with Time

1. Know that twenty-four hours is no longer experienced as twenty-four hours, for time has been *compressed*.

2. Keep in mind that time is not a material thing. You can't lose it or misplace it like you could a clock. You never have time to begin with, because it's simply an arbitrary measuring stick devised thousands of years ago to define motion and events.

3. Time can be experienced differently depending on who you are and your reference point. An hour of your favorite pastime can feel much shorter than the same hour laboring at learning a new and challenging task. If you are fifteen and your next birthday is six months away, it can seem like time has slowed to a crawl. If you are sixty-five and reflecting on your life, you may wonder how the years have passed by so quickly.

4. If you approach the distant future in a linear way—worrying about what may happen—you will be setting up a needless cycle of anxiety, pressure, and dissatisfaction.

5. If you employ conventional views of time when viewing your own potential—basing future possibilities on your past experiences—you will limit yourself. To move into your full potential, you must be able to see beyond what you have already created. If you have failed at something in the past, this does not mean you are locked into failure. Likewise, if you have succeeded at something before, you want to be open to new ways of success. When creating anything that's really new, it will not be a carbon copy of what has come before. Be open to new ideas each time you do something.

6. Look to the natural world for clues about how to work with time in a less linear way. Animals allow their own body rhythms and sense of time to guide them. When the sun rises, most animals awaken and begin their day. If they are

hungry, they find food to eat. There are no rigid mealtimes. Animals such as squirrels store food for the winter, not because they have a calendar reminding them to do so, but because they naturally know to do it.

7. View your personal relationship with time in a more expansive and flexible way. That includes how you approach deadlines, whether artificial or real. It can be helpful to set your intention to forge a brand-new connection with time. As part of that, you will want to let go of the illusion that time is either your enemy or your friend. That is a dualistic approach and is out of step with the multidimensional being that you are. Time is just time. It is up to you to decide how you will relate to time.

As you are redefining your relationship with time, you will want to keep in mind your personal needs as well as your interactions with others.

Personal Needs to Consider

1. Do you often eat when you are not really hungry, simply because the clock tells you that it is time?

2. Do you sometimes have a time focus when you eat, hurrying your meal and then later realizing that you ate twice as much food as you really needed?

3. Do you ever feel like a slave to a rigid schedule you set for a project, trying to force creative ideas at a predetermined time when your energies would be better utilized doing something else at that moment?

4. Do you honor your personal needs for downtime and self-reflection?

5. Do you know how to be in tune with yourself at a deep enough level to tell when you need rest, food, companionship, alone time, or a specific activity?

6. Do you factor into your busy schedule enough time to focus on spirit and your spiritual growth? Do you step back from the minutiae and happenstance of the day often enough to get a larger perspective that exists beyond the short term?

7. Do you find it's easy to ask others for the time you personally need—whether it's alone time, more time to reflect on a key issue, or simply to be released from an artificial deadline?

Interactions with Others

When you update your relationship with time, you will want to do so responsibly and without doing harm to others. To be responsible with time means that you consider how your actions impact the lives of others. Examples include your attitude and actions as you interact with other people on the road, in the market, on the phone, at work, or in other public places.

Consider some of the ways that you interact with others. Here are some examples.

1. Do you tailgate when you are driving and in a hurry?

2. Do you get angry when you must stand in line at the grocery store at the end of your workday?

3. Do you have a habit of being late for meetings with others?

4. Do you arrive late at the movies and disturb others in the audience?

5. Do you make plans with a friend and then change plans at the last minute without regard to how the change impacts your friend?

6. Do you commit to projects at work without a realistic view of how long they will take, your delays setting off a series of other delays for your coworkers?

7. In your most intimate relationships, are you respectful of the time of your loved ones?

Being Where You Are

To simply be where you are—without a preoccupation with past events or future outcomes—is easier said than done. Even though a part of you knows that the present is the only point of real power, it can feel challenging to keep your awareness present focused. That's especially true if you don't like your present reality!

To be satisfied with your own existence is no easy task. Arriving at a peaceful coexistence with yourself and your outer world is not automatic. You don't achieve this by reaching a certain age. It doesn't come from where you live. It cannot be reached through fame or fortune. No other person can give it to you.

This state of peacefulness is only to be found deep within you, when you access your true nature. That eternal part of you exists beyond time and space. The eternal you is unaffected by the world's chaos; it is able to simply be, no matter what. You can discover how to connect with this aspect of yourself. You can learn how to be satisfied, peaceful, and free. You can discover how to feel comfortable with uncertainty. This is your divine birthright.

You are here during this pivotal time to help influence the upward movement of human consciousness. To be most effective, you must find intelligent ways to work with the regular input you receive from the outside world.

Open your eyes to how you allow others and your worldview to influence your thinking. Discover a balanced approach to the constant influx of ideas from all types of media. This is a challenge when you have learned to be connected to media almost nonstop.

The Media—Blessing or Curse?

Powerful media messages, which now can be accessed 24/7, will remind you of the uncertain state of the world. You can see that as a blessing or a curse.

Your ancient ancestors had no Internet or cell phones to give them the kind of global perspective of change you now have. They often did not know about the sufferings of people beyond their small villages. It was common to be ignorant of the connected web of life on Earth. History was not viewed globally, but regionally from the perspective of what the local peoples were experiencing.

You can choose how the media and technology will affect you. You can discover how to be accepting of evolutionary change. It is as though you and other humans are living in a construction zone. As humanity and the Earth undergo the process of massive reconstruction, you may feel like you want to run, yet there is no place to go.

The changes are under way all around you while you continue to live on the planet you call home. If there were another planet you knew to go to right now, you might be tempted to go there. Because that's not an option, you are like the homeowner with a house needing repairs. You can choose to make the repairs while also adjusting your view about life and living in a home that doesn't fit your current needs.

The key to empowerment in these chaotic times is to develop more self-awareness, to train your mind to switch off the fear channel, and to fully develop your intuitively guided reason and ability to question.

You will want to question what others say will happen in the future. You will want to question your own views of what is possible, determining where your blind spots are.

✻

Questions: What to Ask Now

1. Have I ignored something that is important to my soul's growth?[20]

2. Have I forgotten to make sensible plans for some aspect of my future physical existence?

3. Am I taking adequate care of my body?

4. Am I waiting for someone or a certain event to change my reality?

5. What deep-seated fears are being triggered by the world's doomsday messages?

---

20 The soul is typically thought of as the spiritual part of a person. In some traditions, it is linked with a person's essence or core. Throughout history, the word "soul" has been used in numerous ways, in part depicting the views of the tradition. As an example, soul is sometimes used interchangeably with terms like "spirit," "mind," or "self." For the purposes of this book, soul relates to a person's spiritual nature or true self.

6. What about this great shift will be different from those of the past?

7. Am I subjecting myself to an excessive amount of fear-based media?

8. Am I connected enough with the world to effectively determine what my ideal next steps are?

9. What is the key element of truth in the futuristic film I just saw?

10. What presented in that film is a fantasy or a scare tactic?

11. Which books, films, and other informational resources provide the highest levels of truth about the future?

12. What is the biggest future-oriented doubt that I have right now, and is it based on anything real?

On a regular basis, inquire within to determine whether your view of the future is based on perspectives that are sane and balanced. Get in touch with any views that need updating. These include fantasies you once embraced and now recognize as ill founded. Acknowledge pessimistic views, too, such as doubting that your efforts can be worthwhile.

To create the kind of future in which you want to live, you must believe it is possible to change your present reality. You must embrace your role as a divine changemaker.

Role of a Divine Changemaker

Remember that you are a divine changemaker, creating not only your own present and future but that of the world around you. You change it by taking conscious actions in the present. You change it by becoming more aware of what's needed and of what needs to fall away. You then take steps to help create changes, and you bravely do the inner work to release old energies.

Rather than simply focusing on what's wrong with the world, you recognize what needs to change, and then you focus your energies on making changes within yourself. Your priority is to live as fully and consciously as you can while also finding out how to be the loving and peaceful being you want to see everywhere you go.

You catch yourself when you dwell in the past, remembering that the replay of old ideas is draining your energy and preventing you from moving forward. You know that to repeatedly remember how someone or something hurt you is only reinforcing a painful past. You recognize that your only power is in the present moment. Realizing this, you shift your focus to the present and to what you can do to be happier right now.

Chapter 3

Times of Great Change

Right now you live in the midst of a revolution in human consciousness. This involves such significant changes in how people live and view life that we don't yet have language for it.

You are having some previews of coming attractions in those fleeting moments when you know what's going to happen before it happens. It occurs when you lose track of time, and when you discover that some projects typically taking you an entire day are accomplished within a single hour.

It occurs when you meet people for the first time and feel strangely comfortable with them, as though you have known them forever. It happens when you contemplate a troublesome issue before sleep, inviting a divine resolution, and you awaken with fresh insights that can help you turn things around.

It occurs when you go beyond reason and discern a truth with your heart and intuitive knowing. It takes place in the moments when you let go and simply allow yourself to see what was there all along.

Seeing What Was There All Along

What you find may astonish you! An example is your sensing the presence of a benevolent, nonphysical spirit guide. This guide may have been around you for your entire life, yet perhaps now is the first time you have had the readiness and willingness to recognize its presence.

Another example is when you are able to suddenly connect the dots in a longstanding puzzle of pain. You may have had realizations about your issue many other times, yet none of them led you out of the maze that kept you hopelessly stuck. This time, though, you really understand the root of your problem. A flash of insight and divine grace, coming seemingly out of nowhere, helps you to illuminate the root of your pain. This brings you clarity about the connecting pieces. You grasp the big view that spirit has. Your expanded understanding allows you to let go of old hurts. You can see the past with fresh eyes. Your new view changes how you respond to what happened, and you finally find peace.

In general, as you grow in awareness, the truth that was there all along comes to the surface, and it becomes easier for you to recognize it as truth. This happens on a more conscious level as you question what you were taught and what you are being told today by authority figures. This questioning is vital if you are to discover what is real. Indeed, the more that you can recognize truth, the more quickly you can advance out of human ignorance.

Personal Awakening

During these times of great change, people from all walks of life are beginning to awaken from a very long sleep. The planet's evolution into a higher consciousness is under way, and this movement will proceed even if the majority of people are not ready for the shift.

This last point is something to remember on those days when you feel concern for the plight of fear-based masses of people in all corners of the world. On those days you may question whether there is hope and whether the majority of people really care about anything beyond mundane concerns. When you are feeling like that, rather than dwell on the negative, focus your energies in positive ways that can help yourself and others. *Regardless of what others are doing, decide that you will be ready for the next stages of the shift.*

Remember also that upward spirals of growth can occur either very slowly or seemingly in a flash of time. This applies to both individuals and the planet as a whole. How quickly a person evolves is directly related to the level of willingness to change. There must be openness to seeing things differently, questioning one's own status quo, responding with radical new approaches, and fearlessly making different choices without a road map. Although this approach may sound like an impossible feat to someone mired in a life crisis, even the ordinary person can succeed if there is enough self-love.

The quality of self-love is developed as you drop conditioning that says you are not enough. This happens in stages as you discover how to be patient with your own perceived shortcomings. You move into more self-acceptance when you discard the habitual pattern of judging yourself and comparing yourself to others. As you rediscover your divine perfection, you will naturally love yourself more. When your self-love is strong enough, it will be unshakeable even when troublesome life events occur.

Self-Love Is the Key

Set your intention daily to develop even more self-love than you had yesterday. Decide that you will be willing to look closely at those patterns within you that prevent you from being unconditionally loving. Notice when you are overly critical of yourself. Pay attention to how you worry about being enough or being okay. Monitor your self-judgment and the learned habit of self-doubt. Notice when you compare yourself with others and when you set impossible standards for yourself. Listen to your internal dialogue about yourself and watch for words that sound punitive or doubtful.

Approach your inner work with fearlessness, kindness, and patience. During this process of transformation, set your intention to nurture yourself just like a loving mother would do with her young child.

It is not selfish to love yourself and to create a lifestyle that allows you to transform and progress spiritually. In fact, you harm yourself and others when you neglect your own growth.

Discovering how to love yourself is not easy to do. Most people have little training in how to love unconditionally. Our society focuses a lot on love, but it's usually the conditional kind. You learn to be critical of yourself if you don't fit into society's standards of beauty, talents, or wealth. You learn to think of yourself as small and less than others. You learn to look for what's wrong about yourself.

You can discover a new, gentler way to be with yourself. You can change the pattern of your thoughts from self-criticism to acceptance and self-love.

Each time you choose thoughts and actions coming from love, you impact countless other sentient beings with a wave of uplifting energy!

Moving into more self-love helps to facilitate your ascension too.[21] This means that you are raising your frequency. Ascension is a natural process of unfolding for the planet and its life forms.

Because you are alive right now, you have unprecedented opportunities to advance spiritually, in part because of your presence on Earth at this auspicious time. These opportunities begin to present themselves as soon as you have a sincere desire for positive change and take appropriate actions.

---

21 Ascension is a process of spiritual growth during which a person raises his or her frequency of thought and emotion. Humanity today is in the process of raising its frequency out of a fear-based existence. More information about ascension is in this book's glossary.

Unique Opportunities of This Life

If you have been on the path of expanded awareness for some time, you have had glimpses of just how precious this life is for your progress as a soul. Your ancestors did not have the same opportunities that you do. Most likely you have had experiential evidence of some key opportunities not available to your ancestors.

For example, to live today offers the opportunity to have real-time access to world events, providing learning about diverse cultures and new ways of thinking and being. The ability to know about the sufferings and celebrations of people halfway across the world helps you to move into an expanded awareness of the interconnectedness of all life.

Rather than simply focusing on your own problems of the moment, you discover that people everywhere are actually quite similar. Underneath their false egocentric exteriors, people on all continents want the same things—to love and be loved, to be happy, to feel secure, and to feel empowered and appreciated.

When you really get what this means in practice, beyond the words, it can begin to change your life. First, being exposed to humanity in this way and realizing these simple truths can help you to be more accepting of yourself. Developing more self-love is the first ingredient needed to advance spiritually.

With more love and compassion for yourself, you can then extend that outward to others. Remembering that other people are also learning how to love, it is easier for you to be kind regardless of circumstances. This kindness is your love in action.

Timing of the Shift

Many of the old-paradigm structures of humanity's past—including fear-based institutions of control and hierarchical governments—

could not change before now because the consensus reality did not support it.

The consensus reality is formed by individuals over time, each person shaping it by how he or she views the world. A person's views include countless belief systems held within the DNA. These beliefs include those inherited from one's ancestors many generations back, those taken on from the mass consciousness, and those formed from life experiences. All of these reside in the subconscious, out of ordinary awareness.

To change the consensus reality, then, requires that sufficient numbers of people change their worldview—from the inside out—and then apply that new view to actions in the world. This change is within one person at a time, and yet the inner change of even one person can impact countless other people.

On an individual level, the process of awakening into a higher consciousness is often accompanied by feelings of urgency and strong desires to change the status quo. You see things increasingly as they really are. You begin to understand just how out of balance things have become.

A part of you knows that you will need to become more balanced, more whole, and more self-accepting before you can see the world clearly. The next big jump that you are preparing to make in this life can only be taken successfully when you have that clarity.

For this reason, the force of spirit within you is guiding you into avenues of potential transformation and nudging you in the direction of positive change. It is in your highest good, therefore, to discover as much as you can about decoding the messages of spirit, and to develop a deeper and more tangible connection with your inner spiritual guidance.

As part of that, it is essential to become practiced in acting on the intuitive guidance you receive. Know that even the seemingly trivial intuitive messages, when acted upon, can lead you to great leaps in personal growth. Therefore, as you become proficient in decoding the messages of spirit and appropriately act upon them, you can greatly accelerate your personal transformational process.

Energetic Shifts and Physical Symptoms

For those who tend to process energetic shifts physically, this current cycle of change is likely to catalyze physical symptoms. Your body is ascending into a higher frequency of operation. As this occurs, you may experience symptoms, such as periodic aches and pains, sleep disturbances, headaches, a lack of energy, feeling ungrounded or spacey, and unexplained sensitivities to foods and other things.

For example, all of a sudden you can have indigestion or another physical response after eating a food that's long been a part of your diet. Sometimes this will have to do with the food's preparation or with how it's treated with chemicals. At other times, your food reaction will have nothing to do with these things, and your body is simply rejecting what you ate for a host of possible reasons.

On some days, as your body processes unseen energetic shifts, certain foods can set off a physical reaction. If what your body really needed was just a glass of water for hydration, and you ate your favorite rice dish, you could have a reaction. Likewise, if you were starting to feel a bit spacey and ate a calorie-laden snack instead of grounding yourself with a walk barefoot on the grass, you could end up feeling tired instead of centered.

Get into the habit of discovering how to intuit what your body really needs and giving it that. Become practiced in asking yourself questions—in both everyday situations and when experiencing a health crisis. Here's a brief checklist of questions to ask yourself to confirm what your body needs in both types of situations. To ask these, become still for a moment and invite your intuitively guided reason to show you what is most appropriate. Then listen with relaxed, focused attention to determine the optimal course of action.

Tips: Tuning into Your Body

1. Is my condition serious enough to require immediate medical attention?

2. If professional help is warranted, where do I go?

3. Is the discomfort or other physical sensation I'm feeling due to what I recently ingested?

4. If so, what about the food or drink is impacting me (how much I ingested, ingredients, method of preparation, etc.)?

5. If my body is having a physical reaction, what is the optimal remedy (alter the diet, wait a while to eat or drink anything else, do a detoxification or juice fast, etc.)?

6. Is my reaction temporary only, or do I need to stop ingesting something in my diet?

7. How do I take better care of my body to prevent disease and improve my well-being?

8. Does my body need hydration?

9. Does my body need grounding and centering?

10. Does my body need sleep, more rest, or to de-stress?

11. What kind of exercise would help?

12. Does my body need food, and if so, what type is best?

As you progress on the path of personal transformation, you will find that your body requires adjustments in diet, rest, and self-care. You will want to keep up-to-date with what you personally need at each stage. No outside authority can give you the in-the-moment wisdom that your own body can!

Understanding DNA Changes

Your very DNA is changing during humanity's great shift. These DNA changes impact you on all levels—physical, emotional, mental, and spiritual. As this happens, you will benefit from a higher-vibrational diet. In fact, as your vibration increases, your body will have a harder time assimilating the typical Western diet of processed foods and mind-altering chemicals like alcohol and caffeine.

Many of the things you enjoyed eating and drinking in the past will simply be out of harmony with your new energy. If you still eat some of these foods, your body may have difficulty processing them. Similarly, if you have grown accustomed to a very stress-filled life and don't give your body enough rest and quality sleep, you can slow down your own personal transformational process.

As you evolve, you will shed the density of your human form, which includes dysfunctional patterns held within you on a DNA level.[22] Many patterns will drop away as you do personal inner work. Sometimes your shifting will be catalyzed when others around you with a similar pattern begin changing in significant ways, and your readiness to transform facilitates your own leap forward.

One of the biggest changes on the planet today is how rapidly

---

22 Clearing of DNA-level patterns is addressed through energetic healing. Intuitive healers trained to see and work with subtle energy fields are able to identify and clear sabotaging patterns in the DNA. More information about this type of healing can be found in this book's glossary, on the recommended reading list, and on the author's website.

people are able to shed their long-held negative patterns. The releasing still happens in layers. That's because this is the natural way energy moves. As people grow in awareness, the clearing of the layers can happen more quickly. Shedding these layers allows you to hold increasing amounts of light and to greatly accelerate your progress as a soul.

If you did transformational work some time ago, you will sense a difference when applying current energies to today's evolutionary process. New healing methods are available, but it is much more than method; it's really about the energy available to you during these times, and how that energy connects to the higher consciousness that is developing within people.

Things are accelerated with a lighter feel and are accomplished with greater ease. Even old methods, when applied today, can yield much faster results than were possible in earlier times.

Change can be fast, but each person will have his or her own timetable for change. Sometimes, it may appear like no progress is being made. If you're having one of those moments, realize that changes may happen in stages over time. Know the importance of divine timing and learn to develop patience.

As you discover how to be patient and kind with yourself, your road to change becomes less rocky. On some days it may still feel like a roller coaster ride, yet your self-love can help you to have the necessary inner steadiness.

Discovering how to love yourself can be challenging, especially when your parents didn't teach you how. Don't judge them; they didn't know how to love themselves either. They simply did the best they could. In fact, your parents were less prepared than you are for success in these pivotal times of change.

Living with Ongoing Uncertainty

Your parents could not prepare you for the sort of ongoing uncertainty experienced in your modern world. In fact, no generation alive today has the earthly training to fully address the chaos you now face.

To be sure, many of the instructions given to you by parents, teachers, and fellow spiritual pilgrims are now out-of-date. Revisions are needed to address the shift in paradigms.

Realizing this, you may be asking how a person can safely navigate these times of change without a reliable map. Where will the innovative solutions come from? Very simply, they will come from that divine spark inside each person, and they will be born out of a need to create a new and more enlightened world.

Every person on the planet has this divine seed, even if he or she doesn't recognize it or act upon it. It's just waiting to be discovered. Those people now in the process of awakening are creating the needed changes, one alteration at a time. It is happening in increments, reflecting the fluid and moving nature of life itself.

Humans are birthing a radically new consciousness. Because the shifting must first happen within individual people, there often is a delay in seeing measurable changes in the world.

Making Sense of the Shift in Your Own Life

How can you make sense of the shifting in your personal life? The awakening process happens experientially as you move through life—questioning what you see around you, discovering how to understand yourself on very deep levels, and inviting spirit to guide you on a higher road. The higher road is the road connected to the soul rather than the ego. It involves the middle path of spirit rather than the extreme highs and lows of the personality.[23]

---

23   The middle path is one of balance. The Buddha is known for originating the idea of the middle way or path. The idea is to avoid extremes. Humans are conditioned to exist in a world of extreme highs and lows. When a person connects with his or her true spiritual nature, a middle point of balance is found. The Buddha called the middle way the path of wisdom, for it led to his enlightenment.

The journey is a gradual path of discovery, leading you into greater and greater amounts of awareness. What happens over time is that you increasingly travel the higher road of balance and wholeness, and your personality becomes aligned with your soul.

Instead of feeling at war with yourself and the world, you begin to feel increasingly at peace. Experiences of struggle are replaced with letting go and allowing the force of divine grace to create effortless movement and miracles.

It's easier to let go and relax about change when you accept that ongoing uncertainty is a normal part of life. Your intuitively guided reason knows this is the sane approach. However, you've been conditioned by the world to respond to uncertainty with denial, resistance, judgment, and negative emotions, such as anger and fear. It's normal to want to maintain the status quo, even if a superior way were obvious and within reach.

Creating the Life You Want

You have heard that you can create the life you want. If that's really true, why don't you have the life you want right now?

The following explanation will help you to see the gap that often occurs between what you desire and what manifests.

Energy—There is an energy created by your thoughts, emotions, and actions. The energy of doubt tends to cancel the energy of hope. When you are fearful, you draw to yourself situations that fuel even more fear. Being unkind to yourself is an action of sabotage, and you are the one who suffers. Discover how to better understand and manage your own personal energy.

Beliefs—The beliefs you hold about yourself and life are a direct link to what you will experience in the world. These beliefs, sometimes called "agreements" or "values," relate to what you have decided is true. A substantial number of your beliefs are inherited from your ancestral lineage. Your beliefs are recorded within your DNA, silently influencing you. Beliefs about a countless number of topics can impact your ability to make positive and lasting changes. Examples include commonly held beliefs such as "I am not good enough," "Life is full of struggle," and "Ordinary people have no power." When beliefs like these are discovered and cleared from your DNA, you can begin creating more of what you want.

Focus—One key obstacle to creating a joyful life is a lack of focus. The more aware you become of what makes your heart sing, the easier it will be to manifest that in your life. When you are placing your focus on your desires, consider the specifics of what is involved. This includes how your desired life looks, sounds, feels, and tastes. Don't forget to include the other people and circumstances needed for the creation to take form. If you want to change what you are manifesting, consider taking some time to meditate or reflect on your dreams. Invite spirit to help you in this process, providing you with realizations.

Tapping into Your Divine Power

You have grown up in a world dominated by ego-based power and greed. The message from the media is that the people with money and political influence are the ones who have the power. The ordinary person is made to feel powerless over his or her circumstances. Is it any wonder, then, that most people have little awareness of just how powerful they really are? Consider a time when you've felt tangibly connected to spirit, such as in meditation or when in the presence of others also focused on spirit. Experiencing such higher states of consciousness helps to build a bridge to recognizing one's own divine power.[24] As you find out how to get in touch with your natural divine

---

24 Divine power is authentic power that is free of ego, fear, and the need to control. It is the opposite of ego-based power, the type of power that humans have long prized and wielded. Ego-based power involves manipulation, power plays, and the need to be superior and win. Power is energy. To express divine power means that a person is connected to the inner spiritual self and expresses that self and light in the world.

state, you realize that you are connected to an unlimited source of creation. You are then able to see yourself as the divine changemaker that you are.

Finding the Sacred During Turmoil

A part of you knows how powerful you really are. This aspect of self needs no reassurances; it trusts that you are whole and okay, regardless of how much change occurs and what happens in your outer world.

What about those times when you feel overwhelmed by the vast amount of changes and are unsure about how you will cope? Sometimes life gets so rocky that even the most experienced spiritual practitioner can feel disoriented and confused about what to do next. The known path forward may turn into a fork with two or three directions. The path may even appear to be leading to a dead end with no other options in sight. It's clear at that point that there is no going back, yet the path ahead seems an unsolvable mystery. When a course correction is indicated, there are often no directions about how to approach it or how to move in a forward direction. Quite often, the only known factor is a realization that things cannot continue as they are.

When you experience rocky times such as these, remember to let go and step back, allowing for some space between you and the situation. The place you inhabit with your energy can be experienced as sacred regardless of where you might find yourself.

Sacredness is anywhere you are because you are divine. You can discover the sacred and live it regardless of your circumstances. Do not wait for a particular time to connect with the sacredness of life.

Invite in the quality of sacredness, whether you are happy or distressed. Return frequently to your heart and to your own divine wisdom so that you can become practiced in connecting to a sense of stability and sacredness. Doing that frequently when you feel calm will help you to access the same state when you feel unbalanced.

Ask for the intervention of spirit to help you see past confusion and into the truth. Do this when you're feeling blocked in moving forward, confused about where to go next, or simply bored with how things are.

This cycle of human history involves unprecedented amounts of change and chaos. Every human being will be impacted in some way. Previous generations did not contend with this amount of upheaval in a lifetime.

People often are conditioned to believe that if they work hard and live a good life, they will experience smooth sailing. Old notions about everything from relationships and work to health and aging now must be challenged. Belief systems from earlier generations have been passed down in the DNA, and many of them have no validity or application in a world that is shifting into a brand-new paradigm.

To access and remain connected to the sacred during these pivotal times of change is certainly a challenge. It can be done, however, and if you are reading these words, you are on Earth now to do just that.

As you take on this challenge, you are being given an abundance of assistance from the world of spirit. You are being helped, but it's not because you are weak. It is because you are strong, and this is a team effort! This team includes your own inner spiritual guidance and a host of benevolent forces in the spirit world. Do not underestimate the potency of this.

The assistance you receive helps you to let go of old programming and pain. This creates space within you to house more light. As you hold more and more light within yourself, your natural strength shines forth, and there are no limits to what you can create. Your innate goodness comes into manifestation, allowing you to experience the world in a more light-filled way.

Tips: Staying Sane in Chaos

The following are some guidelines that will help you to stay sane regardless of how crazy everything around you becomes.

1. Remember to step back from any stressful situation long enough to breathe. Go into your heart and reassess it from the perspective of your intuitively guided reason. Even if you're in an emergency situation, you can still stop the panic for a few seconds and connect with spirit's wisdom. In fact, in emergency situations, it's essential that you do this. Otherwise, you may go into fear and separate yourself from the intuitive guidance you need to navigate successfully.

2. Resist the temptation to make people or situations so important. Whatever a person in your life is doing or not doing is rarely a matter of life or death. Tell yourself that nothing is *that* important; refuse to take things so seriously. Ask for divine guidance to show you the truth of all circumstances and to give you clarity about people and events. Ask to see the lighter side of situations, and for humor and laughter to be a part of each day. Make it a habit to notice things that make you smile; you can't smile and be in panic mode at the same time!

3. Remember that when you are under stress, it is important to slow down. Your body will need more sleep and more relaxation time to compensate for your stress. Your mind will function with more clarity when you cross a few things off your to-do list and declare a time-out to reflect on what is truly important. When you do this, it is not wasted time.

It is very useful to slow down. Your added reflection time helps you to connect with intuitive insights about your dilemma. Having more quiet time gives you space, and with that space you can notice spirit moving in the happenstance of your life. The divine, in response to your prayers and intentions, will speak to you in countless ways, giving you a clear picture to replace the foggy one you had before.

4. Consider that there is a brand-new way to approach wellness and aging. You live in a time when discoveries are being made daily about the aging process and the real causes of disease. We all have the potential for the longest life span humanity has known in modern history. If you have elderly parents or grandparents, some of the current scientific discoveries may sound like science fiction to their generation. Keep in mind that many amazing inventions and scientific discoveries of humanity's past sounded crazy when first unveiled. Experts and the media often labeled as impossible many inventions that were later proven to be quite workable. Examples include machines that can fly (airplanes) and electrical speech machines (telephones). In today's laboratories, scientists have identified specific genes within human DNA that are responsible for longevity. Researchers have also concluded that people carry within their DNA ancestral belief systems that can impact their experience of aging and growing older. These discoveries open up a whole new way to look at the human body, how it ages, and what can be done to live healthier and longer. While all of this has great potential during these times of a growing senior citizen population, it remains the task of each person to address and clear DNA-level patterns that have been inherited. These limiting patterns include belief systems from ancestors who believed growing old

necessarily involved things like pain, loss, aloneness, and dependence.

5. Be open to the new and the undiscovered. Set your intention to consider a wider range of options than you've ever dreamed of before! Creativity occurs when you travel into new territory with an open mindset and a willingness to do things a different way. Your path may look very different from the one others travel. In fact, if you find that your way begins to look too much like that of the mainstream consciousness, consider that adjustments may need to be made. You haven't been born at this time in history to sit comfortably in the old-paradigm ways. You aren't here to run away from the chaos either. You are here to make waves that will break open new vistas as they meet the shore. To see what this means for you personally, take a few moments right now and invite your heart's wisdom to speak to you when contemplating the following example.

※

Process: Imagining a Brand-New World

Think of the Earth as a huge spaceship on a voyage through space. You are one of the crew.

When you started your voyage, there were lots of rules in place, made up by people who had learned some very old-fashioned ways of navigation and travel. Their conditioning led them to see life and possibilities in very limited ways. One example is the hierarchy you see on the ship.

A majority of those navigating the ship are fascinated by ego-based power. Their attraction to this archaic method of relating is connected to past conditioning involving control. Most of those on board the ship have no idea that they chose to take part in the voyage or that they can change direction in midcourse. They are simply along for the ride, wanting to make it the best trip possible.

At some point on the voyage, you woke up to the nonsense you saw and realized that there was actually a purpose to it all. You could see that there was a divine purpose for each person on the spaceship too. Your heart told you that everyone there was connected and that the group would need to work in unity to steer the ship in the most favorable direction.

Over time, you began connecting with others on board who also started remembering their divine heritage.

In recent times, as this ship speeds through space, you have become aware of potential threats to a successful mission. The climate on board has become unstable, and no one can agree about what to do. Supplies of key resources, including food and water, are uncertain. Fights among those on the spaceship are a regular occurrence, and people can't seem to agree with one another.

Every day there is some kind of craziness or fear-based energy to contend with. Growing numbers of people on board are restless, dissatisfied, afraid, and downright angry.

You notice that most people will believe anything an outside authority figure tells them is true. That includes what they hear on the news channels and from the ship's captains.

You sense that the ship soon will pass through another magnificent window of energy with great potential to transform consciousness. There have been a number of these windows so far. You are enthusiastic about this, focusing your intent and energy to help accelerate the positive changes. You know that each person on board has a role to play, and you are determined to play your role regardless of what others do.

You have an inner confidence that the shift you seek is not only possible but attainable. You have that confidence because of an intimate relationship you have developed with spirit. You have discovered how to step back from the chaos, go into your heart, and discover the truth of each situation as it unfolds. This gives you great peace.

Coming Back to What You Know

In the days ahead, when the world seems to be spinning out of control, reflect back on this idea of the Earth traveling through space. When you remember to view the chaos and shifting in this big-picture way, you have the fuel to step into your authentic power. You acknowledge that your choices decide what you will experience next. You embrace your role as a divine changemaker.

Chapter 4

Choosing a Light-Filled Path During Crisis

The world is in crisis on multiple levels, and you are likely wondering how long the instability will last.

How do you understand what the global disarray and challenges mean for you personally? What do you need to know in order to find your balance during these chaotic times? How can you consistently choose a light-filled path during crisis? The answers to these questions are explored here.

You live during times when local dilemmas can escalate quickly into global ones. During the last two generations, the world has gotten smaller, with a sense of planetary connectedness not experienced before. The sources of your food and other consumer goods are multiple. A crisis within a key country like the United States can soon spread into multiple countries. The growing list of problems includes imbalances in how power is wielded and disparities within key sectors, such as finance, natural resources, health care, shelter, and education.

Shift in Global Power

Adding to the complexity of these issues is the shift in global power. Just twenty years ago, there were only eight countries negotiating to resolve thorny issues involving the world economy. Today, the G8 has become the G20, a group of twenty superpowers.[25] That means lots more players, and country leaders oftentimes want different things. Even when it's clear that the stakes are high and agreements should be reached, politics and special interests frequently lead to stalled or failed summits.

Countries may bicker. Citizens may bristle. The world's overhaul, however, is fully under way. No one knows the final outcome, but it will involve significant foundational changes in how people coexist.

People across the world are feeling the effects of the mass reconfiguration. Although all sectors will eventually get an overhaul, it was the financial system that came up for review first. The catalyst was the US financial market collapse in the fall of 2008, which led to a global economic meltdown, impacting citizens on every continent.

The financial system got the spotlight first in part because of how interwoven it is within society; it impacts everything else. The other systems, of course, are also having their reviews—some of them in tandem with money—and yet each of them will be affected by how the key issue of money is addressed.

Because of how dysfunctional humanity's relationship with money has become, it will not be a quick fix. Healing remedies are now being put in place worldwide by people, businesses, and countries, but these are works in progress. As we put them in motion and implement them in our lives, the remedies will become a medicine for many related dysfunctions that prevent people from being whole and empowered.

---

25 The G8 and G20 are political conferences attended by finance ministers and central bank governors from the world's highly developed economies. The number of countries represented has grown over time to be more inclusive. These superpowers meet to discuss global economic problems and related issues. More information about these groups is in this book's glossary.

The Tipping Point—Economic Crisis

Although comparisons have been made between this most recent financial crisis and America's Great Depression of the 1930s, today's economic predicament is quite different. The world has reached a tipping point, and the out-of-balance structures will need to be addressed in order for humanity to move forward. Band-Aids will not suffice; the global distress cannot be resolved through local measures that are isolationist, protectionist, or elitist.

What you are witnessing and experiencing is part of the great reconfiguration under way as humanity births a new-paradigm world. This crisis is really not personal, yet it certainly can feel quite personal when your income, your bank account, and even your sense of long-term financial security appear to be uncertain. Separate from this, you may well have suffered economic losses on a number of fronts since the fall of 2008.

In addition, you may be dealing with a variety of other types of loss, some already manifest and some possible in your near future. This is like a magnification factor, potentially heightening conscious and subconscious fears of the unknown. You may even feel anxiety when simply contemplating the prospect of how much really needs to change on the planet.

These feelings of anxiety and loss can be overwhelming and can trigger a sudden episode of depression. Even if you don't typically become depressed, you can feel like a black cloud is obscuring your happiness, hopes, and dreams.

A wise part of you knows that change and loss are normal elements of the creation process on Earth. You likely have witnessed or directly experienced countless losses, big and small, throughout your life. You have probably developed coping mechanisms for handling loss. Your wise self knows that the changes happening now are a part of the great shift in consciousness that you are here to help create. The road is rocky, but it leads to a place from which you can soar!

Opportunity of This Unique Window

Given this unique window of time, right now is an excellent moment to contemplate and perhaps update your responses to change and loss.

During these historic moments, you have an opportunity to catapult into a more enlightened state. Your ability to shift out of past limiting patterns and to remember the truth of who you are is profound beyond measure, especially in this particular cycle. The acceleration and magnitude of what is before you cannot be quantified in human terms. Never before has there been so much cosmic assistance or such a collective global shifting in consciousness as you will witness during this window of time. Therefore, taking a close look at your relationship with change will be well worth the effort it takes.

If you lived at the seashore and it was hurricane season, you would naturally want to take precautions to protect your home and family. You and your neighbors would certainly consider boarding up the house and packing the family car with provisions as needed.

Similarly, right now with the massive reconfiguration happening in plain view, you and other people are being nudged to discover more evolved responses to change.

The typical human being has become like a fat man wearing a suit three sizes too small and trying to fit his oversize body into a standard-size chair designed for people of his grandparents' generation. This man, to be comfortable and healthy, has a number of options, each one of them involving some sort of change. The key for this man is *how* he approaches change. This has everything to do with consciousness and where—literally and energetically—the man sits in each moment as he responds to the happenstance of his personal life and the events of his world.

The energy of how the man sits is the key. The man can choose what sort of cushion he sits on, impacting how he sees and experiences his world. However, this ordinary man tends to forget that he has this choice. Perhaps he simply has not learned that he even has a choice. After all, this vital training is nonexistent in most cultures focused on outer-world success.

Like that man in the too-tight suit, you are faced with choices that will necessitate changing your thinking. It will be your view of situations that will determine your response to difficulties and your ability to find peace.

Choose Your Cushion

If you sit on a cushion of fear and hate, you will face great obstacles during these times of massive change. The old-paradigm ways involving fear and blame will not get you where you want to go. Judging yourself and others for how things are will put you in a negative energetic spiral. You will feel worse instead of better when you become judgmental.

Expecting others to rescue you or to magically fix your problems will leave you feeling even more disempowered. Viewing the disassembly of your broken systems as disaster will add to your sense of loss and hopelessness.

Each person, to thrive in the coming months and years, will need to discover more innovative and light-filled ways to respond to what is happening.

Process: Checking in with Your Heart's Wisdom

For you personally, that means getting to know yourself more intimately. If you think you already know yourself, remember that the path of self-awareness is an ongoing process of discovery. To succeed at the more advanced levels, one must be willing to go deeper and to look at oneself in new ways. This sometimes means revisiting topics that seem like a rehash of old news.

Consider opening yourself to some radically new options and ideas. Check in with your heart's wisdom. Begin the flow of a more positive energy that will begin shifting your current experience. Here are some examples.

1. Decide today that you will find a fresh approach to working with change and loss.

2. Ask your higher wisdom to help you become more comfortable with the process of change and to stay more positive when you lose things and people dear to you.

3. Invite in the help of spirit to lovingly point out unproductive responses to change.

4. Imagine or visualize regularly throughout your day that you are surrounded and supported by a benevolent universe.

Remember that the needed changes will come from people like you who make different choices and find their center amidst the chaos.

A part of you, existing in the future, has already done this. Call upon this part of yourself now as often as you like as you travel the uncertain road ahead.

Your Personal Response to Financial Crisis

As you are investigating more evolved responses to change, remember to include your views about money.

Regardless of how you are impacted by the world economic predicament, you will want to use the opportunity of today's rocky financial situation to develop new approaches to money. After all, the world's financial situation is in devastating disarray because of a need to totally revamp humanity's relationship with money.

Changes are needed on a large scale involving the masses, but also on a very personal level. To positively impact the whole of the planet and use the opportunity of the planet's financial upheavals for your greatest spiritual advancement, you will want to explore your relationship with money. As part of that, you will want to update your DNA-level programming about money with more enlightened perspectives.

How DNA Patterns Affect You

All people, regardless of culture and income level, carry limiting belief systems about money in their DNA. It doesn't matter whether you have one million dollars in the bank or whether you live paycheck to paycheck. The beliefs will be there in your DNA, and all it takes is some sort of catalyst to make them operable.

For many people, the current economic chaos is that catalyst. Examples include concerns about where the economy is headed, personal financial losses, and fears about coping with unknowable factors. Any of these things can trigger the playing out of limiting belief systems about money.

Where do these beliefs come from? Many of them you inherit from your lineage. They come from ancestors who might have lived a very long time ago, perhaps during a depression or famine. Some of your ancestors could have taken vows of poverty during their lifetimes. Still other beliefs come from the mass consciousness, meaning that great numbers of people collectively believe the same thing.

All people carry outmoded beliefs in their DNA, representative of old-world perspectives about money and a host of other topics. Most of the limiting belief systems involving money are fear-based. They include ideas involving lack, struggle, and never having enough.

Medicine has not yet developed a test to prove that you have these beliefs, but they are there. They exist within the subconscious mind, and the beliefs affect how you respond to crises such as the economic meltdown. These beliefs are like dinosaur worldviews that silently influence how you react to financial uncertainty, causing you to worry and to doubt that you will be okay. They put you into survival mode, a low-frequency state of consciousness that blocks your ability to envision success and to manifest abundance.

These old worldviews of money are outmoded and unworkable. That is the reason for the collapse that you are seeing now. Revolutionary approaches are needed to create new-paradigm models for working with money.

Humanity's Relationship with Money

The overhaul of humanity's relationship with money is a rather broad topic relating to a complex web of elements. These include the obvious things like resources, markets, and business. However, there is much more to the picture.

It is shortsighted to view the international crisis as an impersonal problem affecting only the stock markets, financial institutions, and investment funds. To be sure, you will experience the world's economic predicament differently if you don't have a retirement account or other types of financial investments. Likewise, you will have a different impact if you now have a steady job or a regular source of income from a pension, rental property, or other source.

People Everywhere Have a Role to Play

The key here is to remember that all of humanity is connected. There is an intricate set of links between countries, markets, the diverse populations of people, and the businesses that provide the services and products that you consume.

Remember that humanity and the Earth are in the midst of a massive paradigm shift, the likes of which has never been experienced before. People everywhere are being affected on countless levels, including in ways that cannot be sensed or seen. Whether you live in America or some other place across the globe, you are part of the mix of change.

As society is reconfigured, outmoded approaches to money will be replaced with more enlightened views. Today's concepts about success—now tied in a linear way to how much money or power someone has—will shift into a new model. As you and others redefine what success means, you help to transform the old models.

The changes that you want will come about through efforts of individual people like you who are focused on creating a more enlightened world. Some of these people you will elect to office. Others will be found at the helm of businesses and institutions involved with progressive approaches. Still others will be leaders of private oversight committees charged with the overhaul of broken systems.

Each person has a role to play. There is so much at stake on the planet right now. The world's economic crisis is not something that you want to leave in the hands of bureaucrats, elected officials, and other authority figures.

To give your power to others—without also taking an active role—is an old-paradigm approach. This will not get you and the world out of the quicksand of financial collapse.

What You Can Do

What can you do? The following are just a few of your options. Each one of them adds to your potency to create the kind of world that you want. When you exercise a combination of the options, you catapult yourself into the forefront of a revolution in how humans relate to each other and to the world.

Your Role as a Divine Changemaker

Embrace your role as a divine changemaker. That means moving into your authentic power, being willing to look at what is going on, and then taking actions based upon what you find. It also means taking actions that reflect your own truth rather than someone else's truth. To do that requires more courage than the everyday person typically expresses.

Instead of complaining and viewing circumstances as something unfortunate, use the opportunities of the chaos to create what you want. Trust that you can do this and refuse to buy into doubts that tell you otherwise.

Educate Yourself about the Big Picture

During a world crisis, educate yourself about the big picture. Look beyond the mainstream media newscasts and discover the underlying reasons for what is happening. As you look at the modern-day financial crisis, become educated about the history of humanity's experiences with money, power, and control.

Investigate what has worked and what has failed during past cycles of financial turmoil. When investigating this, look beyond the oftentimes incomplete historical data presented in the media.

In order for humanity to shift into the higher-vibrational ways of being, people must be willing and able to gain awareness from the past. That includes an understanding of how hate and greed have fueled the growth of wars, dictators, protectionism, prejudice, and monopolies.

Let the Past Be the Past

The key to shifting into the higher frequencies is to stay firmly in the present. Obsessing about difficult past events will not help you to create more light-filled experiences. Complaining about slow progress will keep your perspective limited and block your ability to manifest something new that is more positive. Focusing on what you did not like in the past will keep your mind fixed on the negative. Instead shift your thoughts to what you prefer to manifest, giving those things your full attention.

Avoid Fantasy Thinking

It is vital to avoid fantasy thinking. This is not easy, especially when you live in a world that is enmeshed in illusions of all shapes and sizes.

People around you are projecting their fantasies into conversations. The media saturate your senses with fictional tales and superstitious prophecies. A deeper level of questioning will be needed in this cycle if you are to stay sane. Practice being the observer of yourself and your reality as often as you can, inviting a larger view that can steer you out of fantasy and into truth.

Take Better Care of You

Of any cycle in your life to date, this one requires better self-care and being more awake to yourself. What does that mean? It means putting into action the library of research that you have inside of you from years of hearing about wellness and healthy living. If you sense that there are gaps in your knowledge about creating and sustaining well-being, take responsibility for keeping up-to-date.

To practice good self-care means paying close attention to your body and what it tells you. To do that successfully, you must discover how to listen deeply to your body's messages and develop skill in interpreting your body's communications. The next step is acting on what your body tells you; it takes practice and retraining to do this well.

Your conventional training tells you to reach for a painkiller when you wake up with a headache. Pain is your body's red-alert system, showing you that something is out of balance. Rather than immediately reaching for the painkiller, investigate the underlying causes of your pain. With that understanding, you may still take the medicine, but you will do so with a greater awareness of what your body needs. By having this information, you will be able to discover other remedies that will be more than short-term Band-Aids. That is how you honor your body and take better care of you.

Good self-care also means becoming more aware of your thoughts, feelings, and actions as you go about your day. It means making different types of decisions about what you will or will not do with your energy. That includes setting healthier boundaries.

Put Spirit First

In order to skillfully navigate the shift, you will need to put spirit first. This may mean reprioritizing some things. You have learned to focus more on outer-world concerns and on what you need to do, be, or get; you have also learned to seek answers from others before you act. The world offered you little training in how to access your spiritual self, which is so vital to your wholeness.

You are now moving out of your conventional conditioning and discovering how to more fully integrate your spiritual self with your human self. The two are meant to be joined. This was always true. Your path as a divine changemaker involves the art of joining these two energies.

Benefit from Understanding the Success of Others

Discover examples of individuals who have prospered and created innovative humanitarian approaches during both boom times and depressions. Remember that the media typically place more focus on failures and crises than on successes and other news with a positive spin. However, if you look for examples of past successes, you indeed will find them.[26] You will find inspiration by discovering how ordinary people, facing insurmountable odds during hard times, were able to thrive. You can connect with a new way to look at your own successes and failures by learning about the ups and downs of others.

Identify Your Patterns of Self-Sabotage

Become more aware of your self-sabotaging patterns, which include your belief systems involving money. To become more awake to your subconscious limiting programs is the first step in becoming free of them.

One way to begin getting in touch with limiting beliefs held in your subconscious is to pay attention to what you think to yourself

---

26 Success is seldom as instant or simple as it appears. Most people who succeed do so when they face their obstacles and find creative ways to overcome them. Throughout history, people encountered numerous obstacles and failures before becoming successful. For example, Bill Gates dropped out of Harvard and failed at his first business before launching Microsoft. Albert Einstein, the genius known today for shifting how the world views physics, did not speak until he was four and did not read until he was seven. Inventor Thomas Edison was told as a child that he was too dumb to learn anything. As an adult, Edison was fired from two jobs. Later on, as an inventor, he failed a thousand times at inventing the light bulb before finally succeeding. Harry Potter author J. K. Rowling became a huge success after being nearly penniless and living on welfare.

and say out loud. In particular, notice your negative thoughts about things in the past, present, or future. What you think repeatedly will give you clues about the themes of the belief systems in your DNA.

For example, how often do you say to yourself that you never have enough money to pay your bills? What do you say to yourself when contemplating your cherished dreams? Do you think that you will be able to achieve what your heart tells you is your life's work?

※

Tips: Moving from Fear to Abundance

Begin to face and examine your fears and doubts involving money, prosperity, and success. Those include doubts about your personal financial stability as well as fears about the world's economy. Refuse to let these life-defeating thoughts determine what you say and do next.

When fears and doubts aren't fully examined, they begin to take on a life of their own. Remember that what you focus on repeatedly, you will create more of! If you allow yourself, for even brief periods of time daily, to buy into the fear and allow it to fuel your next thoughts, feelings, and actions, you join the ranks of the masses that unknowingly are creating more suffering for themselves.

Your challenge is to remain positive. Make a conscious effort each day to reinforce within your own mind the new kind of world you want to create, have, and live in.

How can you do this when the world tells you that everything is falling apart?

Use these remedies to stay positive during challenging times.
- Persistence
- Patience
- Believing in yourself

- An ability to screen out society's fear-based negative spin
- A willingness to change
- Ongoing inner work to clear self-sabotaging patterns in your DNA
- Surrounding yourself with others who also are focused on creating a new-paradigm world

Focus on Conscious Creation

Consider, daily, the specifics of what you want to create. The more conscious you can become about what it is you want, the greater the likelihood that you will be able to create it.

Don't limit ideas to today either. Think long-term. Keep your imagination and wonder alive by contemplating a new-paradigm world that you know will feel like home.

Don't try to make your dreams fit in with society's doomsday mindset. Reach beyond that rigid view and into a higher way of thinking. Trust that you can create something brand new!

Decide, daily, what kind of energy you want to experience, setting your intentions for what you will manifest and how you will treat yourself and others. Visualize yourself experiencing what you have intended. As you do this, connect with the feeling of this experience as though it's happening right now. Acknowledge how this makes you feel.

Give Your Gifts

Give yourself permission to express yourself in an empowered way.

That includes giving your gifts—whatever they are—without hesitation and without being attached to outcomes. An example of a gift is the ability to have empathy with animals. Remind yourself that the gifts residing within you are meant to be given. Let go of concerns that your gifts aren't enough.

Decide to give them even if no one but you understands their value. Remember that when you allow your precious light-filled energy to circulate in everyday activities, you are helping to create the kind of world that you want to inhabit.

Remind yourself of these things daily. Accept the power you really have to change the course of your own life and the future of the Earth.

Remember the Time Frame

What you do right now is pivotal to your successful positioning during the coming decades. You are creating a new way to view and live life. There are planetary forces at work and also factors that will be personal to you.

As the unworkable elements of society come to light worldwide, countries will be exploring new types of options that would have been unthinkable a decade ago.

On a personal level, your success will come from facing your challenges when they arise and discovering new-paradigm solutions. You will have opportunities to pinpoint and resolve many longstanding issues during this cycle. The key here is staying in the present and addressing what is there when it is in front of you. This means avoiding the temptation to procrastinate. It means developing more self-trust and more in-the-moment connection with your inner wisdom.

Today's Unprecedented Challenges

Remember that you live in unprecedented times. No previous economic downturn, controls on your freedoms, or the sagging reputation of a major superpower such as America could prepare people for what's happening now.

The current financial crisis is not just another challenge or a situation your old-world leaders can resolve with bigger and bigger Band-Aids. Also, regardless of the people you elect to office, they will face tough challenges as they attempt to restore balance and prosperity.

The changes that you heard were coming are rapidly unfolding, one right after another. Though no one knew exactly what these changes would look like, there was a realization that the outmoded would need to be disassembled to make way for the new.

Some of the changes you are now seeing may seem to be sudden, but they have been building for a very long time. The world economic crisis is just one example. Because the world's financial systems are integrally connected to society's other outmoded structures, the economy is the first to have the spotlight. Other sectors will also come up for review and reconfiguration. These include energy, climate change, planetary resources (including water, food, and forests), treatment of animals, education, religion, health care, the aging population, business models, politics, and the military.

It will take some time for the economic overhaul to take place. Some of the outmoded approaches to money have come to light. More of humanity is now aware that a lot must change. However, it will take time to sort out the complexities and find a new sort of balance. Meanwhile, countries, businesses, and everyday people will be in reeducation mode.

As part of your own reeducation, contemplate how you can update your views to reflect the new-paradigm reality. Start with money, because that is the area under the microscope now.

Refuse to go along with pack mentality on this or any topic, even if the views come from people whom you respect. Come up with your own ideas.

Punish the Wealthy?

As an example, there are those who delight in seeing the wealthy lose their great fortunes. Wishing others bad luck and suffering is not an enlightened perspective. This view is rooted in hate, jealousy, comparison, competition, and punishment. You don't want to fuel more of these fear-based approaches.

Do not try to punish those who have money; do not envy their success. Instead, work to change consciousness on the planet. When those with great wealth choose the spiritual path, they will naturally want to share what they have with others. Only those in ignorance of how to apply the spiritual laws of abundance hoard and take what belongs to others.

You do not want to perpetuate the oppressive cycles of punishment humanity has had in force for thousands of years. Punishing the rich does nothing for the poor.

Keep in mind that some of the world's wealthiest people are also the most inventive, having been willing to take risks, to live a dream no one believed in, to come up with something new, and to magnetize the support of others in seeing their dream come true. Discover how to embody some of these positive approaches in your own life.

A New Model for Success

Remember your role as a divine changemaker. You are one of the pioneers involved in creating new models for how life is lived. One of the models in need of overhaul is the one involving success.

People have learned over many generations to associate success with linear concepts involving climbing ladders, rigid goal setting, and advancing past others to feel important. This old-fashioned view is based on the illusion of lack and insufficiency. These reference points have kept people enslaved in cycles of endlessly seeking more. The greed fostered in such an approach can never be satisfied.

This dream of success needs to be challenged and changed.

Changing Your Dream of Success

Changing the dream of success will happen first on an individual level, as increasing numbers of people begin to question what it really means to be powerful in the world. The questioning may come after a job loss or other career setback. It may come from exhaustion or ill health that can accompany climbing to the top.

To change your own dream of success will require more than simply asking the basic questions that have been asked in recent years by a growing number of unsatisfied people. These questions include things like "Why don't I have what others have?" and "What is holding me back?" and "Why has all of my hard work not paid off?" These questions typically come from a reference point of competition, doubt, insufficiency, and lack of clarity about one's real purpose and spiritual path. This view is rooted in limiting belief systems that impact how people view and respond to life.

People asking these ill-founded questions oftentimes don't have the larger view of why they were born during these pivotal times. For those who do understand this bigger-picture view, there can still be lack of clarity about their lives and how to move into more fortunate circumstances.

※

Tips: Remap Your Path to Success

What are some productive questions to ask so that you can understand your path to success? And what is the way to most appropriately ask these questions? Here are five tips to remap your path to success.

1. **State of mind and energy flow**—Be aware of your state of mind and energy flow when inquiring about your success. Asking questions about success when you are tired, hungry, or depressed will not give

you the same level of clarity you will have when feeling energetically balanced and in positive spirits.

2. **Whole-brain approach**—Be sure to invoke your intuitively guided reason and your heart's wisdom when asking questions. A whole-brain approach involving both left-brain logic and right-brain intuition will lead you to the greatest understanding of life's questions.

3. **Divine timing**—Keep divine timing in mind. Asking the same question over and over, simply because you want to know, is not the most productive approach. It is a universal principle that truths are revealed at the appropriate time and not a moment sooner. Also, remember that divine timing is fluid and not linear.

Here is an example. Just because you earlier intuitively sensed that a certain success would come by next year, when that date arrives and the success hasn't materialized, it doesn't mean that your information was incorrect. When this happens, it can mean many things.

What you predicted may have been pushed further into the future because of a host of factors, some of which may have little or nothing to do with you.

Another possibility is that what you wanted may no longer be your best option. Buying a new home is an example. Imagine that your dream home is nearby, and you take initial steps to purchase it. You are certain that this is the perfect home. There are delays in concluding the purchase. Meanwhile, you receive a promotion at work and discover you will relocate to a new city. As part of your promotion, you receive relocation expenses and financial help in purchasing a dream home in the new location. You discover that something even more wonderful than your original plan is manifesting effortlessly!

4. **Looking deeper**—Remember when asking your questions to follow up any unclear or unsatisfactory answers with additional inquiry. So much of how you will progress is in your questions. Skillful means are needed to get the clarity you seek. If, for example, you ask a yes-

no type of question, and the response confuses or disappoints you, ask other types of questions to inquire deeper. The more that you investigate beneath the surface, the closer to the truth you will be.

5. **Questions for self-inquiry**—Consider questions such as these in order to understand your path to success.

- What part of my self-image prevents me from acknowledging the success I already am?
- What are some of my gifts that are a natural part of my success?
- What belief systems do I subconsciously hold that block my success?
- How can I make better use of divine timing and other opportunities in my life?
- Who are the people in my life who have helped mold my ideas of success?
- Who in my current life is a positive influence on my being successful in the new-paradigm world?
- Who in my life is a negative influence on that success?
- What habits could I change to be more successful?
- What skills could I develop to be more successful?
- How does my attitude of gratitude impact my forward movement?
- Who or what in my outside world have I given my power to, blocking my success?
- What am I not seeing about myself, others, or the world that gets in my way?

When You Question Your Progress

When you find yourself questioning your progress, step back for a moment and remind yourself that you are on Earth at this time to birth a revolution on both the personal and the global level. This involves a fundamental transformation of how life is lived.

Success is but one of countless concepts and structures up for a radical overhaul. As you and others personally address and reconfigure these things, you help to create a significant ripple effect of positive transformation in your outer world. As you heal yourself, you help to heal your own lineage and the connected lineages of humanity. Do not underestimate the significance of this—it is vast.

When you have moments of doubting, know that much *is* shifting, including things that you cannot yet see. The grand shift of all time is unfolding, and that is what these times are about.

A Quantum Shift for You and Humanity

Humanity as a collective can evolve quickly in a seemingly brief span of time—just as individuals can. The quantum shift into higher consciousness can be achieved when a critical mass of aware individuals holds and acts upon enlightened views.

Today there are more people alive on Earth than at any other time in history. An awakening is occurring on every continent. More and more people are shifting out of old ways of thinking. There is a growing desire to move away from fear-based reality and into a more light-filled existence.

Once a significant number of people embrace the same probable light-filled future, that outcome is more likely to happen on a planetary scale.

It is very useful to focus each day on the more enlightened world you want to birth. Keep in mind that there are plenty of people who focus daily on doomsday views involving terrorism, devastating Earth changes, Armageddon, mass starvation, and governmental oppression. You can create a much different probability with dramatically softer effects, bypassing the alternative harsh realities.

Trust that humanity will find a way to reconfigure the unworkable to something very effective!

This is a precious time frame for you as a spiritual being. Decide each day that you will utilize this great crossroads of humanity to progress spiritually and to live the principles that you have spoken about for so long.

The ideas of the new-paradigm world must be more than mere words. You must incorporate your cherished principles into your life and act on them. You have an abundance of assistance from your higher self, and from fellow travelers on the path of light, to achieve what you were born to do.[27]

---

27 Sometimes referred to as higher wisdom, the higher self can access clarity and higher understanding. In some circles, the term is used as a synonym for true self. The person's higher self is also viewed as the divine spark within. This relates to that part of a person naturally at one with the divine. It is often differentiated from the lower self or personality, the part of a person conditioned by habitual patterns.

Chapter 5
The Art of Making Choices

Imagine that you could step into the shoes of your future self in 2025. In that future you will exist within the reality of choices you are making now. Your present reality in 2025 will have been formed by your past choices.

The idea that your past choices help to create your future is not a new concept. Quite often, though, you can forget this principle when in the midst of personal and planetary chaos. With today's accelerated energies, it's common to feel overwhelmed and challenged by the constant lineup of choices you are asked to make. A still greater challenge is that you have learned to distrust yourself and to look to outside authority figures for answers. This is one of the biggest dilemmas for all of humanity.

To understand this on a practical level, it is helpful to demystify the process of choice.

Demystifying the Process of Choice

Each day you are making choices and setting into motion a cascade of events that will determine your future.

As an example, consider that one day you leave your home a bit later than usual. You are on your way to an appointment and do not want to be late. You may find yourself in heavier traffic at this later time, and perhaps you decide to take an alternate route to your destination.

Along the way, you discover a shortcut that you had never seen before. Not only do you make up the time, but you feel more relaxed traveling this other way, and you enjoy the different scenery.

The alternate, less-traveled street has more trees and less concrete. Because there are fewer cars here, you are able to slow down your mind enough to notice the colorful flowers on the side of the road. These flowers are also in bloom on your normal route, but somehow you pay more attention to them here. Seeing the yellow ones especially seems to brighten your mood.

When you arrive for your appointment, you feel more fresh and creative, having had a change of scenery and a respite from the usual stress.

Later on when you have time to reflect on your day, you realize that you had been traveling your old route for ten years! In one moment, you had made a different choice. You had paid attention to an intuitive nudge to change course, being open to how things would unfold and letting go of your old habit long enough to experience something brand new.

Imagine what would have happened if you had chosen to travel the same way you had traveled for ten years.

It is much easier to go with what you know, what you are sure of, and what feels familiar—right? That is the habitual response. You know the route already. You know that it will lead to your destination. Besides, it just feels comfortable because you are used to it.

On that day, if you had ignored your intuition to change course and had opted for the comfort of your regular route, what you created would have been based on past conditioning. Your choice would have reflected your habitual route.

This is an example of making choices with a past perspective. People do this all the time and then wonder why they continue to experience what they did in the past. Your inner wisdom is aware of a much bigger picture, however, so it can guide you in present time to the most appropriate choices.

New Times, New Choices

You are now living in much different energies than before. The cells of your body are registering quantum leaps of energetic shifting, even if you can't yet wrap your mind around what it all means. In some ways your life experiences may appear similar to those you had last year or even several years ago. Some of the same people may be in your life, you may live in the same house or city, and you may still be focusing on manifesting some of the same dreams you had for yourself before.

Although some things may appear to be the same, the new paradigm is coming into reality, and with it a radically new approach to life. A new way to look at choice making and choices is needed for these times.

To embody this new approach and apply it in your life, you must become present and conscious when making choices, recognizing the power you have to create in the world. Choices involving the use of force, blame, and victimhood will only accentuate any disharmony you feel in these uncertain times. Likewise, to be really empowered now, you must be willing to break free of habitual responses, judgment about past choices, and worries about your future options.

Choice and the Divine Changemakers

If you are reading these words, you are here to help create a brand-new template for choice making. The old one is unworkable.

As a divine changemaker, you are here to bring light and consciousness into choice making. You do this as you make the needed changes—first within yourself, and then in your world—so that you and humanity can move into an enlightened consciousness.

To change how you make choices will not be easy, but you can do it. In fact, your DNA is encoded to take on this task! Part of your challenge will be the other encodings—also in your DNA—that can sabotage your best efforts. Some of these are belief systems.

Beliefs about Choice in Your DNA

You carry a host of belief systems within your DNA that relate to individual choice. Some of them are inherited from your ancestors. Others are on a mass-consciousness level, meaning that they are in the field of energy created by all of humanity. Everyone is connected with that field, which changes over time to reflect new worldviews.

Belief systems that you will find on the mass-consciousness level of your DNA are those relating to ideas of a predetermined fate and an unchangeable destiny. These types of beliefs can be traced to long-ago times when the masses were convinced by those in rigid religious orders and other societal power structures that the average person had no power to create. People were taught that they had to accept what some outside force decreed was their fate. When people accepted these teachings as true, they formed limiting beliefs that became an integral part of how they experienced life. These beliefs, passed down through the generations, are in your DNA today.

Belief systems like these silently influence you as you make choices. Because they are stored within your subconscious, outside of everyday awareness, you likely don't know that they exist.

On a conscious level, you may believe that you are at the helm of your own ship, able to create the future that you want. Simultaneously, on a mass-consciousness level, you may also believe things like the following.

- The end of the world is coming.
- God will decide who survives the shift.
- Once the signs of Armageddon appear, there is nothing that can be done.
- It is your destiny as a believer to be saved when the end comes.
- Nothing bad can happen to someone who is good.

Beliefs such as these come from ancient times, when people thought that they had no power to change their world. There is a fear-based quality to these beliefs, often combined with fantasies about who survives and who gets saved. These fantasies and fears play out in the minds of ordinary people who hear doomsday prophecies and predictions of a coming mystical rapture.

Consider for a moment that you have some of these fear-based beliefs about pivotal times like these. Imagine that these beliefs, encoded within your subconscious in your DNA, are influencing you right now as you try to make sense of the changes. Consider that even one fear-based belief about Armageddon can obscure your clarity about what is really happening.

For example, if you believe that you have no control over what happens—that some authority outside of you decides whether you survive—you may make much different choices. Feeling that your fate is already sealed, you may pull back your energy and become a bystander. You may become complacent and hold yourself back at the very time when you most need to be an active participant!

When this pattern occurs, it is quite a dilemma. On one level, you are fully aware of your power of choice and of how you create your future through moment-by-moment choices. On another level, hidden from view, you are being influenced by the outmoded belief systems in your DNA.

Making the appropriate choices during these times will be problematic when you are operating from oppositional viewpoints. You see yourself as a divine changemaker. On the other hand, belief systems in your DNA may cause you to think that someone or something else is in charge of your changes.

You cannot explain why, but when you are about to make a significant decision, you feel powerless to choose. Perhaps feelings of doubt creep in or a sense of impending doom colors what your inner wisdom shows you is the optimal course.

Sometimes you simply feel as though you have no choice. The view of being without choice is false and ego-based. You always have a choice, even if that choice is how you respond to life's circumstances.

At other times, you feel very clear about your optimal choice, and you plan to take action on it. Something blocks you, though, and you fail to follow through.

For example, imagine that you decide to learn a new skill in order to advance professionally. You research classes you could take, find the perfect one, and even select a date. You tell yourself that you will register for the class by the deadline next month; it's the only such class offered this year. The next month comes and goes, and you have not registered. When you realize it is too late to register, you become puzzled about how you could have missed the date. You may even go into self-reprimand mode or worry about how you will advance without the skill. The deeper issue, however, is the battle within your mind that prevents powerful choice making.

What really happened here? Your subconscious mind—which is millions of times more powerful than your conscious mind—was running the show, and it chose something else! As you can imagine, this is quite a dilemma. The key is learning to work with your DNA and your subconscious so that your mind works for you, not against you.

Feeling Frozen and Powerless

Have you ever felt frozen when considering what to do about something? How many times did you simply wait and do nothing, even when your intuition prompted you to take a specific action? Have you ever looked at a series of similar relationships or jobs in your life and told yourself that it was simply your fate to suffer with the same type of dysfunction again and again?

If you can identify with any of these questions, know that you likely carry within your DNA some limiting belief systems that keep you imprisoned in a false sense of powerlessness.

※

Tips: Checking in with Your Heart

Because you learned to abdicate power to outside authority figures, it's normal to sometimes feel that you have no choice. Begin to question this every day. To feel without choice is to be disconnected from your true divine power.

Check in with your heart regularly and ask what your options are as you consider what to do and how to spend your time. You likely will become aware of fresh insights. You may also acknowledge some of the helpful whispers your intuitive guidance has been quietly sending your way. Do this check-in about the things you feel you *must* do, too, like going to work. Add to your check-in process an inquiry about what options or choices you would *like* to have in the given situation. When considering this, don't be concerned about whether the option you prefer is possible or acceptable to the authority figures in your life.

Take the following hypothetical example of going to your job. When you begin to explore the answers coming from your heart, you may get in touch with a train of thought like the following.

Do I have to go to work today?
Remember that you chose to take this job and that you are there because of that choice.

Can I change that choice, just for one day?
Know that the choice you speak of here is the original choice to take the job. If your work situation allows for an occasional day off, and you feel it's appropriate to take the day off, consider it. If you don't feel you can take the day off, you can choose how you view going to work and how you respond to being there. You can refuse to allow petty power plays and ego-driven colleagues to rock your boat. You can set your intention, on the way to work and while there, to stay in your center regardless of what happens. That's where you have choice. That is powerful.

What other options do I have besides this job?
For example, right now you have resumes in the hands of two other companies. You sent those out last week in a moment of exhausted desperation. Consider whether either of these other places is really much different from where you are now. Look into both of them in more detail before you waste your present time and energy in fantasy about something that may simply be a carbon copy of your current job. Sit in a state of quiet inner inquiry to explore other options that you would like to create. The key word here is *create*. This word implies action, and it is you taking the action. Your perfect job may not exist at any company right now; it may be up to you to create it.

Decide What You Want

To make a choice is to decide how to express your energy. You are choosing all of the time, from the moment that you awaken each day. How you decide to express your energy impacts you and a multitude of others around you. Choice is an energy set in motion that affects both present and future. Who you choose to interact with, and how you choose to relate to others, sets the stage for a continually unfolding sequence of events.

It is now common knowledge that one choice of a single individual can impact the lives of many. You are that one person and your choices do matter.

✴

Process: Seeing the Gifts in Relationships

Consider someone you have known in the past. It could be a life partner, a child, a friend, a work colleague, a parent, a neighbor, a sibling, or an acquaintance. Imagine for a moment that you never met this person. How would your life be different today? Reflect on how your choices involving this one person have altered your life in positive ways, helping you to grow and evolve. Invite your intuitively guided reason to show you some of the ways that this person has impacted your life. With the following questions as a guide, allow yourself to discover the interconnected circumstances that have arisen from your knowing this one person. Reflect on how the choices you made in relation to this person have been a force for change within you.

The Child You Birthed
If your child had not been born, for example, what would that mean to you? What would you have missed? How would you have lived your life differently? How would your priorities have shifted? What people did you meet as a parent to your child? How did those people impact your life? What if you had never met them? What have you learned about love and life itself by having this child? Consider at least

three things you value today because of birthing this child. How have these things helped you to become more whole?

A Life Partner

Think of a life partner, either your current one or someone from the past. Contemplate how your life would have unfolded if you had never met him or her. How would your life be different? When you form a partnership with someone and it involves your heart, there is always at least one gift you receive. Reflect right now on what that gift is for you. Consider the value of that gift in your life and how you would not be the same person without having received the gift. Being in an intimate relationship with another has the potential to teach you something very profound about yourself. Do you sense that you have fully learned what you could have from knowing this person? If this person is no longer in your life, how has the energy of this person shown up in your other relationships?

A Work Colleague

Consider someone you have worked with. You may think of this person as a pivotal force in your life, as a source of inspiration, as a cause of distress, or as simply an annoyance. Visualize the face of this person now. Reflect on how knowing him or her has changed something within you or changed the external circumstances of your life. When you think of this person, you may be reminded of the supportive words you heard or of the positive role model that guided you to later successes. On the other hand, perhaps even imagining your colleague's face causes your stomach to tighten. In an imaginary interaction with your colleague, do you doubt yourself or change your behavior in any way? What are the ways you give your power away when interacting with your colleague? Reflect on what this person has taught you over the years.

A Parent or Guardian
Think of one of your parents. The parents who birthed you gave you physical life, and with that they also gave you DNA. The DNA that is in your body's cells today includes belief systems you inherited from your parents and family lineage. This means that you share a lot with your parents, regardless of how you learned to identify with each of them. During your life, you may have sometimes felt close to your parents and at other times either estranged from them or simply neutral. If you are like most people, you have on more than one occasion felt quite different from one or both of your parents. You may have wondered why you were born to these particular people. Perhaps you even questioned whether you were adopted!

Ask yourself the following questions as you consider the impact a parent or guardian has had in your life. What are three things a parent or guardian has taught you, either directly or indirectly? How is your lifestyle healthier than the previous generation's because of choices you made after observing this person's self-destructive habits? Before you left home, what decisions did you make because of what you witnessed growing up? When friends describe your positive traits or abilities, which of these attributes do you share with a parent or guardian? Consider five things you can be grateful for today because of having had this relationship. What recent insights about life are the direct results of developing a more enlightened view of your childhood?

An Acquaintance
How about one of the many acquaintances you have met? Consider what doors have opened to you since meeting someone at a workshop, in line at the supermarket, or on the street as you walked your dog. It may have seemed accidental to meet this person, and yet you did choose how you would respond to the meeting.

As an example, think of one time when you exchanged phone numbers with someone you just met, and then a week later you decided to call. As a result of your initiative to make that first call, you began developing a relationship with the person. How did this change your life? Consider the little things as well as the obvious. Sometimes a person comes into your life for an instant only, and other times it can develop into a lifetime bond. From the perspective of your soul's journey, the time frame involved is not as crucial as the gift of learning that each relationship can provide.

Relationships are a kind of barometer of a person's state of wholeness. They are a feedback system, providing data that can be self-examined and utilized to help create greater awareness. Each of the characters regularly appearing in a person's life has the potential to be a powerful force for positive change. The fastest transformation occurs when a person has learned to be conscious of choices involving self and others.

Think about what your life could be like if you regularly utilized conscious choice making in your relationships with others. Reflect on how potent you could feel. Visualize your increased ability to skillfully transcend disharmony with others. Imagine the positive ripple effect, accelerating your spiritual progress and creating more joy in your life. As you contemplate this, remember that people from all levels of spiritual development can benefit from more awareness and from being a more potent force in the world. Everyone is a work in progress.

☼

Questions: Learning from Pivotal Relationships

Take a few moments right now and think of a pivotal relationship with someone who has triggered both happy and sad emotions. It could be a life partner, a sibling, a friend, or a work colleague. Allow your intuition to help you select the most appropriate relationship to explore. The relationship could be one of great conflict, or it could be one that appears harmonious, at least on the surface or until certain situations arise. See yourself having conversations with this person. Picture this person in your mind as you reflect on some recent interactions.

Become still and ask yourself some questions, such as the following:

- How much of the time do I feel powerful when I speak with this person? When I don't feel powerful, why not?

- Do both of us get our needs met in this relationship? If there is an imbalance, who gets needs met more of the time?

- Do I feel confident about how to respond to this person if he or she questions me, disagrees with me, refuses to do what I want, or tries to manipulate me to take a specific action?

- Do I have ready access to my own intuitive wisdom for guidance when the relationship gets rocky?

- On a scale of one to ten, how confident am I about acting on my intuitive guidance when I am with this person?

- What do I do in this relationship when I experience doubt (e.g., question my own intuitive wisdom, yield to what the other person wants, blame myself, blame the other person, retreat, become frozen and unable to act, defend my position, attack the other person)?

- How much of the time does the relationship feel in balance, and how much of the time are we doing the dance of oppositional thinking, feeling, or acting (e.g., clashes of views, feelings of love and hate, speaking words of praise and resentment)?

The answers to these questions will give you more clarity about how powerful you feel in your relationships and how much you trust your inner wisdom. You may want to revisit these questions from time to time to see how your relationships have shifted out of dysfunctional patterns.

In general, it is helpful to remember the power of your choice in each moment of each relationship—the choice of whether and how to respond to the other person, the choice of going within to receive your own intuitive guidance about the next steps, and the choice of acting on your intuitive wisdom. In any relationship, you are making choices continually, even if the choice is to say or do nothing. This is true even when you choose, consciously or unconsciously, to let the other person take the lead. Even choosing to choose consciously is a choice.

It can often feel as though you have no choice about the happenstance of your relationships. It is common to feel like a victim of the other person. It is also common, due to human conditioning, to focus on other people as the source of life's dissatisfactions rather than going inside. Choosing to go within and seeing yourself with more awareness is the solution for healing the disconnected parts of you. To the extent that you consciously make this choice, you become more aware of spirit operating in your life. This happens as you discover how to listen to your inner wisdom. Insights can come from dreams and from an inner knowing you receive as you pay attention to the people, places, and things that show up in your life.

When you are open to the movement of spirit in your relationships, each one of them holds the promise of helping you to become more conscious and more evolved. You remind yourself that there are no accidental relationships and that you can learn from each one of them. Oftentimes, you can learn more from your enemies and those you dislike. To fully embrace this truth is freedom, because you see how silly it is to waste your time in resentment, regret, and retribution. When applied to a challenging relationship, gratitude can help you to turn curses into blessings. A willingness to look at your difficult relationships through the eyes of forgiveness and tolerance can move your personal transformation process into high gear!

To make a conscious choice to evolve through your relationships also means that you will bring to the surface the parts of yourself that are not yet whole. Your splintered self will feel afraid and sometimes angry, resentful, or jealous.

Forgive yourself for having the negative feeling and recognize your choice each time. That choice is to acknowledge and intelligently work with the feeling, or to allow the feeling to influence your next thought, word, or action. Set your intention to make the choice of being conscious of your feelings, learning to question their source, and discovering how to intelligently work with what you feel. When you do this, you will have a greater capacity to heal the underlying issue.

What you will discover is that your feelings and thoughts are directly linked, each influencing the other. Within your DNA are clues about the source of your challenging feelings and thoughts. You hold within your DNA a multitude of belief systems that impact how you respond to life. Healing yourself at the DNA level can help you to move out of pain and into joy.

Each time you examine your fear or other negative response, your challenging emotions will lose some of their power, and you will be more empowered. Over a period of time, your self-examination will have a cumulative effect, and the stranglehold of habitual emotional responses will lessen. You will become freer.

It is useful to remember that becoming whole through relating to others requires a letting go of the many layers of falseness. You aren't alone; everyone has an inauthentic self, just as they have a genuine self, waiting to be rediscovered! The transformation won't happen overnight or through any one relationship. It's a process of becoming more of your own authentic self, moment by moment.

How to Make Better Decisions

As you travel the journey to becoming authentic and whole, you are building momentum with each decision you make.

How can you make decisions more consciously? The first step is acknowledging that decisions or choices are made every day. When you are faced with a decision, know that even taking no action is a choice. You have choices in what you think, what you say, and what you do.

You have a choice about whether to examine what you feel when you feel it. Self-examination is always fruitful, giving you clues about what you feel. If you bypass this self-reflection—taking action on your feelings—you may do something you regret. For example, perhaps you are feeling tired when you consider a task you know needs to be done that day. A bill needs to be paid in order to avoid a penalty. You can choose to recognize the tired feeling and examine the bigger picture. When you do that, you may realize the importance of moving past your tiredness to take care of the bill. Alternatively, you can choose to avoid the self-examination, allowing the tiredness to sabotage you. You may decide that you are too tired to pay the bill. When you choose this second option, you may be forced to pay a penalty fee.

Conflict results when one part of you wants one thing and another part of you wants something else. As you become more conscious and aware, the inner turmoil of these conflicts begins to dissipate.

As an example of a typical inner conflict, imagine that you have a goal of finding a life partner. You seek companionship and like the idea of being in a committed relationship. At the same time you want these things, another fear-based voice inside of you is doubtful. This other part of you is not sure you can find someone compatible. This other part of you may feel unlovable or perhaps undeserving of love. This doubtful voice operates in the background, often outside of your awareness. It can cause you to sabotage yourself. You may tell yourself that finding someone to love is not worth the effort. When you hear of opportunities to socialize, you stay home.

You can learn to identify and resolve inner conflicts like this one. Learning to focus the mind, to challenge the emotions, and to make decisions consciously is an evolving skill. There is no single method that guarantees success. Allow your intuitively guided reason to show you how to travel the middle path of balance. It is a universal path that is inclusive and unifies the splintered self. Go gently with yourself as you discover your own unique way to travel.

Meanwhile, know that not everything about your life will be a decision. At age ten, when you observe the freedom of birds in flight and wish to fly like a bird, you can't choose to become a bird. When sitting in your mother's womb, you can't consciously choose your siblings. At age ninety-five, if your body is weak and near death, you cannot choose to live another eighty years. Under such circumstances, you still have a choice of how to view or respond to what is occurring.

No one else but you can decide how you will choose to view life's happenstance. A helpful question to ask on a regular basis is this: "Is my view of this situation bringing me closer to, or further away from, my own enlightenment?" If you discover that your view or thinking about something is creating an obstacle, you can then ask what needs to shift so that you can get back on track.

New Approaches to Choice

Indeed, new-paradigm approaches to choice making have been evolving for some time. The old ways of choosing and viewing one's choices are no longer sufficient. These outmoded approaches were birthed during a kind of sleep cycle that lies in humanity's past. A global awakening is happening more quickly than it may seem. People are remembering that they are divine and that they are spiritual beings with a purpose to be here on Earth.

Simple universal principles of creation are being brought forward in new ways in order to awaken people in mainstream society. In the early part of the twenty-first century, for example, films such as *The Secret* and *What the Bleep Do We Know!?* became catalysts for new-paradigm views. Basic concepts that have long been embraced in esoteric circles are now being explored and accepted in general society. They include the idea that we create with our thoughts and that belief systems are encoded in the DNA of the body's cells. The idea of conscious choice is being embraced globally by growing numbers of people.

Remedy for the Toughest Choices

Understanding and embracing a concept like conscious choice is one thing. How easy is it in practice? What happens to conscious choice making when you are interacting with someone who pushes your buttons? How about a life-stressor event like moving to a new home, divorcing after a ten-year marriage, or being fired from your job? What happens to your ability to make sensible choices when you feel so burdened by the complexities of life that all you want to do is hide under the covers?

To be sure, as the pace of modern life continues to quicken, the average person can feel overwhelmed and stressed with the expanding number of choices available. Each day, people are asked to make choices about an increasing number of things. Some of these choices will set in motion a new career or life path. Some choices will mean the beginning or end of a relationship. Still other choices revolve around the happenstance of everyday life, like the choice of what time to get out of bed, what color sweater to wear, and what time of day to drive or walk to the grocery store.

Consider the impact of everyday choice making. Have you ever delayed making a choice about something, feeling unsure about what to do or simply suffering from being on overload? Have you ever worried that you will make the *wrong* choice?

Do you feel anxiety or another painful emotion because of a choice you made in the past? Have you ever felt discouraged when it appears that you have *no* choice in what happens? Do you sometimes feel so hopeless about changing a painful situation that you feel frozen in your ability to choose the next step?

Have you noticed that you label your choices as good and bad, giving them an interpretation or meaning? Do you feel punished by being stuck with bad choices or prevented from enjoying the fruits of good choices?

If you have ever felt such pain over the choices of life, you're not alone. It is normal to experience suffering when life is viewed as either choiceless or full of difficult choices to make. This is especially true when a person believes that he or she must pick between two painful options. For example, a young woman may consider staying in an abusive relationship if she fears being alone or losing full-time custody of her children. In another example, a middle-aged man may remain in a toxic work environment, doubting his abilities and letting his fear convince him that he will not find a better job.

Both of these people are making a choice either way, regardless of whether they stay or leave. When this happens to people, they are often ignorant of this fact. Also, due to most people's conditioning in negativity, it is normal to bring a very limited and negative reference point into choice making. This incorrect view is innocently assumed by people out of ignorance. The conditioning people have that fashions their thinking—their view of life—is multigenerational, fueled by the similar training received by their parents. When people are conditioned with consistent messages of negativity, the reference point for life's questions and choices is based on this false view.

Some of the pain involved in making choices involves the learned tendency to forget that one *has* a choice in each moment. This forgetting goes hand in hand with the forgetting of one's true divine nature. The more asleep to this true nature a person is, the greater the tendency to be run by the conditioned rational mind that naturally resorts to the painful outlook it knows.

Choices are made whether one is consciously aware or not. However, the more conscious a person is when making choices, the happier he or she will be with the outcome.

There are many types of choices. The choice is sometimes to do nothing, to say nothing, or to refuse to focus on the negativity of the situation. Even if one cannot alter an outcome, it is possible to alter one's interpretation of what happened and, therefore, to change how one responds to the negative situation.

For example, a woman is rear-ended while driving. The fender on her new white car is severely crushed and stained with red paint from the other driver's car, and her neck feels twisted and sore from the whiplash. The impact of the crash causes her body to stiffen, and adrenaline pumps quickly through her system.

To the extent that the woman stays awake and conscious, remembering to remain in the present moment, the more likely she is to view the accident in a neutral way and to avoid judging herself or the other driver. That is the ideal. The reality for most people, though, is that life's accidents and happenstance trigger a lapse into the past or a projection into the future. That is how people are conditioned in the mundane world. Without adequate training and practice, it is very difficult to remain present.

The woman may focus her thoughts on a string of earlier car accidents, remembering a lawsuit or painful recovery that reduced her body's mobility for months. As she gets lost in the sea of past memories, she stirs up unresolved anger and resentment and brings this negativity to her present experience. As she projects her mind into the future, she moves into a negative spiral of thoughts involving filing an insurance claim, visiting doctors, and repairing her car. As is her habit, she lets her mind race from the present to the past, then to the future, going back and forth numerous times. The negativity now created by the woman is projected into her current life experience and into her choices.

These choices, conditioned by her beliefs in victimhood and suffering, involve blaming and berating. The woman may choose to speak hostile words of blame to the other driver, or she may choose to silently berate herself as she fills out the traffic report and calls the insurance company.

Even weeks after the accident, when her body is healed and her car is repaired, the woman may continue her regimen of blame. She may occasionally think about the accident and judge herself as inadequate, unconsciously choosing to extend the suffering of the accident that is now something from the past.

If she were conscious of her choice making, able to see the higher spiritual viewpoint, she would be able to perceive a more enlightened and joyful way to be.

✷

Tips: Making Choices without Pain

When you become more conscious of how you make choices, you can change outcomes in your life. The key is to understand that you have a process and that you can influence that process. Here are a few positive steps you can take.

1. Set your intention daily to walk a spirit-directed path, inviting the divine to be an integral part of your every experience. Make the decision to be present and fully in your body as you experience life.

2. If you are feeling fear or entertaining thoughts of doubt about a choice, ask yourself whether you are operating in the present *and* whether the present reality is a true or

imagined cause for fear. Unless you are about to be run over by a train or you face some other life-threatening situation at this present moment, it's most likely that your fears and doubts are connected to the past or to what might happen in the future. When you become aware that you are focusing on a choice from the reference points of the past or the future, make a decision to set aside the data you just received and to focus instead single-pointedly on the present.

3. Ask for intuitive guidance to help you illuminate the obscurations of your dilemma. Ask to see a higher spiritual view of the available choices, including possibilities that you may not have considered. It may seem, for example, that you have only two options. The abused wife considering leaving her husband, as an example, may see only her choices of leaving or staying. Other options obscured from her view could include how she responds to each situation as it is presented.

    The woman's cycle of pain can be altered by *how* she chooses to stay or leave. The how relates to the way she thinks, speaks, and acts in response to what is occurring. What is she expecting to happen, and what do her fears tell her about each choice? What has she been conditioned to believe about herself and about life that fuel these fears? What is the truth she is unable to see? What could she learn about herself from this situation so that she could break the cycle of abuse in her life? These are the kinds of questions to ask when you want to move through the fog of not knowing what to do.

4. Set your intention to do your very best in each situation, inviting spirit to help you make the most enlightened choices possible in each moment. Remind yourself

throughout the day that you have set this intention, and allow the energy of this intention to fuel your forward movement. As you make choices and experience life, refuse to blame yourself for not being enough. Remember that you are doing your very best and that you are not alone, for spirit is right by your side.

Your life today is reflective of choices you made in the past. You can't change the past choices, but you can change your consciousness.

The key to changing your consciousness is spirit. To be successful, you will need to develop a tangible relationship with spirit. The more that you partner with spirit in your day-to-day life, and the more you allow the divine to show you the higher road, the more quickly your consciousness can evolve. With increased awareness over time, you will discover that your choices lead to a more fulfilling life.

This bright potential is in marked contrast to the harsh reality that results when you continue habitual patterns of unaware choice making. If you truly understood how you handicap yourself this way, you wouldn't do it. It's like there's a blind spot when you are facing key life issues. When these arise, your intuitively guided reason can take a backseat to fear. Before you know it, your choices can land you right back inside a familiar box with invisible walls. You know you're inside, unable to resolve your dilemma, and yet you can't see the walls, much less the doorway that leads outside to freedom.

The following is an example of a man with this dilemma. Consider the business executive who suffers for many years because of unaware choices he repeatedly makes involving his career. Although he enjoys a certain amount of success in his work, he is plagued by an inner, unspoken feeling that he has failed and that he is unfulfilled. He doesn't know why he's feeling like a failure. He's puzzled because he's done all the right things his outer world tells him are needed to succeed. He remembers his family telling him that he would succeed as long as he worked hard and persisted in achieving his goals.

Over the years, each time he is offered a new position or the option of moving to another city, he accepts the challenge and works hard to realize his picture of success. He continues to persist even when something inside of him—a kind of inner knowing he has yet to connect with spirit—tells him that there is another choice he could make. After the man's feelings of frustration and dissatisfaction build to a boiling point, he begins to seriously question whether there is a better way to live.

As part of this man's quest, he begins a search for solutions that are not being presented in the mundane world. He comes to realize that there is a power greater than what he's been able to access. He learns through experience about the power of allowing spirit to show him a more enlightened view of life. More and more, he consciously asks spirit to be a part of his choice making.

Along the way, he realizes that the choice of whether to involve the divine in one's choice making is really *the* key decision a person has in each moment. He understands that in shifting his choice making from the realm of the ego to the realm of the divine, he's also acknowledging that *he* is divine.

This man has seen the futility of seeking success and power from the perspective of ego-based desires. He has realized that his life is more joyful when he's awake to the movement of spirit in his life. He therefore has developed a sincere desire to involve the divine in his choice making. He tells others about how he makes decisions only after considering his highest good. He regularly asks his higher self to guide him in his decisions. Having done all of these things, he convinces himself that he's doing all he can do to involve spirit in his choice making. After all, he's asking for divine input, and his focus certainly appears to include spirit.

To be sure, the desire for spirit is there, and the man's actions oftentimes are based upon that desire. There are unseen factors, though, that are obscurations, preventing him from fully integrating the divine into everyday life. Therefore, many of his choices are still coming from ego and greed. Because of these factors, outside of his conscious awareness, he's continually frustrated by an equation that doesn't seem to add up. Real success, the kind that comes from a life fully fused with the divine, eludes him.

This man suffers because of his choices, and he grows increasingly frustrated, not knowing how to break the cycle. He thinks he's doing all the right things and truly believes that he's fully participating with spirit. He's ignorant to the fact that he often erects roadblocks to spirit's movement in his life. As an example, he has not developed listening skills, so he often misses key clues.

Success measured by worldly standards never lasts long enough at any one time for the man to feel he *is* a success. He feels like a failure inside, even at times when his bank account indicates he's a success, and even when his peers envy his accomplishments. At times like these, he often blames himself, others, or even spirit. Discouragement and lack of trust often follow in such situations, causing even more of an illusory division between the self and spirit.

To be sure, each person's dilemma will look slightly different. At the core of everyone's predicament, though, is a lack of awareness about the obstacles to fully integrating the divine in one's choices.

※

Checklist: Integrating Spirit into Choices

To more fully integrate the divine in your choices, consider inviting your higher self to help you identify obstacles such as those mentioned here. The more that you can identify your roadblocks, recognizing them in present time as they arise in your life, the more successful you will be in changing painful patterns and making conscious choices. As you review this checklist, invite your heart's wisdom to reveal which ones sometimes apply to you. By identifying your own patterns and making them a focal point in your inner work, you can more easily begin to shift your experience.

1. **Independence valued more than interdependence—**Consider the woman who has a strong need to be independent, priding herself on her ability to think and act independently. She may feel powerful only when she's doing something under her own steam, and when it's *her* idea to do it. Due to ignorance, this woman may close the door to spirit, which naturally works with people through interdependence. Decision making involving interdependence with spirit is collaboration; it's a two-way street. The woman invites divine guidance that can reveal a higher view of her situation, receives this guidance, and then takes appropriate action. To receive the guidance, she needs to be willing to listen to her inner voice. To benefit fully from what she hears, she must set aside her own agenda and expectations. Listening is followed by questioning anything that is not clear. When the woman has clarity, she can choose how to optimally respond to the intuitive guidance. It's not about being told what to do; the doorway needs to be open though.

2. **Being out of touch with one's body—**Imagine the man who has been trained to figure out life logically and to use his head rather than his heart. By the time he's an adult, he's grown accustomed to ignoring many of the sensations and messages of his body. He's not in touch with the fact that his body is a divine messenger of wisdom. He doesn't see aches and pains, or even specific physical diseases, as potential instruments of divine knowing. He's been trained to want to fix physical discomfort as soon as possible, without probing into the *why* of the condition. Perhaps a stomachache begins on a Friday afternoon when he's considering working the next day to complete a project that's due on Monday. If he would listen to what his body

is telling him and inquire within about the real cause, he could perhaps make a more enlightened choice.

3. **To question is deemed wrong**—Children traditionally have been taught to look up to authority figures. They learn that others know more than they do. After all, when a child is six, he or she is dependent on caregivers. Consider the young girl who sees through experience that questioning her parents and teachers can have unsavory consequences. Perhaps she's scolded for talking at the wrong time, for asking a stupid question, or for doubting that her caregivers have her best interests in mind. She may decide that it isn't safe to ask questions because of the threat of punishment. In other scenarios, she may continually defer to others without questioning whether they are right, believing that they probably know more than she does. When she matures and begins to seek a connection with spirit, she may fear consequences if she poses questions to the divine. Perhaps she has made spirit into yet another authority figure. She may be afraid of the answers that she will receive, falsely believing that spirit has an agenda like people do. She may avoid inquiring into life situations that seem unchangeable, and she may feel that she has no choice. She may reason that spirit knows the dilemma she faces and that if she's meant to be rid of it, spirit will fix it without her asking.

4. **Numbing the senses with food, alcohol, busyness, or other addictions**—It is quite common to numb the senses with any number of substances or activities. The more that a person disconnects from the present moment with such actions, the less he or she is open to the messages of spirit. Picture the man who meditates each morning before work. He spends a few minutes inviting spirit to participate with him during his day, asking for divine insights into how he

can live a more joyful and abundant life. As part of this, he requests guidance about a specific dilemma he must resolve that week, trusting that spirit will reveal the answer during his workday. Then, as is typical for most people, he obscures the answer by not paying enough attention. Perhaps he has numbed his senses with a heavy lunch, or by a frenetic work schedule that does not allow enough quiet time to hear spirit. He may simply be so disconnected from his present experiences that he doesn't notice when the divine orchestrates the answer he seeks. It's like being stopped at a red light and not noticing that it turned green. Drivers behind you start to honk, and then you notice. In those previous moments of not noticing, what else did you lose sight of?

5. **Fear and doubt color the communications line**—Everyone has fears and doubts that can color communications with the divine. Consider the woman who asks her higher self to show her an appropriate solution to a relationship difficulty. After requesting this assistance, she allows her fear to take center stage, blurring her ability to discern the communications coming from spirit. She pays so much attention to the fear that she begins to doubt that there *is* a divine solution to her dilemma. At times, she even tells herself that she's making it all up and that those messages she's received from spirit must be only from her imagination. At other times, her fears and doubts relate to time and timing. Spirit doesn't have the same timing we have. When the divine indicates a potential solution, the timing of putting that solution into motion cannot be mandated by our will.

Choice and Ascension

As you move through your ascension process, you will naturally make different choices than before. These will be higher consciousness choices that come from holding more light. These new choices will often nullify earlier choices that you made. This is appropriate, for you are now wiser. The key here is to continually update your view of who you think you are, and to remove the punitive energy of shoulds from your choices.

To walk the path as a divine changemaker, you must become awake to yourself and to all of your choices. You must let go of fantasy thinking in all of its forms. Examples include the idea that you need to be rescued. One false notion says that you do not need to choose or to take action because you will be rescued at the eleventh hour.

Similarly, you must learn a new way to view luck and fortunate circumstances. Did you know that there is no such thing as being lucky? You can feel lucky of course, but luck is not the word to describe the outcomes of conscious creation! There really are no random events, no accidental meetings, and no chance encounters. All of the good of this moment was set in motion by what you created in the past. Choose to be grateful for the positive things you have created.

Now is the time to choose to be an active participant in the changes occurring during Earth's pivotal years.

Chapter 6

In Pursuit of Truth

You live during a time of global crisis. The old is quickly crumbling beneath your feet, and the new may be feeling choppy and unfamiliar. The recent decades of accelerated shifting are unique. You don't have an experiential yardstick to measure the amount of change occurring now.

To successfully navigate the changes, you will need to discover reliable methods of knowing what is really happening, what is really true, and what is true for you personally. You will need to learn to recognize the difference between old-paradigm approaches and the new, more light-filled ones that you are here to create.

The old ways were born out of false notions, superstitions, and fear-based manipulation and control. These old traditions, which include much of the conventional paradigm of your modern culture, are broken. Most of them never worked well to begin with because they were the antithesis of what fosters an enlightened society.

Increasing numbers of people across the world are becoming aware that a great shift in consciousness is under way. The levels of understanding of what is really happening, of course, will vary in relation to how evolved people are.

As an example, some people are using most of their energy to complain about problems of society's outmoded structures. They are quick to point out what is not working and perhaps how they personally suffer as a result.

For some who feel victimized and unlucky to have inherited a broken system, the view is one of doom and gloom. For those with the most negative mindset, a common view is that humanity has gone beyond a crucial turning point and there is no redemption. The belief is that it is far too late for solutions to be successful. This is a very dismal picture indeed.

For the more awakened ones, response to the global crisis often involves taking more personal responsibility based on an awareness that each person's energy, consciousness, and actions count.

Within this group of people, more are taking a stand to support innovative change, putting in motion radically new solutions that would have been unheard of during other cycles of history. The ones who are learning to incorporate their intuitive right brain into decision making are finding themselves increasingly guided to connect with others of like mind.

For example, a person's intuitive nudge to attend a meditation group can result in meeting others who also are on a path of awakening. A support network is oftentimes built from such chance meetings and new friendships. There is a life-affirming boost that comes when one finds others who share a sincere desire to create positive changes on both personal and planetary levels.

You know you want change in the status quo. Most likely you want lots of changes, and you would like to see them occurring more quickly and with more ease.

Chances are that you have been questioning the old modes of thinking and operating for some time. You may even sense the undercurrent of dishonesty and secretiveness as you attempt to unravel the flurry of nonsense being presented on the world stage.

Examples include media exposure of shady business dealings and government corruption.

Knowing Who to Trust

Today more and more people are questioning the status quo, seeking to know what is really true and to expose untruths. Truth is on people's minds. Much information that previously was kept secret is now being revealed.

How do you figure out what to trust and who to trust? How do you know when you are being presented a half truth, or even an unadulterated lie? What sort of personal gauge have you developed for knowing truth? How often these days are you finding yourself led astray, baffled at how your own compass of truth failed to discern what was really occurring?

Indeed, in today's climate it can be quite a challenge to see past the myriad of illusions that exist. Even an experienced traveler can be fooled and sent down an unproductive road. Although it's useful to take note of when this happens to you, avoid getting into the habit of judging yourself for not knowing better.

Self-judgment is a waste of your precious energy. When you are harsh with yourself and go into self-reprimand mode, you move further away from clarity, not closer to it. The negative spiral you instigate in these circumstances is probably familiar because of what you learned in your punitive upbringing. Punishment and the threat of punishment have been cultural tools of control for a very long time. Therefore, do your best to shift out of automatic pilot and embrace yourself with kindness and compassion.

A Time of Truths Revealed

As political elections and social reforms take place in key countries across the globe, there likely will be undercurrents of unease and skepticism as concerned citizens question whether they are being given a truthful picture. There have been questions before, of course, yet this current phase brings deeper levels of inquiry. Some of this questioning will come about after fraud and trickery are exposed. These kinds of things have been exposed previously, but they continued because most people were unaware and disempowered.

The cumulative impact of an awakening consciousness in these times is changing all that. As more hidden knowledge comes to light, there will be a natural connection of the dots, leading to a deeper probing into issues and systems that had before escaped scrutiny. One overhaul will lead to another, setting in motion a domino effect that will be felt worldwide.

This is a time of revelations of truth. Massive distortions of information and untruths accepted for generations are coming to light. As this occurs, remember that the whole backstory of an impersonal truth is rarely uncovered all at once or by one individual; the uncovering is more of a process than it is a single event.

In past evolutionary cycles, some truths were partially revealed only to be covered over again by ignorance and fear. Sometimes truths were hidden from mainstream view by secret societies, desiring to limit the precious information to their limited circle.

There are many examples of ancient truths that were discovered and utilized for a time and then forgotten or rejected by subsequent generations. Examples include ancient knowledge of energy fields, healing properties of the natural world, sacred geometry, and the afterlife.

To be sure, an impersonal truth can be revealed fully and have long-term staying power in human consciousness. After all, truth is unchangeable and just is, regardless of whether anyone sees it. However, a complete uncovering of a truth occurs only when there is a readiness within significant numbers of people over sufficient periods of time. Otherwise, regardless of how true something is, the masses of humanity will be unaware of it.

Empowerment through Questioning

You are empowered through questioning. Get into the habit of asking questions that can help you to discover what is going on under the surface. Invite input from your higher self about the significant issues of these times.

For starters, consider questions that focus on three key elements of society: government, religion, and teachers. These questions can lead you to a place of more empowerment as societal structures get a massive overhaul.

After all, when you discover the truth about something, this knowledge will set you free. Only by living in darkness from the truth can you be harmed. Once you see the truth of a situation and live your life accordingly, you are no longer bound by the lie. You can then move into a place of conscious choice.

You cannot be a victim and consciously choose at the same time. Therefore, you free yourself from mechanical living and automatic fear-based responses.

Before reflecting on this list of concerns and questions, take a moment to become still and tune out the noise of outside distractions. To do this, you may want to turn off any background sounds, close the door to your room, and take a few deep breaths. Invite your higher self to give you feedback as you read each item from the list. Pause long enough with each insight you receive to notice whether additional questions or ideas come to you.

Government

Do you believe that you hear truth from the politicians running for office, or from those already in office? When they are speaking, how much of what they say do you question? How do you determine whether they are genuine or simply presenting what they have been told the voters want to hear? Do you question what information they are leaving out or avoiding? Do some things they say simply not add up?

Does it seem that their authenticity wavers when in a debate? What happens when they are firmly entrenched in their seat of political power—do their promises and stances on issues change?

What kinds of powers have you and other citizens given to those in government? What kinds of powers have government leaders taken without your knowing? Have you questioned which powers are appropriate to leave in the hands of government?

Consider what you as a private citizen are doing to be empowered in your own life. Set your intention to notice when you give your power away to authority figures such as politicians. Be willing to take your power back.

Religion

Reflect for a moment on any early religious training you had. You may not be religious now, but what kind of religious ideas were presented to you by your parents or other authority figures? As a young child, your mind takes in new information like a sponge. Much of what you are taught goes straight into your brain.

Even if you have little recollection of it now, invite your higher self to remind you of early training related to religion. What did you take in as true simply because it came from people older than you who were supposed to know?

If you have difficulty remembering anything specific, consider what your parents believed about God, heaven, hell, who gets punished, and who gets saved. You may have decided to trash all of these concepts when you got older. Perhaps you threw them away without examining them fully. These concepts may still be in your personal trash bin, yet some of them will also be a part of your belief systems.

Why?

You hold within your DNA belief systems formed in response to your early-life conditioning. Also recorded within your DNA are belief systems inherited from your lineage of ancestors. These may include religious-oriented beliefs based on superstition, fear-based notions, control, and lies.

If you have studied humankind's history, you will remember that many of the bloody battles between peoples have been in defense of beliefs about religious truths. These twisted notions about which faith or race of people is right are in humanity's mass consciousness.

Most people on the planet today unknowingly carry some of these ideas in their DNA. When limiting beliefs such as these are not consciously detected, the beliefs remain a potent underlying influence in your life. So it will be helpful to discover the outmoded, religious-based beliefs you have and clear them from your DNA.

An example of such a belief is, "It is wrong for women to hold positions of power." This kind of belief—which can be rooted in religious dogma of hierarchy—can be an obstacle to today's woman who seeks to be appropriately powerful in the world.

Teachers

Consider some of the teachers who have influenced you. When you were a child, these teachers included your parents and other caregivers. If you were like most children, you went through a stage in early life of adoring and looking up to these people. They were bigger, after all, and you could not take care of yourself without their help.

You likely learned to do what they told you to do. When you began to question why things were the way they were, you probably received some confusing answers. Perhaps your father simply said you should do what he said because he said so.

Similarly, if you were exposed to religion as a child, chances are the God or deity you learned about had an authoritarian nature. Perhaps God was even a father figure. You were the child, and these authority figures had the answers. You did not know back then, but these early interactions with authority figures had a big impact during your precious formative years. Your experiences in childhood set up a model for your adult life and how you would view the world.

Contemplate what happened as you matured and began relating to teachers and other role models. Did you ever discover that you connected with a teacher in much the same way as you had with one of your parents? Think of an example of how that teacher was able to push your buttons, making you feel small or unworthy just as your parent had.

A teacher can be anyone in your life. Not all will have the teacher title, yet they still are your teachers. Some of the teachers who influence you are outside of your social network. Examples include authors, philosophers, media personalities, and spiritual leaders. They can be living or dead. They can be nonphysical, spiritual beings—even God.

As someone on the path of personal transformation, you will want to actively and regularly question information you receive from teachers, leaders, and role models. This includes what you read, what you ingest from broadcast media, what you receive over the Internet, and information you receive secondhand from others.

Just because a story has been presented numerous times, does that make it true? Consider, for example, what you assume to be true about this period of time. When you see headlines predicting the end of the world, do you question what that means? Do you pay close attention to the sources of information you are taking in? Do you check in with your inner wisdom to discern whether or not fear is coloring the information?

It certainly takes more effort to be awake and consciously aware of the information you accept as true. However, if you digest information on automatic pilot, you run the real risk of being manipulated, confused, and sent off course. Keep in mind that things often are not as they appear! Experts can be misquoted; authors' works can be edited in such a way that the true meaning is hidden.

A controversial prophetic posting on the Internet may have all of your friends chattering and postulating about the planet's future.

Perhaps this posting refers to very specific dates or places involved in a catastrophe. The way it is presented, mentioning other prophecies and well-known sages, may give it an air of credibility. Do you find yourself caught up in the buzz without deeply questioning what elements of the posting are really true? Do you allow your emotions to take center stage, momentarily forgetting to tune into your intuitively guided reason?

Also, when a teacher you trust begins to take a fear-based approach, do you question it? Are you skilled enough to even notice when this happens? When you read a spiritual website or go to a spiritual event, do you assume that all of the information presented will be valid? Although it's not helpful to become jaded and doubt everyone and everything, you will need to develop discernment if you are to progress spiritually.

Remember that you are a student of life, yet you are also a teacher yourself. In order for you to teach others in a sane way, you must have discernment and the ability to tell fact from fiction.

*

Tips: Recognizing Truth—Telling Fact from Fiction

- If something is true, it does not generate fear or create harm.

- Truth exists outside of linear time, yet you access it in present time.

- When someone insists that only his or her religion or philosophy is right, he or she is not presenting truth but energies of exclusion and control.

- If something of supposed merit appears false when you first hear it, or you are unsure of whether to trust it, be open to the possibility that the idea could be partly or wholly true.

- With information that appears to be at least partially true, inquire within yourself to discover what aspect is true so you do not unconsciously digest the whole package as true.

- When someone shares a truth of what has helped him or her personally, be willing to hear the person's sharing without judgment, allowing your own inner wisdom and life experience to show you if and how it applies to you. Be careful of taking in anyone else's truth as your own without first investigating it fully.

- When you are evaluating something to determine its truth, remember to step back enough to see the big picture. Do you know any of the backstory of the truth? Do you understand the implications of the truth, both big and small?

- Learn to ask questions that delve deeper. For example, when you have a feeling that something is true, do not be hasty in jumping to conclusions. Inquire within yourself to find out what part of you believes this (e.g., belief systems you consciously choose to hold or programming you inherited from your early conditioning or ancestral lineage). Ask what personal life experiences validate the truth. Recall where or from whom you first heard the truth. Inquire whether the truth is unwavering or whether it is influenced by dogma or something false. Ask why you believe it is true, and then ask what is at stake for you if it is not true. What are you afraid to see? Finally, ask what other truths you have unknowingly attached to this truth.

When Truth Is Elusive

For most people, truth is highly desired yet very elusive. One factor in this unsatisfactory experience is that people tend to relate to life on a superficial level. Self-examination, when undertaken, is often short-lived and does not go deep enough for complete understanding. It is common to look to others for advice and to ignore seeking one's own inner wisdom. People typically learn to trust others more than they trust themselves.

You Alone Can Determine Your Truth

Remember that you alone can determine what is true for you. Others can point to it, but only you can discover it. You can find it by being willing to live beyond superficial levels and through consistent questioning of your reality.

When something is really true for you, it will resonate with your inner being. The connection will feel so strong that you just know it is correct. It's not easy to be that confident. Knowing your own truth like this involves a high level of awareness and development of keen discernment. That takes time and a learned expertise of being able to sort through the fiction, camouflage, and illusions to get to the truth.

If you sincerely and consistently apply yourself and are willing to do the inner work, the rewards are beyond measure. From doing the inner work, you can become more and more real. As you become more genuine, peeling away the layers of your inauthentic self, you will naturally be able to access more of your true authentic nature.

You have the potential to evolve your consciousness to a state in which all of the senses, including intuition, are wholly utilized to discern truth. When you have learned to use all of your senses in tandem with your reason and practical experience, you will have stepped fully into the light. This light will shine down on you, be fully present within you, and emanate out from you in all directions.

Humanity's Deeper Questioning

Right now more and more people are beginning to question things that they never questioned before. Individuals from all walks of life are seeking new answers and trying to make sense of a nonsensical world.

For some people—who have been asleep to humanity's great current of change—a personal crisis could be the catalyst causing them to seriously question the status quo. The crisis or wake-up call could be anything from a grave health condition to a costly divorce, a house foreclosure, or a job loss. When a person begins questioning more deeply than before and realizes how shaky the traditional means of support are, an opening is created to change course.

A person in crisis must take action in order to shift his or her circumstances. As part of that, he or she must move out of habitual conditioning and choose a different path.

The New Path of Heart

This new path involves looking within for answers and responding to the world with a heart-centered focus. It means giving up, bit by bit, the habitual ego-based patterns learned in the conventional world. Giving these up is not a simple thing to do because there is much resistance and ignorance about the truth of one's real condition. That is a normal part of being human.

The awakening person will need to approach the new path with dedication, persistence, self-love, compassion, and patience. The last quality of patience is particularly important because success in navigating the new heart-centered path will require ongoing actions and choices. The person must be willing to continue choosing the higher path and taking actions that reflect that choice, regardless of what appears to be happening.

Sometimes it may appear as though nothing at all is happening; other times the progress may simply seem to be too slow. No matter what adversity is experienced, discouragement must not be allowed to block the person's resolve. The shifting into an entire new way of being requires tenacity and an ability to continually remember the big picture.

Your Deeper Questions

As you grow spiritually, you learn to ask the deeper questions. You look under the surface of what the world presents. By looking beyond what the casual observer sees, you can discover what is really real.

In today's uncertain world, it will become increasingly imperative to question what you see and hear. Light will continue to shine on disparities and dysfunctional old-paradigm approaches. As that happens, many secrets and much hidden knowledge will be exposed. Some of the information coming to light will receive more fanfare from the media. Be alert also to truths unveiled without the media hoopla.

Know that some of the hidden information coming to light will trigger deep transformational processes. When this happens for you, allow the insights to propel you into a fruitful healing of old, outmoded patterns. If you can approach the process intuitively and sanely, doorways will open to allow for resolution.

Skilled people who desire to eliminate a longstanding concern, therefore, may find that this next cycle provides just the spiritual fuel needed to finally complete the healing.

The Shift on a Global Scale

Each person on the planet is being impacted by the accelerated transformational shifting occurring in this unique cycle. Whether conscious or unconscious, the impact is there. The challenge is to connect the dots and make sense of the oppositional forces. Fear-based agendas and actions can be subtle, disguised as something benevolent. Again, remembering the larger view and making sure to regularly question within are keys to each person's individual progress.

If you feel that your ability for inner inquiry needs to be strengthened, there has never been a more important time to further develop this skill. Having this talent in these pivotal times is not a luxury, but a necessity.

This ability is developed by first opening to it and then through lots of ongoing practice. Opening to your natural ability to question will take a very strong desire and a willingness to learn new ways of approaching your reality.

It will also require an inner strength that does not waver when you feel challenged by others, the status quo, or unflattering information you receive about yourself. You must be willing to see the truth behind the falseness in everything, including your own long-standing identity. That, too, must be allowed to fall away so that you can discover your true divine self hidden underneath.

Inner inquiry is also an essential part of developing your intuitive knowing or psychic abilities. Those who have developed their skill of using intuitively guided reason will be in high demand in the times to come. They may call themselves intuitive, or they may use other language to describe their gifts.

Those gifted with intuitive ability will be needed everywhere—from corporations, government bodies, households, and healthcare facilities to the intuitive arts. They will surface to help others not yet skilled in inner inquiry. They also will be able to help other skilled intuitive people, who from time to time desire additional self-understanding. After all, even the most skilled intuitive can be challenged in uncovering personal hidden truths. A person can possess great self-awareness and the ability to see others' dilemmas, but his or her most challenging issues may remain a mystery.

Restoring Atrophied Talents

For most people, questioning and listening are rather atrophied talents. Everyone can learn to do these things, but the conventional world puts little value on them. In fact, from an early age, most people are told what to do, how to think, and what is true.

Education, even at the higher levels, does not teach people to question, to listen, or to really think for themselves. People learn that to succeed in the outer world, they must be first, the best, to fit in with what society dictates, and to be the loudest voice in the crowd in order to stand out. There is tremendous pressure to do and be these things.

When people follow this conventional recipe for success, they are headed for disappointment. The recipe may be all they know, and it may appear that others use it for great achievements. Yet it is based on a lie. At the root of the lie is a tangled web of false notions of the conditional world. They appear real because humanity has given them so much energy and accepted them as a guidebook for living.

False notions must be dispelled one at a time. You clear these errors in thinking by questioning things, listening to the wisdom of your inner voice, and making a conscious decision to update your view.

When atrophied talents are restored and made relevant for these times, a person has an intuitively guided rational means of responding to uncertainty and chaos. Those who are drawn to focus on these nontraditional approaches know, at a cellular level, that this time in history is unique.

The next cycle of shifting will not be a carbon copy of any other time, even though some dynamics are similar. The familiar themes—long part of the human landscape—include war, greed, ego-based control and power maneuvers, hatred and prejudice toward anything or anyone seeming to be different. There are plenty of fear-based messages of doom and gloom, often predicting the end of the world.

The Media during Earth's Pivotal Years

People today are enamored with their gadgets and technology. The multitude of devices and communication networks has enabled storytelling to morph into a twenty-four-hour phenomenon. People of diverse cultures can now communicate instantly worldwide. The media, like all of us, is changing in big ways.

The media has long been a force shaping public opinion. It has been a tool for education, connecting people with the latest news. As the media industry changes, it is becoming a potent vehicle for humanity's shift into higher consciousness.

Ideas that previously percolated among limited audiences, slow to manifest, today can ignite into tangible form with lightning speed. Messages that before might have gone out in only one form or perhaps a single time are now duplicated countless times and reach vast audiences. A person doesn't have to be a geek or social media maven to be influenced by the revolution in how we communicate. Indeed, humanity's paradigm shift would take much longer to occur without these changes.

Right now, we and the Earth are passing through a unique window of time during which the future of generations to come will be determined.

There is a big acceleration of evolution taking place. This means greater opportunities than ever before to create a light-filled world and to personally evolve. Each person living today has the potential for a huge leap in consciousness, leaving dysfunctional past patterns in the dust and moving forward without the heavy baggage.

The acceleration, along with its unique prospects for positive changes, is worthy of your attention. It is not your imagination. It is real. You will want to approach these times with your heart open and with sanity. You will want to become skilled in making appropriate choices quickly and with harm to none.

Steady Parade of Information

It will be important to develop discernment as you take in the steady parade of information available to you from all directions. You will be hearing predictions about the future from other people, at conferences, at the movies, in alternative media, on websites, and through social media.

Some of what you hear will be true. Some of the information will be based on truth, yet it will have a heavy dose of fear thrown in. Examples include Internet postings that misinterpret natural cycles, declaring that the end of a cycle means that all life will end.

A portion of messages about the future will simply be false, disseminated by well-meaning people who have misinterpreted what is happening. Some information will come from those who live in the shadow of the dark side, not yet having chosen the path of light. These people will warn you of inescapable devastation, catastrophes punishing evildoers, and conspiracies to control your very soul.

The Legacy of Earth's Great Sages

The real truth, of course, always comes out. For someone like you, wanting to make sense of things now—to fully utilize this unique window—you won't want to wait for the entire world to wake up to what all the fuss is about.

Humanity indeed has come a long way in embracing new ideas that are still in the birthing stage. A majority of the old-paradigm thinkers, however, continue to demand physical proof before even peeking at options outside the accepted norm.

The legacy of the Earth's wisdom keepers is available when one looks for it. Ancient cultures left instructions for future generations in their architecture, their writings, and in the oral stories they handed down from generation to generation. The people from these cultures understood the cycles of time and also the natural process of endings and beginnings. They knew about the kind of energy quickening occurring now on Earth.

The momentum of this evolutionary shifting will be increasing incrementally over the coming years. This is the time that many scientists and wisdom keepers of diverse cultures are linking with a great quantum shift. This time is referenced in both Eastern and Western traditions as a period when the Earth's cosmic cycles reach the end of one very long period and the beginning of something brand new. Such cycles are quite long by their very nature, spanning thousands of years. Specific dates aren't as important as the process that is involved.

Your Pivotal Choice Point

Decisions you make right now will determine how this cycle impacts you. The time of importance is now, when the decisions you and others make can dramatically change dire prospects into manageable situations. Choices made now will set in motion the seeds of your new future. This applies both individually and collectively.

Remember this the next time you feel that you can't make a difference or that you are being held back by a world that doesn't seem to care. The key here is that you can decide to care. You can care what happens to you, to your loved ones, and to others living on the Earth—and you can act on that caring as you go about your everyday living.

Connecting the Past with the Present

When you study the natural cycles of Earth's past, you can begin to understand more about your place in the universe.

Utilizing your intuitively guided reason in your research, you may feel a subtle knowing, or even a deep remembering, of what earlier humans did during such times. As part of that, when you hear about the Earth changes of humanity's past and what people did to cope, you may feel it's somehow familiar. If you seek understanding in a fearless and discerning way, without agenda, you may have an inner validation of the similarities between the past and the present.

There is ongoing research about humanity's past cycles, undertaken in these times to understand how and why previous great civilizations ended. As more of this research comes to light, you may then begin to connect the dots between these long-ago times and the precipice upon which you now stand.

Humanity Seeing Itself

Humanity in these cosmic moments can choose to see itself, its history, and its past cycles. As a collective, humanity can spark a grand shift into higher consciousness that impacts all of life.

That shifting is occurring right now, as you read these words!

You came to participate in this great shift. At the deepest levels of your being, you know that you are living now to be here for this. You came to watch the shift unfold as well, but not as a bystander. Your watching is meant to be active, participatory, intuitively intelligent, and visionary. You came to observe the world in a new way—seeing from the expansive perspective of an active cocreator.

You came to see countless unworkable societal structures fall away, and to be instrumental in helping to create a more enlightened world. If this seems like much more than you signed up for, consider that you indeed have the resources to pull this off. Remember that you are a divine changemaker, here to help create the needed changes.

You may describe yourself as a person on the path of light, but you are no lightweight.

You see your human self when you look in the mirror, yet that body is merely the temporary housing for your eternal spirit. Your spiritual self knows that this pivotal time involves a quantum spiritual leap. This part of you, speaking through your own higher wisdom, can help you to navigate the choppy waters and make sense of these times.

※

Tips: Gathering Information Sensibly

How do you apply discernment to the plethora of information about the state of our society and our future? How do you see through all the hype to discover what's genuine and true for you? How do you tell when a piece of information is merely someone's attempt at profit mongering? How do you know whether something is merely a rumor, repeated so many times on the Internet that large numbers of people believe it? Being able to answer these types of questions will help you stay sane during these times of great change.

The following are some guidelines for sensible information gathering. They can be applied in general as well as to your discovery of truth about media reports.

1. **Invite your higher wisdom to bring to your attention the information that will help you understand the great shift happening on the planet.** Ask to be guided to media resources and teachers you can respect and trust. Ask to be steered away from fear-based propaganda and media messages with a control agenda. After asking, pay attention to dreams, to people sent your way, and to messages you are drawn to in the media. These could be books, messages in

social media, postings on the Internet, films, and gatherings of people interested in evolving consciousness.

2. **Regularly question what you take in with your senses, not out of fear but out of a sincere desire to discover truth.** Don't assume that because a trusted leader or teacher is saying something that this person has all the facts. Realize that within many of the media's messages are subliminal triggers that can stir fear-based belief systems in your DNA.

3. **Remember that the Earth is a place of opposites, and not everyone will see something the same way you do.** These people are not your enemy, and their ideas are not something you need to fight. Stay centered in your own truth.

4. **Be alert to information saying the future is set in stone.** No one knows exactly what will happen to you or to the planet on a given date. There may be indications of future happenings based on past patterns and current actions, yet your future is something you create moment by moment as you make new choices. The future is so fluid, in fact, that you can redirect your destiny with decisions made even in the final days of a great shift cycle.

5. **Become mindful of the company you keep.** When possible, invite the company of those who have an optimistic vision of what's possible. Spend time with people who are actively working to create positive changes in their lives. If people begin complaining and start going into worry mode, remember that you have a choice about whether you chime in. You can decide in each moment how you will respond to your outer world. Complaining and worrying will send you into a spiral of downward negative energy, which will

deplete your life force, dampen your creativity, and block your real passion for being alive in these times.

6. **Make spirit more of a priority in your life during this pivotal cycle.** There is no time like right now to begin making spirit more real, more tangible, and more integrated within your human expression. Spirit is not separate from you; it is the source of your wisdom. Be open to new ways to connect more to the energy of spirit that is always within you. Allow this divine force to show you the way out of the chaos and into the light. Invite spirit to help you answer questions such as the following when you want clarity about the changes of these times.

Who? Ask who is saying what you are hearing or reading. Who is the source? What do you know about this person? Do you intuitively feel a sense of respect when you think of this person? Another part of who is you—what part of you is listening, caring, judging, or responding? Consider your role as you receive the information. What state of mind are you in as you receive the news?

What? Ask what the message you're receiving is really about. Dive deeper to discern what the film or author or speaker wants to convey. Do the facts seem to have any substance? Does the information appear to be fear-based or to have an agenda of control? As you take in the information, notice whether any relevant data is excluded. Is the message warning you that you have no way out? Does the information seem punitive? Is the focus of the information on helping others? Does the message feel like it's coming from the heart?

When? Ask about the timing of disseminating this message now. Consider why the source would say this right then. Question any underlying agenda at play. Look at the timing of the message and how the source could possibly know what he or she is saying. If it's a prediction, remember that a prediction is only one possible outcome based on current energies. If this outcome is similar to one that has happened in humanity's past, there is still no guarantee it will be repeated now. Do your own investigations into past cycles of history to better understand what happened in the past. For the best clarity, find a number of different types of sources for this history. Be mindful that many times historical accounts are speculation, yet when repeated enough times over mass media circuits, they can seem very real. Spotting this kind of misinformation will take some training and practice. As always, remember to invite spirit and your heart's wisdom into your process.

Where? Ask where the information is coming from. A government with a history of hiding information may not be revealing the whole story. An organization known for radical religious views may have an agenda. Read Internet postings with care, remembering that even spiritual-related websites can include incomplete, inaccurate, or biased information. Consider getting at least some of your news from outside traditional sources. For example, Americans can monitor news about the United States coming from media in Europe and elsewhere. Citizens of all countries can consider looking to nontraditional sources of news, including the Internet. Regardless of where you look to be informed, remember to look under what is presented. You can be discerning without becoming cynical and jaded.

Why? Ask why the information is important. Does the communication fully address the why in your view? Does anything seem missing, and if so, what? As you take in the information, is a part of you suspicious about the motives or hidden agenda of the author? Allow your intuitively guided reason to show you what to be alert to.

How? Ask how the information is presented. If it's a TV talk show interview, does the host seem to have a fear-based bias? If it's a press conference, does the spokesperson invite questions or simply disseminate a prepared statement? Do you wonder, after receiving the information, what was left out? How does the information make you feel? Check in with your heart. Invite your heart to show you what to pay attention to, what's really important, and how you can most appropriately follow up on the information.

Different Skills for Different Times

Becoming skillful with inquiry will put you light years ahead of the average person. These skills are essential for being able to intelligently respond to the steady increase of input. You want to be able to discern fact from fiction. Without discernment, you are vulnerable as you are exposed to prophecies, fantasies, and half-truths.

Becoming practiced in asking probing questions will help you find balance and benefit most fully from being alive now. This is not your ordinary lifetime, so ordinary questions do not suffice.

During these times, the world is being profoundly impacted by the cumulative force of an awakening consciousness. Well under way already, it is the biggest shift in consciousness humanity has seen in so short a time period. Much of this forward movement is difficult to discern, however. That's because most people tend to put their focus on what's wrong during times of hardship. Despite this, the perceptive person can sense the force of awakening that is building and reaching new levels of progress each year.

Right now humanity stands on the edge of the crucial jumping-off point that can allow for a dramatic leap into higher consciousness. This is the leap you are on Earth to make, what you have been working toward—knowingly or unknowingly—your whole life.

The new paradigm of enlightened consciousness is more within reach than ever, despite what you hear to the contrary. It's important that you believe this and that you focus your energies on creating it—mainly within yourself but also in your actions taken in the world.

The more consciously you work to create this new paradigm in the next cycle, the greater your opportunity to shift into a higher-vibrational state and to positively impact the planet. As you do this inner work, you will be assisting others around you and also helping to create a more heart-centered world.

It is vital during these times of great change to stay awake to the lies and manipulation. You will be told that there's no hope for the planet and that future generations will face a bleak existence. You will be told that you must give up your freedoms to be protected from the enemy. You may be told that it's too costly (or some other explanation) to fix our dysfunctional systems involving health care, allocation of resources, and destruction of the environment. None of this is true.

Your Intentions and Actions Count

Set your intention right now to be someone who seriously questions what is happening, and to take conscious responsible action in the world to be a positive force for change. Intend to do this continually, regardless of what seems to be happening. Remember that your intentions and actions count.

The momentum of change is all around you. You can see evidence of it regularly. Noticing the discontent in people and their desire for something brand new can become inspirational reminders that people are growing less accepting of conventional ways of being. When you view it this way, rather than as a reminder of how much everyone is suffering, you shift your vibration higher. This view may also inspire you to be of more service to others.

People in all corners of the world are beginning to have less tolerance of lies, hidden agendas, broken promises, cover-ups, and deceit of all kinds. These ways of being, and public outcry about them, are now more out in the open than ever before.

Differing points of view about truth continue to be a source of conflict on both a personal level and within groups of people. Most of the wars fought between peoples have involved disagreements about truth.

Some cultures teach the idea that there will be a final battle between good and evil, and that only certain good ones—classified by their idea of good—will survive and be saved. Other cultures have very different ideas of truth. The truths at issue will always be relative truths, based on the conventional reality.

Your truth may look quite different than another person's truth. How you define truth is often connected to what you think is real. However, consider that without a full awareness of reality, including the physical and nonphysical, it is impossible to know truth except in relative terms.

*

Checklist: Accelerating Your Personal Transformation

The following are some guidelines for approaching your own personal transformation. Become still and tune out the world's chatter for a few minutes as you read these words. Invite your intuitively guided reason to show you which of these is a priority for you right now. You can come back to this list again later. Notice if your priorities have shifted, and discover additional insights about your personal journey.

1. **Observe your mind**. Become more aware of what you are thinking, what you focus on, and what you say repeatedly to yourself. This will give you clues about what belief systems you hold within you at the DNA level.

2. **Learn to focus your mind**. You can do a number of things at one time, yet your mind can only efficiently focus on one thing at a time. Notice when you go out of focus,

putting your attention on another topic. Practice focusing your mind on something positive you wish to create or experience.

3. **Bring your intuitive right brain more into your everyday experience.** For example, as you focus on something you desire to create, imagine your creation in living color, with the details filled in. Allow your right brain to come up with additional details you may not have included when thinking of your creation through logic alone.

4. **Question.** Set your intention to question things you have never questioned before, and then get into the habit of questioning what the world presents. It could be a television show that glorifies meanness, your doctor giving a dire prognosis, or government officials taking away your freedoms. It could be something personal, such as a relationship challenge, or your doubts about personal progress in recent years. Question these things and more.

5. **Take action on your questioning.** If you inquired within about your doctor's prognosis and received very emphatic, intuitive guidance that your doctor doesn't have all the information—with another more positive outcome being possible—refuse to let the doctor's prognosis decide the outcome. Be willing to take every step you can to create a different outcome. Invite a divine solution and ask to be shown the way one step at a time. Continue to trust what your heart tells you is true for you.

6. **Do not settle for an everyday approach to personal growth.** Conventional approaches do not allow you to progress spiritually. You are not alive today to be conventional; you are here to make a new mold. Ask to be

guided to new-paradigm methods of healing and knowing the self. Find and apply new approaches in ways that suit the particular approach. Have the courage to stick with it, even when your lifestyle seems increasingly foreign when compared with that of the everyday person. Remember during times when your courage wavers that you are not here now to simply continue your cycle of ordinary existence. You are here to rediscover the divine at the core of your being.

7. **Become more compassionate.** Without compassion for yourself and others, you will not be able to realize your true divine nature.

8. **Drop all judgments.** Set your intention that you will become more awake to your judgments. We have a habitual tendency to judge everyone and everything; this puts people and things into boxes labeled right and wrong, good and bad. When you judge, you reinforce the polarity of opposites, and in the process, you limit yourself. Decide that you will judge less and be more accepting of what is.

9. **Reassess and update your relationship with yourself regularly.** Get into the habit of frequently asking yourself whether your life is reflecting the new-paradigm road you desire to travel. At home, for example, you can reevaluate your environment, your lifestyle, and even your clothes. Consider whether some modifications are in order. You may have an extra bedroom filled with things you hardly ever use, and you've been wondering where you would find a quiet space for your meditation practice. Perhaps some reorganization could serve a number of purposes.

Another example could be your quiet time, and the realization that you would like to devote more time to inner reflection and being still. Consider what outside distractions and other factors you would need to address.

A third example involves looking at your use of time and energy in the context of the path you want to travel. One week you may have invitations to become involved in several diverse projects. When you carefully evaluate each one—using your heart's wisdom and keeping the big picture in mind—you may realize that at least one of the projects may divert you from your goals. You may discover that there are much better uses of your time and energy.

10. **Trust that you will be guided to solutions.** Regardless of how hopeless a personal dilemma may seem, it is important that you trust there is a divine solution. Invite in this solution and then be open to how and when it shows up. The solution that is perfect for you may not be the solution that would work for others, yet it will be exactly what you need. If your dilemma remains unresolved after a time, it is important that you are willing to simply *be* with your condition. If you can learn to accept what is and to know that there is always a higher purpose to things, you can find peace.

11. **Use your time wisely.** Remember that each moment and each new day is an opportunity to grow spiritually, to love, and to progress on your path of light. Set your intention that you will make full use of your gift of physical life. Treasure the moments during which you experience love, openings, and awakening to the movement of spirit. Let go of the rest.

12. **Go gently with yourself.** Treat yourself as you would a best friend. When you know you need to rest, don't push yourself needlessly. When you have suffered a major disappointment, be kind to yourself. When you don't meet your own expectations, resist the temptation to criticize yourself.

Chapter 7
Heart-Centered Living

You are in the midst of a revolution in how humans relate to one another. There is a deep yearning for change. What is this change, and why are these moments in time so vital to the progress and survival of humanity? The change involves the most basic elements of what it means to be human. It's like taking the typical human life and turning it upside down!

Moving from "What's in It for Me?" to "How Can I Help?"

The "What's-in-it-for-me?" approach is being replaced by one that asks, "What can I do to help others?" The change is to a brand-new paradigm in which people express unity and connectedness. It includes a remembrance, held deep within each person's inner being, that the heart is the key to being free. It means that people across the planet are waking up to the destructive force of fear. It involves a relearning of how to be a whole human, utilizing both receptive and active qualities. In this new world, the feminine principle joins with the masculine.

For humanity as a species, it's now clear that the status quo cannot continue. The human race is now plagued by a plethora of challenges, each one of them of massive proportions. Most of these problems are rooted in the imbalances humans themselves have created through competition, greed, and exploitation. These crises will not be solved with the tools that created them. They will not be solved, or even fully understood, with fear-based agendas.

The solutions will be found when people learn to move out of fear and into their hearts. This may sound simple, but it is not so easy in practice. It's one thing to grasp the idea of being in your heart. When you learn that this is a key to your spiritual progression, you naturally embrace it. The challenges come when you attempt to live fearlessly in a fear-based world.

Fear is so much a part of your conditioning that it's a difficult energy to banish. It is a bit like the party crasher who comes without warning into your gathering to spoil the fun. Fear is like that, an unwelcome guest within you. The energy of the fear, when not tamed, can prevent you from living in your heart.

Understanding Fear

When you respond to life events with fear, you will generate even more fear. As soon as you go into fear, the natural ability to connect with your heart is obstructed. When this happens, the next interactions you have with yourself and others are clouded by fear. Your energy then spirals downward. When you reside in the lower-frequency energy of fear, it becomes more challenging for you to discern the truth of what is happening.

This can lead to feelings of insecurity and failure. When you are in that state, there is a tendency to expand upon the fear you already have. This expansion of fear is then incorporated into how you relate to yourself and the world.

The Real Threat of Violence

All of the violence you see in the world, whether on a personal or global scale, comes from fear.

Violence is a poison that threatens humanity's survival. There has been so much of it over humanity's history that there is a cumulative impact that is very real. The planet is now showing humanity the results of these toxins.

Although there is a genuine underlying desire for a peaceful world, individuals and countries continue to express violence. It's something that has been learned. Violence is not a natural response of the whole human. New teachings are needed, and these are now in the process of unfolding all over the world.

There are many forms of violence. The most obvious kinds, when you think of conflicts between countries, are war and the loss of life. Other types of physical violence include murder, beatings, and drive-by shootings. Just as poisonous are forms of violence that are verbal or psychological.

It's common these days to see violence in the schools, at sports arenas, and even at markets and shopping malls. Destructive force can also be used against oneself. This self-abuse can take many forms, from injuring oneself with drugs to fatally harming oneself through suicide.

Violence can be something that actually happens to you, to someone you love, or to a stranger shown on the evening news. Violence can also be a made-up story, seen at the movies or on your TV screen, depicting a conflict and themes involving good and evil.

At the root of most types of violence are fear-based belief systems that label others as the enemy, as bad in some way, or as simply a threat. When a person feels threatened by another, there is a learned tendency to compensate by going on the offense or defense. What this means in practice is relating to others in ways that produce conflict instead of peace.

Alienating communications are seen everywhere, from the

bedroom to the boardroom and beyond. They are a product of the old-paradigm approach that says, "If I am right, you must be wrong," and vice versa.

Reversing the Cycle of Violence

To turn this around will require the effort of individual people, each one learning how to relate from mutual respect, honoring, and cooperation. A key element here is compassion, the ability to care for self and others.

When you are compassionate, you have a genuine desire to see others freed from their suffering. This desire is not dependent upon your relationship with another person. True compassion is boundless. You don't set boundaries when deciding whether to extend compassion to this person or that person. You don't have to agree with someone's politics or lifestyle to have compassion for them. You can have compassion for your enemy as well as for your friend.

Developing compassion for yourself will help you to generate this quality to extend to others. At the core of your being, you already have the ability to be compassionate because this is naturally within you. Once you begin to remember this, and to access the related knowing of your connectedness to all other beings, compassion can blossom from within you.

Compassion is a quality you can express more fully as you become whole.

Balancing Feminine and Masculine—A New Paradigm

To be whole involves a balancing of your feminine and masculine aspects. You are now at a pivotal juncture: the new, more light-filled world you seek to inhabit cannot come into being until humanity has a balance of the feminine and masculine. For centuries, the feminine face of the divine has been given a backseat.

In the patriarchal traditions of your ancestors, the natural feminine principles were given a lesser importance. Masculine qualities of conquest, competition, and control dominated the scene.

The fully realized person operates from a balance between the divine feminine and divine masculine. Divine is the key word here. Your ancestors forgot their natural divine nature and moved into ego-based relating.

The outmoded patriarchal society—with its focus on war and fear-based manipulation—is in its death throes. It is collapsing because it ignores universal laws of wholeness and goodness. It keeps humanity in a primitive, machinelike state that ignores the natural union of feminine and masculine.

The heart and intuition are discounted in the old paradigm. The left logical brain is what this dying society prizes, to the exclusion of the heart and intuitive right brain.

Each person is naturally meant to access both masculine and feminine aspects. It is not about gender. This energy, when joined fully in one's life, creates wholeness and balance.

The current state of the world is a reflection of the imbalance of feminine and masculine. Humanity in general has acknowledged the receptive and nurturing roles of the feminine. However, these qualities are defined as inferior to the masculine qualities of action and logical thinking.

The result of humanity's imbalance of masculine and feminine is seen all around you. The Earth itself is crying out for nurturing and respect. The peoples of the Earth are suffering needlessly because of political and social actions of the powerful few who act out of greed, fear, and hate.

What you have on a world scale is a decision-making model that is based on profits and wealth making for an elite group. This egotistical model does not allow sufficient concern for the needs of individuals, the planet's ecology, or the impact on the collective. This off-balance approach is creating an off-balance world.

Choosing Love and Kindness

Progress during this time of the shift into the new paradigm can be made only when people choose love and kindness. These are the natural antidotes to the myriad of challenges you and humanity face.

The choice to be loving and kind needs to be made through intent, even at times when you are unsure of how to express yourself in a loving or kind way.

When you are confused about how to do it, or when you simply feel ill equipped to be loving and kind, continue with your intent to choose the high road of the heart. Take a stand in that instant, deciding you will do your best.

Invite spirit's input to help you when you waver. Remind yourself of the importance of each moment; each choice counts. Think of the big picture, including how your actions impact others.

Consider the progress of your soul. Remember that the choice of coming from love and kindness must be an individual decision, made moment by moment during the course of an ordinary life. Each person needs to make this choice, again and again, even if others continue to choose the old outmoded ways. Without this altered course, the future of humanity on the Earth that you now call home is a big question mark.

Why Relationships Matter

If you are reading these words, it's because you want to be an integral part of the changes now under way. You want to better understand the shift in consciousness and to know your part in it. You also want to accelerate the process of your own awakening and to move forward with less suffering and more joy.

Know that your relationships are a very vital piece of the puzzle.

Each relationship holds within it some of the threads you will need to weave your own tapestry of heart-centered consciousness.

You cannot and do not do it alone. You may discount some of your relationships as trivial or even curse them for bringing you pain, but they matter in the larger picture. Each relationship that you have can help you to see yourself more clearly and to learn how to be more loving. Oftentimes, you learn the most from those who make you feel uncomfortable, angry, or unloved.

All of the relationships of your life are a fertile ground for your growth. You can learn from each one of them, advancing your progress by leaps and bounds.

Consider the many types of relationships you have. For starters, you are in a relationship with yourself. As you work with everyday issues and visualize your dreams, this is always the relationship you are coming back to. You will view all of your other relationships in terms of how you view yourself.

Your other relationships include your connections with spirit and the nonphysical world in general. You are also in relationships with your loved ones, coworkers, neighbors, store clerks, strangers you see on the street, and a diverse set of other people you may connect with from time to time.

You aren't just in relationships with people either. You have a relationship with your body, your home, your car or mass transit system, your computer, your pets (or the pets of neighbors), and even with time. These are just a few of the many people and things you relate to in some way.

Sometimes people move into a phase in which they withdraw from meaningful relationships with others. This can result from disappointments, loss of trust, or doubt in one's ability to create harmony with other people. Long-term withdrawal from significant human interaction is different from times when a person purposefully steps back for self-reflection and inner work to better understand oneself. These time-outs are a useful tool, especially when relationships have been rocky and unfulfilling.

Questions: Discovering Remedies for a Difficult Relationship

If you are now in a difficult relationship, remember to give yourself moments of reflection and refueling by spirit so that you can bring more light into the relationship. Ask to be shown what you are learning about yourself by being in the relationship. Allow yourself to consider a different view by imagining you are in the other person's shoes.

One way to do this contemplating is to become still, to be away from the person triggering the pain, and to visualize your relationship. You want to approach this process as truthfully as you can, without an agenda.

If you are angry with the person, first allow your heated emotions to cool so you won't be looking at the other person from the place of anger. To transmute your anger, it may help to focus on something you like about the other person. When you can connect with gratitude, you raise your energetic vibratory state higher, giving you a more accurate assessment of your relationship.

Once you have diffused your anger, take a few moments to visualize the person causing you angst. As this person's face comes into your awareness, invite your intuitively guided reason to help you answer questions such as these.

1. Why is this person such a pivotal force in my life?
2. What am I not seeing about this relationship?
3. How is my thinking causing disharmony with this person?
4. What about this relationship is a familiar theme in my life?
5. How can I have a more loving relationship with this person?
6. What can I do right now to help improve this relationship?
7. How can I be more patient with myself and this person?
8. What is the biggest gift I've received from this relationship?

The answers to these questions can lead to more understanding of underlying friction, helping you to see what's needed to shift out of suffering. The key here is to be boldly honest with yourself and to honor the inner wisdom you receive. Don't be concerned with whether or not the answers place you in a positive light, or whether or not you think it's possible to change.

The walls you are feeling in this relationship are really your own inner walls, erected one brick at a time as you lived in a world that didn't understand how to love. Trust that dismantling these walls is possible. Know that it will happen when you have understood what the walls represent, and that the dissolution will take place one brick at a time.

Keep in mind that whatever you learn from the current relationship can be of benefit to your future relationships, as well as to your overall spiritual progress. You are discovering brand-new ways of relating that involve a heart connection.

If you are like most people, you did not learn how to do this as a child. This is because the people who raised you and who modeled life for you did not know how to do it. When you grew up and entered the adult world, you had regular feedback about the importance of being smart and successful. You heard a lot about the significance of keeping up with everyone else. The world gave you messages that encouraged you to be logical and left-brained because these things were highly prized. You suffered because your heart was left out of the picture.

As you contemplate your current relationship, inquire within yourself to discover potential new approaches to resolving longstanding problems you have as you relate to this person and other people.

Remember to look for patterns. Humans are creatures of habit, learning over time by repetition the behaviors that they apply in relationships.

Ask your higher self to help you see the benefits of knowing this person, staying in the relationship, or leaving the relationship.

Remember to continually ask spirit to give you more clarity and a higher view, allowing the answers, in whatever form they are given, to lead you to more heart-focused relating.

It is helpful to remind yourself that you aren't alone in experiencing pain in relationships. There is not one person you will encounter who can truthfully tell you that his or her life has been exempt from such pain.

When you consider something you are personally feeling as universal, shared by many beings around you, the pain takes on a different and more manageable energy. You have changed your view of the pain, and this will help you to face it, see it truthfully, work with it, and heal from its effects.

Blocks to Openheartedness

In your everyday world, how often do you encounter two people who appear to be connecting heart to heart in a fearless and nonjudgmental way?

Ask any person whether he or she would like to feel more love and openheartedness in their world; chances are he or she would say yes. Many people will even tell you that having more love is a major priority in life. It's natural to want to feel accepted and connected with others—the alternative is feeling rejected and disconnected. When you feel separate and wounded, the world may seem to be a very unfriendly place.

You may not feel secure enough to be in your heart. The ordinary world conditions you to play it safe, avoiding genuine heart connections except in rare instances.

※

Process: Shifting into Openheartedness

Here's a self-test for heart-level sharing. You may want to work with this now and then revisit the process regularly. You can discover over time your progress in creating more heart-centered relationships.

Right now, consider how many of your typical human interactions involve intimacy and heart-level sharing. Of the many people you see and communicate with, which ones mirror back to you a feeling of being whole and complete?

As you contemplate their names and faces, remember to include the people you love as well as others you encounter in the happenstance of your life. Imagine them one by one, picturing typical conversations and energetic exchanges.

Invite your intuitively guided reason to give you examples of heart-level sharing in your life. Even if only one person comes to mind, focus on that one person for now. It could be a friend you have learned to trust, a romantic partner who helps you to feel cared for, or some other special person who uplifts you.

Picture talking to or being with this person. Imagine both sides of the conversation and think of different scenarios, including the ones that trigger negative emotions. Reflect on how much of an effort it is to relate lovingly and openly, and how much of the time you are able to do it. Let go of blame when you think of the other person or yourself. Simply allow for an honest appraisal.

Invite spirit to help you uncover the patterns that cause you to erect a wall around your heart. These are learned and artificial ways of being. The time to begin dismantling them is now.

Living in a heart-focused way is each person's divine birthright just waiting to be discovered, cultivated, and realized. This state of being, which many would call bliss, is not for a select few who have trained at mystery schools. It is not something you have to earn.

However, due to human conditioning focused on pain and suffering, a quantum shift in viewpoint is required. This involves a change in your very DNA, a kind of record keeper of who you are at every level, including belief systems.

To change and shift into a higher, more loving consciousness, you must be willing to fully excavate the undiscovered territory within. You must become fully engaged with all that you experience, allowing people and circumstances to teach you and to help you grow. Resistance must be recognized, faced, and dealt with if you are to succeed. This simple but intricate process involves developing a quality of fearlessness. You will need courage to fully see yourself. Any deep self-reflection will uncover plenty of good as well as bad and ugly elements.

Perhaps you feel weary at times, even discouraged about your progress. You may sometimes doubt that you are up to the task of returning to your heart and fully residing there as you face life's obstacles. The challenge oftentimes may seem beyond what you can handle.

Even though a part of you knows better, it can be tempting to retreat into a victim role. You have lots of training in how to blame, compare, and complain. You have learned victim tendencies through observation and life experience, and you have also inherited many of these patterns from the DNA of your ancestors.

The victim mentality has been part of the human landscape for so long that it isn't easy to shake, even for the advanced person.

What to Do When You Feel Wronged

When you find yourself feeling wronged, take a time-out. Breathe deeply and let go of the need to figure things out or to change your circumstances in this instant. Remember that the painful patterns did not magically appear overnight. Know that even as you begin to unravel and heal these destructive issues, it can take time for you to recognize the subtle changes within yourself. This means the journey may sometimes appear to involve the same scenery you are used to seeing, when in fact elements have shifted and look identical only to the untrained eye.

Recognizing Your Progress

As you make changes and transform yourself, the road of life you travel on may seem like the same two-lane highway you have traveled for a very long time. It takes a skilled eye to recognize that this road has been resurfaced and widened. As you grow in awareness, you begin to notice subtle clues about how much you are transforming.

For example, as you travel down your two-lane highway, you may notice there is more room and space for the cars to pass one another. Fewer cars honk their horns, and when they do, you are increasingly able to remain centered and unbothered. The signals at intersections are green more often too.

You notice this, connecting this outer manifestation with your calmer inner state. When the light does turn red, you are less likely to take it personally or to become concerned about your important appointments. You realize that you are learning to be more present, including with the element of time. There is freedom in recognizing that time isn't your nemesis. If you have a flat tire, you may find that the renovated road has a new turnout lane. All you need to do is pull over, and help naturally comes to your aid.

You discover that the help you need comes much more quickly when you are grateful for what you have in the moment. Therefore, you regularly remind yourself of your blessings and make mental checklists of things that you are thankful for.

Sometimes you forget the gratitude and just get angry at the flat tire. "After all," you complain, "I shouldn't have to suffer like this!" Remember that even when you travel the resurfaced road, you are still human. You won't be able to control the outcome or prevent the ups and downs that are part of the rhythm of life. You can, however, learn to travel a middle path of balance. You can learn to be the love you have sought for so long, broadcasting that love to others. Over time, the potent force of love you generate within creates a life filled with love!

How to Move into Your Heart

Connecting with your heart is vital in these times of accelerated energy and unprecedented change. It can no longer be an afterthought. The old ways of coping with stress and confusion—involving strategizing and looking to the outside world for answers—will not get you to a place of peacefulness. These are new times. To achieve more balance and harmony in the midst of today's chaos will require a firm heart connection. When you come from this heart-focused space, you can learn to connect with your heart's infinite wisdom.

In order to be in your heart and to come from your heart as you experience life, you must be grounded. This is a challenge for most people, having been trained to intellectualize. Your mind and heart cannot be fully integrated if you reside mostly in your head. The head-focused approach will leave you ungrounded and unable to access your heart. You will feel disoriented, spacey, or unable to focus your thoughts.

How do you get grounded? One way is to get in touch with your breath and to focus your energy on your feet. Imagine that your feet are connected to the ground and that you are receiving a powerful red energy from the Earth. Visualize that red energy coming into your feet, up both of your legs to your waist, and then circulating back down into the Earth below your feet. Imagine that this red energy is bringing vitality into your body. If you do this a few times as you breathe deeply in and out, you will begin to feel more centered and connected with your body.

Additional tools for grounding include eating something nutritious and drinking some purified water.

As part of your grounding process, it's helpful to pay attention to your body and emotions for any messages they give you. For example, your eyes may remind you to rest a few minutes away from the computer. You may also recognize that you are feeling needlessly anxious about a deadline. When you acknowledge these things and take a brief time out from your stress, you can again find your center.

Spend a few moments focusing on this grounded connection several times a day. Do it even if you think you are already grounded. This will help you to get and stay more present in the moment and will help you to focus intuitively from your heart rather than from fear-based thoughts in your conditioned mind.

※

Checklist: Connecting to Your Heart

It can be useful to regularly run through the following checklist in order to be more connected to your heart in everyday life. Allow your intuitively guided reason to show you the answers to each of the following.

1. When I interact with the world, am I grounded, or am I feeling disoriented and unfocused?

2. When others are speaking, am I able to focus on what they are saying and let go of my own thoughts?

3. When I am speaking to others, are my words expressed without judgment?

4. When I interact with others, do I let go of the need to receive their approval?

5. When I am considering an important decision and I get an uneasy feeling about moving forward, do I honor my intuitive knowing?

6. When I am under stress, am I able to let go of worry and find something for which to feel grateful?

7. When I feel angry or hurt, do I pause long enough before acting to get in touch with how I am feeling and acknowledge the feelings?

8. When I have a task to do, am I able to keep my focus on the present, or do I obsess about the past or future?

9. When I receive bad news of a personal nature, do I let go of the temptation to act on it before I've checked in with my heart and my own intuitive guidance?

10. When I hear bad news broadcast in the media, do I avoid responding in fear and turn inward to seek my heart's wisdom?

To the extent that you can truthfully answer yes to these questions, you will have a validation of how much you are connecting with your heart.

If you get no to any of these questions, ask your higher self to show you what needs to shift within you so that the answer becomes yes. Ask to be shown how your thinking and belief systems prevent you from fully accessing the wisdom of your heart. Ask for help in developing more patience, acceptance, and self-love.

After inquiring about your personal transformation and asking for help from your higher self, remember to let go of the need for an immediate fix. Go gently with yourself. Trust that the help is coming to you even if you can't yet see the results. Use this checklist whenever you are experiencing disharmony in relationships too.

Creating More Joy—Having More Love

It is a natural human desire to want love and loving relationships. Creating joy in these times will be directly linked to your ability to develop, build, and sustain loving relationships. This includes your romantic love relationships as well as the many other types you have.

Each of your relationships is important because each presents a potential for your growth and evolution. Every time you relate to another human being, you receive feedback—whether you recognize it or not—that can be useful to your journey. There are learning opportunities with even seemingly insignificant people like your landlord, webmaster, and pet sitter. Each of them can teach you something new about how to love.

Your most intimate love relationships can provide a kind of crash course in love. One reason for this is the amount of time you spend with him or her, as well as the intensity of your interactions. The feelings of intensity can be heightened if you have known him or her for a long time. Another factor is similarity. It's common to attract a partner with some of the same agreeable and disagreeable traits exhibited by former love interests. As an example, if you like outgoing people, you will attract extroverts. Likewise, if you have unresolved trust issues from former relationships, mistrust may continue to be an issue in your relationships.

People living during earlier cycles did not feel the sort of discontent you now feel. Relationships went sour just like they do now, but people had little understanding of the underlying causes. Few people understood the nature of repeating patterns. There was more acceptance of the status quo, in part because people were unaware that there were solutions for relationship challenges. People in modern relationships are dissatisfied and want more.

Why? You are living in the midst of a giant leap, of an alteration of paradigms. You haven't lived through anything like this before. The new paradigm you are helping to birth involves finding a more enlightened way for people to relate to one another. That includes humanity remembering how to love unconditionally.

Yes, you are a part of this shift, even if you don't yet accept that you have the power to dramatically change the course of human history. Because you are a part of the shift, and that shift is happening all around you, you may feel an irresistible desire to heal your dysfunctional relationships and painful patterns.

On some days, the volume of your pain may seem to have been turned up so high that you question whether you can go on. It's natural that you would feel this way. However, know that what you suffer from is not fatal. It's the accelerated blossoming of consciousness, and there will be growing pains.

Each person has a slightly different path and a unique way to bloom, but the eventual destination for everyone is the same.

What can you do to lighten the load and have more joy birthing the new paradigm?

※

Tips: Finding Inner Peace

Fuel of discontent—Allow your discontent to fuel the positive change you seek. Remind yourself that your discontent is a symptom and is not to be feared. It's showing you the need for transformation; it's bringing to light truths that you would not otherwise see. Allow your inner wisdom to show you what to do next. In each moment, there is a part of you that knows exactly what to do. That wise part of you has all the answers that you seek. Begin to trust these answers when they come to you.

Self-appreciation—Make it your priority to love yourself more each day. Start with wherever you are right now. If you haven't yet begun to appreciate yourself, today is the perfect day to start. *Consider writing a list of five things you appreciate about yourself.* If nothing immediately comes to mind, think of things others have said to you in praise. It doesn't have to be current. Perhaps your mother complimented you for a good grade when you were ten, or your best friend told you why he or she liked being your friend in college. If you still can't think of something to appreciate, consider the things you do well. This can be a source of appreciation too. Everyone does something well. Simply record the first ideas of appreciation that come to you, add to this list daily, and refer to it often.

Appreciation of others—In order to help build a more loving relationship with anyone in your life, consider making a list of things you appreciate about the person. This works with best friends as well as with adversaries. If you look deeply enough, you can always find something to appreciate. After all, there's something good in everyone. Reminding yourself of what you appreciate about others can help you to maintain a more positive focus. In the process, you may observe that the person does something causing you to appreciate him or her even more!

Giving—Shift your focus from what you want to get from others and give instead. The joy of giving to others without strings attached cannot be measured. Consider what you would like others to give to you and then go ahead (within reason) and give it to yourself.

Setting intention—Set your intention daily to be more observant of the happenstance of your life, to look within yourself for answers to life's problems, and to learn to listen more effectively.

Being a conscious observer places you in present time. This allows you to have current information. When you don't observe carefully, you could miss important clues about the optimal next steps. Become like a scientist studying your own life, your observations leading to self-questioning that can lead to self-correction and an ongoing self-renewal.

Know that looking within yourself for answers is an approach that will take lots of practice to be successful. That's because society has conditioned you to believe everyone except you has the answers! It will take time and lots of experiences before you learn to value your own inner wisdom.

As part of observing, it is vital that you learn the art of effective listening. Becoming a good listener makes you a much better observer. Effective listening involves sincere attention to what is being said, without interrupting or interpreting. As with other skills a person develops, listening requires patience, practice, artful timing, and self-observation.

Clearing belief systems in your DNA—The limiting belief systems you hold in your subconscious are like a weight on your shoulders, preventing you from living a life of joy and fulfilling relationships. Everyone has limiting beliefs about something; they are in your DNA. These beliefs are hidden from ordinary view but impact you nonetheless. For people who are married or living together in a romantic partnership, the three topics argued about most are money, intimacy, and work.

✳

Checklist: Sabotaging Belief Systems in Your DNA

The belief systems in your DNA can be positive or negative. Each of us carries both types. There is no reason to have concern about positive ones. If you believe that you deserve to be happy, then of course you want to continue thinking that way. The beliefs that sabotage you are the negative ones that you don't know are operating in your life. You may recognize that you associate love with pain. However, you may not realize that you have specific beliefs in your DNA that continually reinforce that experience.

The following is a checklist of negative beliefs that are common within people.

- No one understands me.
- Life is a struggle.
- Money is hard to come by.
- I never have enough.
- I get hurt every time I love or trust someone.
- It's weak to show I need anything.
- People never consider what I want.
- No one has time for me.
- Love is painful.

In order to navigate the paradigm shift with more ease, it's helpful to begin uncovering and clearing these types of beliefs from your DNA. Positive thinking and wishing won't make them disappear.

Clearing these patterns at the cellular DNA level will greatly speed your journey into wholeness.

Right now, as humanity moves into an even more accelerated cycle of energy, more and more people are focusing on clearing up painful patterns and healing troubled relationships. As part of that, people are increasingly seeking to leave the past behind and to create something more wonderful in the next phase. What would you like to leave behind right now?

Chapter 8

Shifting into a Lightness of Being

Some people say humankind is in its darkest hour. Others insist that humanity at long last is moving from darkness into light, with increasing numbers of people becoming more conscious and seeking enlightenment. There is some truth in both ideas. In fact, both conditions can exist simultaneously, as odd as that might appear.

To be sure, each of these viewpoints is born of a human perspective and comes with a kind of labeling that people attach to things based on how they see their world. In any one moment, a person can choose to see these times as dark and devoid of hope. In another moment, that same person can choose to see these times as hopeful and full of the promise of enlightenment.

Spiritual Awakening—From Darkness into Light

To see humankind as being in its darkest hour is to focus on the hatred, pain, and suffering experienced in daily life. Yet we can also see humanity as being in the midst of a spiritual awakening that involves a shift from darkness into light. When we choose this second viewpoint, we are able to see through the eyes of love. This radically changes how we experience what is happening on Earth now.

People choose in each moment, knowingly or unknowingly, to come from the viewpoint of love or hate. When there is a focus on love, with a desire to experience more love and an ability to receive love in the world, the energy of love expands and reverberates to all sentient beings. Likewise, when there is a focus on hate, with a desire to attack others and to seek retribution, the energy of hate grows and is broadcast to others. Due to the law of attraction, what is sent out to others will naturally return to the sender. This means that the person who broadcasts the energy of hate will attract that energy. Likewise, the person who focuses on love will receive love from his or her world.

Did you know that an unlimited force of light lies within you? This light, naturally existing from the time when you were born, awaits your discovery, remembering, and reclaiming. It is your birthright to contain this light within your being; it is not separate from the essence that is you! Keep in mind that you will naturally awaken to the existence of this light at the appropriate time in your evolution. As part of your spiritual progression, you can fully reclaim this light while you walk the Earth as a human being.

Why Are These Times Different?

If you have always had this light within you, then how are these times different? Why should you care about this light? What do you need to know in order to more fully express this light in everyday life?

To begin with, there is a significant influx of light energy being received by humanity and the Earth as the shift in consciousness gathers momentum. This is helping to stir the pot of transformation like never before! Everyone is affected by this greatly accelerated pace of life. Farmers and rural shopkeepers are impacted, as are business executives and social reformers.

Change is in the air. People in cities all over the world are feeling the impact of the evolutionary shifting from old to new. This includes the masses of humanity not yet on a conscious spiritual path. On a personal scale, this means that unfinished negative patterns are being brought to the surface for clearing, sometimes at a dizzying pace. The other impact is a sense of urgency that is generated on a personal and global scale. Each person, depending upon his or her unique path and level of consciousness, will respond a bit differently to these energies.

What's really happening is a shifting into more lightness of being, as each person and humanity as a whole shed the many layers of denseness and outmoded ways of living. This alteration of paradigms has never happened so quickly before; it's as though human evolution is on fast forward.

It's common to complain about time and not having enough of it. Have you ever felt like time is speeding by too fast? It's normal to view time as the enemy and to want to slow it down. There is so much to do, so much change to assimilate, and so much more change desired.

What People Are Asking Now

Consider the following types of questions that are voiced regularly by those like you traveling the spiritual path during these times.

1. How can I make friends with this process of accelerated transformation?

2. How can I progress more rapidly with the least amount of difficulty?

3. How can I benefit the most from these fortuitous times, accelerating my awakening?

4. How can I help myself more?

5. How can I connect more with help from the universe and my own inner wisdom—receiving assistance with guidance, healing, and shifting?

One way to make friends with the process of accelerated transformation is to develop the quality of patience. Imagine that you're traveling as one of several passengers in a car, and that car is speeding along so fast that you lose sight of road markers if you're not paying attention. If you're busy talking with the person next to you, it's likely you'll miss seeing the sign when you cross the intersection.

The Practice of Patience

The practice of patience is the ability to be still. Sometimes it's about being silent. Patience is about pulling back and stopping for a moment. You wait and observe. Life is speeding by around you, oftentimes pulling you this way and that way, but you wait and let go of the need to act. You let go of the need to judge, to figure things out, to respond with anger, and to make things happen. You simply let go. Patience helps you to do this.

When you are patient with your process, it also means being patient with yourself. It does take a lot of patience to see your perceived shortcomings and learn to treat yourself with kindness. If you just failed at something, give yourself a dose of self-love. Realize that you did the best you could and resolve that you will do better next time.

If you find yourself impatient with your ability to transform quickly, remember that impatience won't make you transform any faster! Go gently with yourself, allowing yourself downtime that is unstructured.

During this quiet time, give yourself permission to be curious about your process, your negative patterns, and your soul's journey. Allow this healthy curiosity to bubble to the surface, guiding you in an investigation into the nature of who you really are.

The more that you develop the quality of patience, the easier it is to see yourself, your process, and the path ahead clearly. Another benefit is that the more patient you become, the more easily you can sense and connect with the divine timing that facilitates positive change. It makes you more present to life's subtleties, so you can benefit more from synchronicities.[28] Instead of forcing something to happen or responding in anger when your needs aren't met, you patiently sit still and allow your intuitively guided reason to show you the next steps.

As you sit in the middle of your dilemma, you become more comfortable with yourself and allow for resolutions that come from the world of spirit. This will save you time. A focus on spirit will also help you to become more empowered. If you act on ego-based needs, however, you continue in cycles of pain and suffering and miss out on opportunities to shift into a higher consciousness.

The great shift in consciousness is the reason you are here now.

These are times of revolutionary change. Humanity now has the potential to create a brand-new type of world. The expanded energies you now experience were made possible by the steady leap in consciousness occurring over the past several decades. People over time have helped to create these more light-filled energies. They did this as they remembered that they are divine.

You live now so that you can consciously take part in this great shift of ages. You are evolving exponentially now and are also contributing to the positive changes occurring within humanity.

The great shift energies will be present for some years to come, yet right now is the pivotal moment. Do not wait for a specific date

---

[28] A synchronicity is the coincidence of events that seem related but are not obviously caused one by the other. The term was originally used by the psychologist Carl Jung. An example of a synchronicity is when you think of an old friend you haven't seen in years and the person calls you soon after.

on the calendar to address the changes you sense need to be made. Invite your higher wisdom to guide you, step by step, into a brand-new way of being. Decide you will continue to strive for the light-filled world you want, even if your outer-world reality seems stuck in the old-paradigm energy. The changes you want are happening, but many of them are occurring on subtle levels first. Trust that a positive momentum is building. Know that you play a key role in creating what happens next.

Come back to these thoughts regularly, especially at times when you feel your life is in chaos. Remind yourself that it's normal to feel overwhelmed and out of control when so much is happening, so many decisions are required, and so little time seems to be available.

※

Tips: Moving into Your Power

How can you work with the new energies in positive ways that move your evolution forward? To answer this question, consider what it means to be empowered in the new paradigm.

Here are four suggestions to reflect on.

1. Remember that true empowerment is based on spiritual power and not worldly force. Spiritual power, the birthright of every human, comes to life when you walk with spirit and allow spirit to guide your life. This true source of power, your connection with the divine, is found within. No one outside of you gives it to you.

Think of it as divine power, a natural resource that is available by opening to it and working with it. It isn't about pushing and making things happen, but about allowing and receiving spirit's input about the optimal course of action.

Likewise, it's not about needing to win and control others. That's the old paradigm, now outmoded and in the process of falling away. Spiritual power is about being present and focused, learning to pay attention to hidden messages found in life's synchronicities.

Being awake to spirit in your life, in very tangible ways, is the key to empowering actions.

2. **True empowerment cannot exist alongside ego-based comparisons.** Let go of them. Know that it is futile to habitually compare your progress with that of others. For one thing, each person's path to enlightenment is unique.

This means that if you are comparing yourself with another person, keep in mind that you don't know everything about this other person. Appearances can be very deceiving! Consider suspending judgment until you are fully enlightened and have the bigger, more eternal view.

When you have that level of awareness, you will see both yourself and others from a much different perspective. Therefore, at this stage of your path, it's more useful to focus on your own evolution, discovering how you can progress in positive ways.

3. **Allow for divine timing in all things**. To operate from this view means to be patient about change. This relates to both the new wonderful things you want in your life and the painful situations you would like to end. Perhaps you would like a new romantic relationship, for example.

When you embody genuine power, you live your life with the knowing that you are complete with or without a partner. You get to this place of power by doing the inner spiritual work involved in developing self-love. There are no shortcuts, and no one else can give you self-love.

Once you have developed this inner confidence, you naturally radiate a glow of self-acceptance. If your potential new love partner encounters this beaming energy, and you have allowed spirit to orchestrate the timing, the magnetic effect can be profound!

Similarly, consider that you've been in therapy and have done substantial healing of an old relationship from ten years ago, and you simply want the chapter closed so you can move on to a new partner. Wanting this and consciously working toward this are one thing. Demanding that the healing be completed now, just because your ego insists on it, is something else. To be in your power means accepting where you are in each moment, even if it doesn't match where you think you should be.

4. Regardless of where you are in life right now and what goals you have achieved, there can be a nagging question of whether you are doing enough or whether you are carrying out what you were born to do.

If you are having questions like this, know that this is normal. Your purpose is fulfilled in stages, and even at the most advanced phase, you are not a finished product. You continue to learn and evolve. Wake-up calls may continue, too, as you travel your spiritual path.

The purpose of wake-up calls, contrary to how they might *feel* when occurring, is to softly nudge you onto the path and then to help guide course corrections along the way. Softly is the key word here, because spirit operates in subtle ways.

There is a tendency, especially in earlier stages of awakening, for a person to be confused by wake-up calls and to feel like a victim of bad luck or painful circumstance. It's common to blame others, or the life event itself, and to go into fighting mode. Judging something as wrong or bad doesn't make it disappear.

Also, when you fight or resist your difficult circumstances, the pain you feel can be intensified and even prolonged. A more useful way to work with wake-up calls is to allow them to teach you about yourself and the human condition. Sometimes the nudge is simply to show you when you are out of balance or when you need to pay more attention to something.

If something in your life has diverted you from what would be in your best interest, allow spirit to show you how you got off course. Invite spirit to open you to the realizations, healing, self-love, and other qualities you will need for self-correction.

Give spirit permission to help you disarm the booby traps you find on your path. You can give permission in this way. Demanding is futile, though; to demand and to force are the energies of the old paradigm. The new way, fueled by spirit and lived in partnership with the divine, is about cooperation and allowing.

As an example, perhaps you feel ready to do whatever is next in your spiritual mission, so you ask spirit to show you the plan and its overall purpose. Don't be surprised if this question leads you to a dead end. If you did receive an entire plan of some sort, realize that it is only one probability of many based on numerous actions taken one by one in current time.

More likely, spirit reveals pieces of your plan in a sequence of appropriate, divine timings. Spiritual maturity involves learning to trust in what you can't see and discovering that a life fueled by spirit will naturally lead you where you need to go. A spiritually mature person doesn't insist on having instant answers to all questions, and he or she realizes it's futile to demand guarantees of how things will turn out.

When you become a seasoned spiritual traveler, you find it easier to grasp the importance of opportunities when they are presented, and to make appropriate use of them. You realize that each day you have the potential of embodying more light and consciousness. It is a day-by-day experience, and yet there is also a momentum building!

Because of this momentum, the coming times will offer great potential to shift into a more tangible experience of being the light you seek to embody. A very wise part of you remembers that each stage of the shift in paradigms comes with opportunities to express your light in new and more expanded ways.

Sometimes the part of you having the human experience judges the opportunities, seeing them as obstacles and things to avoid. Indeed, some of your opportunities could be catalysts for reconsidering your values. Other opportunities could teach you to be more accepting of your gifts and of the light you have to share with the world.

Rethinking Your View

The following are two examples of how life challenges can prompt a rethinking of your view.

In one case, your partner's income is dramatically reduced because of workforce cutbacks or some other change at his or her job. Because you are a two-income family, you know you'll need to make alterations. When something like this happens, the crucial thing is your response.

Do you respond with fear, anger, or resentment? Do you allow the unstable and unpredictable situation to throw you off balance, saying or doing something you regret later? Or do you remember to look to spirit for a solution, allowing your intuitively guided reason to show you the way? As part of this, do you remember to connect with your inner wisdom for a higher view of the situation?

On another occasion, you plan a long-awaited vacation to a tropical island. A week before your trip, you are in a car accident. You are hospitalized and require extensive physical therapy for several weeks. You are unable to drive and must restrict your physical movement, so a vacation is out of the question.

While you heal, the doctor agrees you can work for short periods from home, but only after a three-week recovery. In practical terms, this means no communications—not even e-mail or calls from your cell phone. Just as with the previous example, this challenge brings opportunities.

You can choose to use this opportunity to heal. While your body recovers, you can allow yourself time for inner reflection about what's truly important in your life. Perhaps some priorities are in need of updating. Be open to this possibility. Invite spirit's input about the underlying purposes and potential benefits of this situation.

Both of the example opportunities can be the fuel to further investigate what you truly value. Sometimes these reminders are just what you need to get and keep on track. After all, wake-up calls are what first caused you to begin consciously traveling a spiritual path. As you continue that journey, additional wake-up calls are orchestrated by spirit to gently nudge you forward.

Those who have chosen the path of light are indeed facing many challenges in these uncertain times. Keep in mind that for someone on the path of light, the desire for the light is stronger than the desire to stay in ignorance. Once you make the decision to travel this path, you really do not go off the path, but progress depends on you.

One big roadblock to progress is self-doubt. This can get in your way at any juncture along the path. Even experienced spiritual practitioners have moments of doubting themselves, the path itself, or their interpretation of truth.

The Poison of Self-Doubt

Sometimes it can feel challenging to simply accept your own gifts, typically because you doubt yourself. You may have dreamed of having or doing something very wonderful, yet when the opportunity arrives, you sabotage yourself with self-doubt. You want to say yes to the opportunity, and a part of you really does say yes. However, another unaware part of you doesn't yet fully accept your light. That part of you is unable to embrace your divine capabilities.

For example, you take a series of classes designed to open you to your natural, intuitive abilities. In the classes you have validations of your intuition, and you are enthusiastic about being able to utilize your gifts in everyday life. When you are not in one of the classes, though, your doubt often speaks louder than your earlier enthusiasm. You allow that doubt to get in your way.

You forget or discount the importance of applying what you learned, and you quickly lose the momentum you started. Even when you are faced with a difficult life situation your intuition could help you to resolve, somehow in that moment it feels like too much to reach for the tools you already have.

You are not alone; many others do this too. In today's society, knowledge is highly valued, but experiential practice is often discounted as busywork or something befitting novices.

Perhaps your resistance takes the form of the question, "What's the use?" Your human mind can trick you into believing that it would be futile to expend effort! You retreat back into your logical left brain that wants proof of each step's value before you will take the next one.

You forget that although intuitive development classes are different from what you would learn in a business school, some basic principles still apply. Learning any new skill involves applying yourself to what you have learned in the classroom. This will mean lots of practice and taking the time to develop a growing comfort level with the skill. This applies even to skills you feel you know by rote.

The more that you work with something, the more confident you become. There are nuances that you won't notice until you have gone deeper with your practice. Intuitive development requires building on sets of skills and expanding your trust in what you cannot see with your physical eyes. That takes time, practice, and patience. In order to accept your gifts, you must be willing to take the steps and walk the path.

Your Spiritual Transformation

The path you are on is a journey to becoming whole. Once you begin waking up to this fact, it's normal to want to quicken your progress. It's helpful to remember that your evolution will continue with or without your conscious knowing. However, you can and do impact how quickly you move through the process.

One of the key factors is your ability to be present and accepting of yourself and your circumstances. The more that you resist what is happening, the more fallout and delays you will experience.

To resist the current moment is to deny the truth of what that moment is communicating to you. When you fight your circumstances, making them wrong or making yourself wrong for experiencing them, you block your ability to move into the real truth of your being.

Therefore, whenever possible, move into a space of surrender or yielding, being willing to accept your life without judgment. Whatever problem you are facing, when you move into the state of surrender and simply let go, you open up a huge reservoir of positive energy that can alchemize the suffering.

When you tap into this reservoir, you have access to an unlimited supply of healing solutions.

Help for Your Journey

Shifting into more lightness of being is a personal process, but it's not accomplished single-handedly. You have lots of help! Remember that all of us are in this process and that we impact each other in many direct and indirect ways.

For example, each time you discover more love for yourself, the impact of this increased self-love ripples out into the world, touching other people. When you learn to love yourself more, the DNA in your cells broadcasts a higher-vibrational song into the world.

The people you interact with benefit energetically. This includes your family, neighbors, people you see at the market, other drivers on the road, and even strangers you speak with on the phone.

On those days when you feel the most burdened by your personal clearing process, remember that you are not alone. Other people have their own struggles and frustrations. Chances are many other people currently have a problem similar to yours.

Realizing this can help you to reframe your problem and downsize its looming importance. A slight change in perspective can help create the inner peace you need to get back on the middle path of balance.

Reaching Out to Others

Sometimes you feel so discouraged by your own problems that you become self-absorbed, feeling unable or unwilling to reach out to others in distress. If you've been focusing on your own personal dilemmas for a time and feel at an impasse, consider letting go of your preoccupation with self for just a bit and see what you can do to brighten someone else's day. It doesn't have to be complicated or time consuming.

Oftentimes loved ones simply need the reassurance of knowing that you are there supporting them. A few words of encouragement may be all that's needed. When you help another person out of sincere caring and without strings attached, you shift your energy and focus. This shift can help you to return to your own problem solving with a lighter perspective.

Regardless of where you are with a dilemma, remember to include the divine in the resolution process.

You have an abundance of assistance available to you from the nonphysical realms as you do your personal clearings. If you feel you lack the desired intimate connection with spirit, take the steps to develop this connection.

The first step is to be open to the help and to invite it into your life. As part of that, it's useful to maintain an ongoing two-way dialogue with your higher self, asking for input and inspired solutions each step of the way.

The next step is paying attention to how spirit moves in your life, bringing you the thoughts, people, and situations that can show the way to healing and wholeness. Following the path that spirit lays out will get you where you want to go!

Reclaiming Your Light

Has there ever been a better time than this moment to begin fully reclaiming your light?

One way to make the process more tangible, and to feel that you are doing something, is to work with the method of conscious intent. To do this, you contemplate how you would like to express your light. You remind yourself that you have a right to shine that light in the world. You remember that you are here on Earth to be a physical manifestation of that light. You then voice your intention to reclaim your light.

When you voice your intent, you are expressing what you will be, do, or have. This is potent. Stating your intention is a way of connecting with your true power to create. When you do it with feeling and positive expectation, the intending catapults your energy into a higher-vibrational space. As you intend something for yourself, visualize yourself in present time, having or being or doing what you are intending. Allow it to become real. It can also be helpful to write down on a sheet of paper what you are intending, reading the words as you say them, and then keeping that sheet as a reminder of what you are creating.

☀

Process: Setting Intention to Reclaim Your Light

Take a few moments right now and set your intention to reclaim your light and to participate in the planet's energetic openings as fully and consciously as you can. It's not necessary to understand the process with your rational mind.

In fact, it's ideal that you allow the logical left brain to take a backseat, freeing the imaginative right brain to guide you into more clarity. Allow your intuitive mind and intuitively guided reason to take you beyond logic and beyond the stereotypes the world presents.

Invite your higher self to assist you in connecting fully with your light and with the many blessings available at this time. Make the conscious choice to be awake and responsive to the messages and gifts you receive.

Remember that the movement of spirit is subtle. You can connect most tangibly with the movement of the divine by becoming still and quiet, and by allowing your life to become very simple. Allow the divine to provide the catalysts you personally need now in order to move into greater clarity.

Remind yourself to be openhearted as you respond to these catalysts, refusing to allow your fears and doubts to color your view.

Accelerate Your Enlightenment with a Light Journal

Start a light journal to document what you learn about the positive force of light in your life. You may want to date each entry and to note where you were when you recorded it.

For example, you may return from a walk on the beach with an inspirational idea from spirit. Perhaps you were reminded, as you gazed at the water and reflected on a current personal dilemma, that your issue is universal. You may have visualized how people from all parts of the world have struggled with this issue.

Perhaps you were reminded of some very simple solutions people could apply if they would just remember them in the moment. Your reflections on these solutions and how anyone could apply them gave you encouragement to remedy your own dilemma by accessing your light.

When you record your insights in your light journal, along with decisions of how to apply them, you can quicken your enlightenment process. Recording where you were when you received insights, what time of day, and whether you were alone or with others can help you to better understand your own rhythms of receiving input from spirit.

You may begin to notice a pattern. Some people connect more easily with intuitive guidance when they are in nature. Other people notice that they connect more when they spend time with certain people. Still others notice they receive the most input when alone, regardless of where they are.

※

Process: Connecting with Your Light

There are many methods that can help you connect with your light. A very simple approach is to spend a few minutes at the beginning and end of each day to become mindful of the light that naturally shines forth within you.

Sit quietly and close your eyes. Invite in your higher self. Ask to feel the presence of your light. Be still and relax.

Next, ask to be shown how your light naturally attracts a positive force. Imagine or visualize yourself in activities where this positive force plays out. Be still once again and receive divine input.

Ask to see past the darkness of any current difficult or limiting situation by calling forth your own light to illuminate it. Regardless of how painful or distressing a scenario may seem, take a few minutes to contemplate how the light within you has the power to bring a peaceful resolution. Trust the divine to give you a sense of this power you have.

Remember to get all of your senses involved—sight, sound, touch, scent, taste, and emotion—and allow the divine to bring you an experience that is personal to you.

Contemplate how you want to more fully express your light. Ask your higher self to help you have increasingly tangible experiences of being the light you know that you are. Imagine for a few moments embodying this light in the world.

When you feel complete with the experience, affirm to yourself, "*I am the light, and it is this light that sets me free.*"

Chapter 9

Creating within the New Energies

There is a new energy on planet Earth; a quickening of evolution is occurring. Humanity's progression, in full swing long before you were born, is now in an accelerated wake-up mode. A speeding-up process has been in motion in a tangible way since the 1980s.[29] It was then that a cultural waking up began to occur across the planet.

The decades leading up to now were talked about even in ancient times. Elders of diverse traditions, including the Maya and the Tibetans, spoke of massive changes. They documented great cycles of change, providing us with clues about previous and imminent climatic shifts and humanity's repetitive remembering and forgetting of universal truths. They reminded us of our eternal nature. They told

---

29 The 1980s has been referred to as the dawn of a new age. During this decade people in society started to become more aware of world problems. There was a growing understanding of the interconnectedness of the world. This was fueled in part by computers and increased access to information. This decade was the beginning of the information age, with personal computers and cell phones making their first appearance. Other noteworthy developments included the collapse of traditional communism and the end of the Cold War.

us about a time when we could take a great leap forward and create a light-filled existence.

We live during that unique window of time that the ancient ones foresaw. Exactly how things play out is up to us. We are the ones who will decide our own fate. We, as divine changemakers, can create a brand-new start for ourselves and our planet. That is why we are here right now.

You are being impacted even if you know nothing about cycles or humanity's past. It is helpful, however, to become acquainted with these things and to learn how you are personally affected. When you have that understanding, you can make wiser choices and feel more connected to the bigger picture. You can become skilled in creating within the new energies.

What Are the New Energies?

The new energies are a frequency, a higher-vibrational state of being within which you naturally connect with your light. They represent a radical shift in consciousness, for they are fueled by love rather than by fear. These energies are life affirming, and they are free of the harshness and struggle that have long been dominant in human experience. When you reside in these new energies, it is much easier to access your joy!

During humanity's great shift, as you become more awake and make more conscious choices, you will find yourself residing in the new energies more and more of the time. Know that the higher energetic state is a vibration and not a location. To remain in a higher state requires ongoing effort.

The power you have to create at those higher levels is profound. This power comes from within you, from your own mind. Your own thoughts carry such weight, with their energy manifesting so quickly, that you will need to become very skilled in mastering your mind.

Even brief moments of worry or fear will send your energy into a downward spiral.

For most people, the progression into the higher-frequency energies is a bit like a roller coaster. In some moments you may feel very connected with the new, more light-filled energies. At other times, you may revert into old habits and find yourself caught up in fear-based patterns. Don't be concerned about this, but do learn to pay attention to where you are energetically.

Accelerated Momentum of Cause and Effect

The universal laws of cause and effect play out at an accelerated pace as you advance spiritually. The boomerang effect of actions and expressed emotions can be almost immediate.

When you express negative energy, consciously or unconsciously, you draw to yourself negative experiences. Likewise, when you express positive energy, you magnetize positive experiences.

Examples of the negative include expressions of anger. Imagine you are driving home from work after being fired by your boss, a longtime friend. You feel so angry at him that you want revenge. You wish that he would be jobless too and that he would lose everything that he has. Without thinking things through, you call him on your cell phone and say some very mean things. You tell him that the friendship is over. As you speak to your boss, you crash into the car ahead of you on the freeway. Things get even worse when you get home. Your mate, to whom you have been faithful, accuses you of having an affair and threatens to leave you.

Similarly, your positive actions can bring positive rewards very quickly. For example, ahead of hip surgery you work with the power of your own mind. Doctors tell you that the surgery has only a 40 percent chance of success, but you stay positive anyway.

You visualize your body as healthy and whole. You imagine unconditional love moving into your hip area. You see it healed—

right then. You continue to hold to this vision before and after your surgery. You visualize sending healing energy to your hip and pelvis. You imagine a quick recovery, a full regeneration of your hip, and an active life without joint pain.

During your post-surgery appointment several weeks later, your fast recovery from surgery baffles doctors who told you to expect a long recuperation! When they see that your surgical wound has healed several weeks earlier than projected, they may wonder what you did to beat the odds. They are amazed again six months later when you show no signs of limited motion or pain.

How to Create Powerfully

You can learn to create powerfully. You can discover how to tap your inner resources to create more of what you want. You can become skilled in your role as a divine changemaker.

To be skillful in creating the changes you seek, you will need to work with, not against, universal laws. You will need to become more aware of how energy works, not only within your own body and energy field but between you and the world. You can consider this in two categories:

Your own energy—your physical body, your mind, your emotions, and your connection to spirit

Your energy that interacts with other people and the physical world—the interchange between you and the people and things in your environment

The more that you can become awake to these energy flows, the easier it will be to consciously shift yourself into balance. After all, you cannot change something in your energy system if you are unaware that it needs attention. Awareness of imbalances can lead you to fruitful investigations of the solutions that will be most appropriate for you. Then, as you learn to intuitively apply these solutions, you can facilitate the healing you need. Remember that even if the ideal solutions include help from a healer or other source, it will still be you who applies the remedy to shift yourself back into balance.

※

Checklist: Managing Your Energy

The following are some guidelines to help you better manage your energy. You may want to review these regularly, as well as any time you feel that you have gotten out of balance. Begin with your body, a sacred container for your soul's experiences on Earth. Then look at other elements such as thoughts, emotions, and your relationship with other people and spirit.

Body

Nutrients—Consider your diet and to what extent you are giving your body enough nutritious foods and pure water. Learn to become skilled in giving yourself intuitive physical readings to determine the best nutrients for you. Your own body is your best resource for this information. Nutritional needs can fluctuate widely depending on a host of factors individual to you. If you honor your body by giving it the specific nutrients it requires, it will serve you well.

Movement—How much exercise, and what type, is ideal for you? What happens to your energy level when you forget or neglect this exercise? Can you find some ways to make your exercise time more fun? Have you thought of partnering with an exercise buddy to make it more enjoyable? Consider experimenting with some moderate forms of exercise to discover or rediscover the types that work best for you. Then take steps to incorporate these into your routine.

Rest—When your body has adequate rest, you will have more energy for the activities of your life. A rested body helps your mind too. Your mind will be able to function with more alertness, better emotional balance, greater creativity, and increased intuitive sense. Are you honoring your needs for rest, downtime, and sleep? If not, consider what you can do to allow for these needs.

Thoughts

Your mind produces all sorts of thoughts, and these thoughts will determine what you experience. Your thoughts are real and have energy within them; each thought carries a vibration. To master life, it is essential to become adept at working with your mind. Set your intention to become more watchful of your own thoughts, including those you think silently to yourself and those you express out loud to others.

Notice how much of the time you focus on low-vibrational, fear-based thoughts involving worry, lack, and anger about something in your past. Fear does not come from outside of you; it is generated within your own mind. If you dislike something about your life experience, become determined to get to the root cause buried within your own limiting thought patterns.

These thought patterns, also known as belief systems, are carried within your DNA. Beliefs are created when a meaning is given to something. Sometimes it was you who assigned the meaning as a result of a life experience. Other times, it was a member of your family's lineage who did so, and the meaning-connected belief was passed on to you in your DNA. In other cases, the meaning-connected belief was born out of the powerful field of humanity's mass consciousness, and you took it on as your own.

Begin changing these patterns, and you can change your life. To do so, you must first change your mind about your mind. Instead of allowing your mind to carry you forward like a wild horse, you can decide to tame it. You can learn to tame your mind and to teach it to work for your highest good.

Emotions

In order to manage your energy effectively, you need to learn how to consciously and intelligently work with your emotions. How do you do this? Get into the habit of checking in with your own feelings; as much as possible, do this in present time. When you can begin noticing how you feel when you feel it, you can develop discernment in emotional response.

To name your feeling right in the moment can help you to work with and safely release it, with harm to none. Let go of any self-judgment during this process, remembering that everyone has challenges with feelings. Consider what you do with feelings of anger, doubt, fear, and resentment. Through self-observation you can become skilled in recognizing which emotions tend to get you off balance and which emotions are most dominant in your experience. Everyone has challenging emotions like anger; that's part of being human. The key to being in balance is learning how to intelligently respond to what you feel.

✷

Tips: Relating to Others

Your energy that interacts with others is a direct reflection of your own consciousness. Learning to manage this energy flow begins with a more intimate understanding of you. The more self-awareness you develop, the more you can master your responses to the people and situations of your life.

The following are a few tools that can be helpful.

Consider the example of how you are troubled by interactions with someone you see often. When someone consistently pushes your buttons, decide that you will discover a more positive way to respond. Making that decision is an important step in reclaiming your power. Remembering that you have a choice of how to respond is liberating.

Pay attention to your thoughts and emotions, receiving clues about the pattern being triggered within you.

Approach yourself gently and patiently. Issues such as self-doubt, for example, involve a complex set of internal causes. Know that if you continue to be plagued by self-doubt when interacting with someone, it means that you have not eliminated all internal causes.

Open your mind to the possibility that you have a blind spot. Being unaware of something you have not yet discovered is not the same as being stupid. Make that distinction and then let go of your self-reprimanding.

Set your intention to leave no stone unturned as you investigate your pattern. As part of that, let go of demanding to know how many stones lie on top of your issue, hiding it from your view. Remind yourself that you may not see all the stones at once, but that when you do notice a stone, you will fearlessly address it. Decide that you will act with fearless determination, continuing your efforts until the very last stone has been removed.

Remember throughout this process to put your trust in spirit and your own intuitive wisdom. Allow the beneficial force of spirit to guide you and help accelerate your learning.

Be willing to view the person pushing your buttons as a gift from the divine. Let yourself see the person through the eyes of gratitude. When you can be grateful to those who cause you pain, you can soften the sting of the pain. Seeing the person as your teacher helps connect you with an ability to respond to them with your light.

Spirit Connection and Energy Mastery

Your connection to spirit is the vital ingredient needed for energy mastery. Your true nature is spirit and without form. That part of you is intuitive, telepathic, and multidimensional; it operates beyond linear time and space. You access it when you learn to use your intuitive right brain and when you discover how to express yourself from the heart rather than from the ego. Your intuitive knowing is the key that unlocks your deeper wisdom and brings the divine into your physicality in a tangible way.

Think of your spiritual self as a kind of inner knowing. It is like a compass that shows you which direction is optimal. It helps you to manage your time and guides you to the best uses of your energy. It prevents you from making mistakes. It alerts you to real dangers. It helps you to find clarity and truth.

Sometimes, when you are very busy and faced with a myriad of tasks, you can forget to check in with your intuition. It may seem as though you do not have time to sit still and listen to the voice of spirit within you. However, the treasure to be found by doing so will allow you to move through your troubles much more quickly.

As you develop your intuitive knowing, you are able to express more of your light in the world. When you are facing a personal crisis, your intuition and connection with spirit can guide you safely through the minefield of difficulties.

Switching Out of Worry Mode

When you catch yourself in worry mode, step back from your situation long enough to remember the big picture. Your life is not a random accident; you are here now for a purpose. You were naturally drawn to be here as part of the human collective for the great opportunities of these times. You are interconnected with people in every corner of the world—each of you moving into juxtaposition in order to take part in a quantum leap in consciousness.

If you have felt that you are in waiting mode or that you have had a setback, remember the massive amounts of preparations you and others are making and have made. Put away your linear yardstick. Acknowledge that there is an accumulation of efforts involved. Sometimes your human self doesn't see the whole picture.

To be sure, your efforts are individual, yet they are also cooperative as great numbers of people wake up and begin to connect energetically to create positive changes.

The initial phases of humanity's transformational shifting, under way for a very long time, have led you to where you are now. You come from a long line of ancestors who evolved over time. Those living during the earlier phases helped one another to progress spiritually. This progress occurred as they learned from one another. You evolve in similar ways today while also benefiting from the wisdom and shifting of your ancestors.

Your Catalyzing Life Event

In your life you have encountered one or more wake-up calls that caused you to seriously challenge the status quo. There is no one correct way for this process to occur, so avoid the temptation to label your experience or compare it with that of others.

Your catalyzing life event could have been losing a job, experiencing a financial reversal, moving to a new place, divorcing your partner, facing a debilitating illness, or experiencing some other major change in circumstance. Any one or a number of these could have stirred a deep, inner discontent and questioning of things you never before questioned. When this happens, it's really a nudge from your soul, waking you up and guiding you to travel the path of spirit.

In today's upheaval, people are oftentimes receiving what may appear to be more than one wake-up call simultaneously. Also, people can have supplemental wake-up calls a long time after their initial one. Think back for a moment and consider what your own wake-up calls have been.

Understanding Wake-up Calls

To understand and optimally respond to your wake-up calls, keep in mind the following.

First, know that the typical progression from a wake-up call to full awakening is anything but usual these days. You live in very different times, never before seen on the planet.

Humanity and the Earth are ascending in a process that is leading to a more enlightened existence. You and others like you on the path of light are creating a new way to coexist and be. People did not have the same opportunities for awakening in earlier times.

Likewise, people born in earlier cycles did not share the planet with so many people, nor was it possible for such a significant shift in consciousness to occur for the masses. Wake-up calls in previous times had a different meaning, scope, and potential impact.

Second, know that wake-up calls in modern times are the soul's way of preparing you to succeed on your path of light during humanity's shift. Your first wake-up call tends to set the stage for what follows.

If you pay attention to the first one, taking the opportunity to assess your life and noticing the nudges of your soul, you are redirected to a different course. The actions you take in response to that redirection will help to determine your forward spiritual progression.

As an example, if you respond to your soul's nudges with an attitude of willingness and acceptance, your road ahead will have fewer bumps. The learned tendency, however, is to resist change and to want to maintain the status quo.

When you are in resistance, you are likely to be blocked from receiving your inner guidance from spirit. The guidance is there, but you cannot access it. Instead, you may simply feel anger and alienation. These responses can leave you feeling disempowered and victimized by your outer circumstances.

Third, know that despite how willing and accepting you are, and how connected you are to the nudges of your soul, your awakening is a process and not a single event. Remember that during this most precious human life, you have the potential of quantum levels of awakening not before possible!

This means that you may be a seasoned spiritual practitioner—familiar with wake-up calls and practiced in responding effectively—yet your awakening journey is not complete. That journey is a process. Maintain your discernment here because you can fool yourself into thinking you are fully enlightened, with no more awakening to experience. Your ego can and will try to convince you that you represent a finished product.

This ego-based response is particularly prevalent within circles of spiritual practitioners who compare themselves with the general populace. Certainly, when you compare yourself on a surface level with the masses that remain asleep, you are leaps and bounds ahead. Comparisons are a trick of the ego, though, and they can derail you when you least suspect it.

Fourth, know that your readiness for the changes is instrumental in how you will experience them. How ready do you feel, on an everyday basis, for the big changes about to occur? Is your enthusiasm for positive change waning as you envision what's ahead? Do you feel prepared to take on the challenges that are sure to come? Are you willing to go deeper within yourself to access the more stable sense of empowerment you will need to navigate the unpaved road ahead? Are you able to step back from the world's fear-based messages often enough to stay in your center?

To be enmeshed in such a gigantic shifting process as you face today can take its toll. You likely are feeling impacted on a number of levels. The obvious levels include outer conditions involving your home, work, finances, human relationships, and physical health.

Other key elements include your emotional stability and repetitive thought patterns. These will determine the meaning you place on current events and will trigger limiting belief systems recorded in your DNA. Examples are commonly held beliefs involving lack, failure, and authority figures having power you can't access. As belief systems such as these are catalyzed, your ability to successfully respond to crisis is compromised.

Most likely you are being challenged beyond what you think your limits are. The world around you is becoming increasingly dysfunctional, and society's overhauls are triggering your own. It's not just the world financial system, which went into meltdown mode in 2008. It's every sector of your old-paradigm society that has been based on fear, greed, and ego-based manipulation. Each of these worn-out structures will need radical reshaping over the coming years.

This cycle of the Earth's history represents a turning point and a time of great societal reconfiguration. The reshaping involved is both personal and global.

Fifth, know that you have a higher role to play than simply living out an ordinary life. This is not the time for a mundane approach; it is a time of waking up to your wholeness, your fullness as a being, and the unique gifts you alone can offer. Discover your own niche and learn to find a balance between fantasy and doom and gloom.

That means letting go of fear-based human conditioning that tells you some outside force is coming to the rescue. That same conditioning tells you that you are flawed, need fixing, need to be told what to do, and are lacking in what it takes to succeed.

It may feel comforting to think that a force or people outside yourself can save you and the planet. Is it also comforting to imagine that, without such intervention, you would be helpless and fail at what you were born to do?

Have you ever wondered where you came from? Has anyone ever told you that you are divine? Have you ever associated your humanness with a divine imprint that is eternal?

Remember that you as a divine changemaker are an integral part of the shift. The key changes involve shifts in consciousness within individuals such as you. As you make these changes and interact with others and society, there is a domino effect.

Underneath the layers of falseness you unknowingly took on

in human form, you really know the truth. At the core of your being, there is really no doubt about who you are, why your human experiences are such a gift, and how you are meant to be on Earth now to forever change the landscape for humankind.

At this pivotal juncture, world leaders and people everywhere are taking stock and choosing what will play out in this next phase. Some of this choosing is conscious, with people aware of what they are choosing. On other levels, the choosing is taking place under the radar, masquerading as something like inaction or avoidance.

※

Process: Imagining a New Start

Imagine that each day you have an opportunity for a new start; yesterday is gone, and tomorrow is not yet here. What kind of life would you like? What would you like the next few years to look like? How do you see yourself taking your place alongside other divine changemakers?

Consider the following questions as you envision what you want to create next. Invite your heart's wisdom to guide you as you reflect on these ideas. For starters, you may want to select a question to focus on from each of the lists below. Keep your questions handy and reflect on them throughout the day. As ideas come to you and you record them, you will open a door for your higher self to expand upon the thoughts. You may find, for example, that the simple process of recording your insights creates a flow of additional ideas that you might not otherwise receive.

Your Biggest Obstacle
- What is my biggest obstacle?
- What can I do differently that will resolve this?

- What resources have I not yet used fully that could help me resolve this?
- How can I involve spirit more in resolving obstacles such as this?

Your Biggest Choice
- What is the biggest choice I must make now?
- What's the big picture surrounding this choice?
- How will my making this choice, and acting on it, change my life?

Your Greatest Allies
- Who are my greatest allies on my path of light?
- Who helps me to find my center when I get off track?
- Who in my circle connects me with laughter and lightness of being?
- Who teaches me the most about myself?
- Who helps me to connect with spirit?
- Who helps me to connect with my inner truth?

Your Greatest Opportunities
- In what direction will I find expanded opportunities?
- Who are the people I am meant to serve?
- How do I find and connect with these people?
- What can I change in what I offer to be of most service to these people?
- What is the one thing I need to let go of for greater success?
- How do I get in the way of my own success?
- What can I offer that will be in demand in any economic climate?
- What do I need to know or do in order to successfully offer this to the world?

Keep this list of questions handy for the times when you feel stuck, uninspired, worried, or fearful. These types of questions are meant to be asked on a regular basis. You will receive different answers depending upon your circumstances.

Invite your higher wisdom to reveal the answers to questions such as these as you go about your day. Ask spirit to reveal other types of questions that you could add to the list. Trust that the force of spirit within you is very wise. Allow this force to communicate its wisdom through your own thoughts and through the people and happenstance of daily life.

Chapter 10

Living Your Mission of Light

There is a stirring within humanity. An awakening is occurring across the planet, and even the Earth is in the midst of an initiation into a higher consciousness. On some days you likely feel the shifting of energy at very deep, cellular levels.

As part of that, you may notice a subtle remembering that there are more pieces to the puzzle of existence. When you get in touch with this, you may begin to question your teachers, politicians, religious leaders, and other authority figures.

Understanding Your Role in These Times

Chances are you have more frequent questions about who you are, what you are really doing here, and what your role is on your path of light. You likely have heard that you have a mission or purpose for being here, and you naturally want to know more about it. Questions tend to percolate from within your consciousness, sometimes in words you can recognize and other times in a more subtle way that leaves you simply feeling unsettled.

As you grapple with the answers to these questions, you may feel a sense of even more unrest. And sometimes it may appear as though there really aren't any answers. The flip side of this is when you receive information about something you are to do, and then you are puzzled when opportunities to do that fail to materialize.

Right now as you read these words, it is more important than ever that you continue questioning. Ask the deeper questions even when you think you are receiving no response. Ask them even when it appears that you have hit a brick wall, and when apparent delays cause you to go into cycles of fear and doubt.

Continue your questions, remembering that an inquiring mind is one of the qualities necessary for your enlightenment.

Others around you may seem to be asleep, but do not allow their forgetfulness to delay your own awakening. The Buddha and other great enlightened beings from humanity's past did not stop their inquiry simply because others around them weren't yet ready. They asked questions that others weren't asking, and they kept asking even when others accepted the status quo. They certainly would be asking lots of deep questions right now!

Consider What Will Matter in Three Hundred Years

People oftentimes spend great amounts of time focusing on routine questions about life. Chances are they are more interested in the hows and whys of mundane happenstance than they are in the deeper meanings of being. It's typical to obsess over job interviews, disappointments in love, and new cars. However, all of these things have only transitory importance. The job not taken, the love affair, and the shiny new car will not matter in three hundred years.

You want to consider the big-picture perspective as you assign importance to life events. Jobs, cars, and romances will come and go. What really matters to your spiritual progression is your ability to grow in self-awareness and to develop qualities like kindness and patience. To be sure, it is helpful to ask questions about your key relationships, jobs, and other opportunities. Consider deeper questions about these topics, however, so you can grow. As an example, when in a troublesome love relationship, you can explore what you are learning about how to love.

You and Your Relationships

When you are in a relationship, for example, you will want to know what you are learning by knowing this person and what this teaches you about yourself. In your earlier stage of growth, you may have simply wanted to know what you could do to cause this person to treat you more favorably.

Without realizing it, you may have manipulated the other person, trying to get him or her to change. You may have tried to force yourself to fit a mold that is not true to your authentic self. You may have considered eliminating this person from your life, but without first considering whether you had learned the lessons offered by the relationship.

You now are willing to look more deeply than before, acknowledging your role in the dance of the relationship. You want to understand, and put to use, the gifts of knowing this person. The more you learn to do this, the easier it is to take actions that fuel your growth. Sometimes this means giving yourself or the other person more space. At other times, it means releasing a person from your life. In those cases, you realize that you have learned all you can from the relationship and that it is in your highest good to move on.

Considering Your Perfect Work

Regardless of what kind of job you have, you will want to inquire about how your work can be more in alignment with your highest good. Keep in mind that your highest good may not equate with the highest paycheck or praises, and it certainly may not look the same as some other person's highest good would look.

Each person has his or her own unique path.

The more you awaken, the more you do things in the world because an intuitive voice inside of you says they are appropriate. Think of your job or work in terms of your service to others. Think of it in connection with what you are learning about yourself. The work doesn't have to involve a paycheck to be of value.

Some of your work will be comprised of things you do simply because it feels right to do them. In fact, all of your work may be without compensation if you are retired. You do these things because your heart guides you to act, not because others pay you.

It will be important to know whether you are fully utilizing your gifts and your potential for service as you carry out your work. If not, you then question what you can do or avoid doing to change the situation.

Discovering What Matters

Perhaps you dislike your job or feel unfulfilled by a key relationship. You may question why you exert such effort, why you remain in a job you despise, when the work of your life's mission will arrive, or why the thorn-in-your-side person won't give you what you want. These are all questions of a surface nature and won't get you deep enough to change things.

In fact, the lack of real solutions available from this sort of inquiry is likely to make you feel even worse. When this feeling gets triggered within you, there can be a tendency to falsely believe you aren't enough as a person or that you don't have the resources to affect true transformation. You can feel at the mercy of your situation, setting off old familiar patterns of victimhood.

Your fear can lead you into a downward spiral of waiting for some outside source to come to the rescue. In the moments you buy into the fear, you convince yourself that you need more of something before you can shine your light and live your purpose.

Perhaps you even feel abandoned by God and wonder if your prayers will be answered. Sound familiar?

Knowing How You Fit In

In today's chaotic environment, you may be asking yourself how you fit in with the world and what your role is to be during humanity's great shift into higher consciousness. You have many opportunities for growth and for being of service in these uncertain times, yet perhaps you question how to identify and use them.

Sometimes when you focus on the magnitude of change under way, you may even wonder if you are fully equipped to take on the challenge. There is so much that needs changing. Where do you start?

More important, how do you keep your sanity and be personally empowered as you serve as a divine changemaker?

What does it really look like to be a potent force for positive change in these times? When you live in this transformational role, what are the outward signs of manifestation? What are some of the hallmarks of the new-paradigm approaches to work and living one's purpose? Where are the like-minded people you are meant to befriend, learn from, and serve?

These questions and more are addressed in the pages that follow.

Unique Opportunities Available Now

The following is some background on these unique times. To be alive now offers unprecedented opportunities to evolve and change your path of destiny. In no other historical period could you advance so much as you can now.

The potential you have for spiritual transformation is profound.

You make choices daily, knowingly or unknowingly, that can help you to create positive energies and let go of negative ones.

As you uplift your consciousness with inner work and outer actions, you help yourself in ways that are beyond human linear measure. In addition, your higher-vibrational consciousness impacts your loved ones, strangers you meet on the street, and even the global mass consciousness.

Your path of spiritual transformation involves clearing away layers of falseness and remembering your natural divine nature. Though that is easier to conceptualize than to do, you indeed can succeed. You can learn to fully express your soul on Earth and to integrate spirit into your everyday reality. After all, you are divine, and your spirit will naturally express through you as you advance.

Seeds for the massive planetary shifting now under way, including those you have personally planted in the past, are sprouting at lightning speed. Because of this, you are now witness to the most revolutionary shifting humanity has ever undertaken.

Right now, you are in a process of being awakened to the truly dysfunctional state of the world and the need to change the outmoded status quo. This is happening in phases, your own higher self bringing to your attention untruths and awareness about timeless and multidimensional approaches to reality.

Connecting More of the Dots

If you have been on your path of awakening for a while, you are now able to connect more of the dots of the bigger picture. This is because you have an understanding of humanity's history and age-old patterns involving ego-based power and control. If you are one of these more seasoned travelers, you are no stranger to many of the universal truths now featured in best-selling books and on Internet sites.

Some of these ideas, voiced in earlier historical cycles, were relegated to specialized interest niches. The masses didn't hear about them. The fact that these secrets are now revealed in a more mainstream way is a sign of humanity's great shift in progress. Each day, somewhere in the world, more people wake up to be your companions in the most exciting journey you could ever take!

Finding More Like-Minded People

As more people awaken, you will find increasing numbers of like-minded people to work and play with! Some of them will seem to come out of nowhere, and you will wonder where they were before. They may wonder the same about you! As this happens, simply move into gratitude and a knowing that divine, perfect timing has been and is at work.

Pay attention to your dreams. When you wake up in the morning, you may have an idea to take a class. When you act on this idea and sign up for the class, you may meet a new friend.

Realizing You Cannot Do It Alone

When you embrace the need to radically transform yourself and the way that life is lived, it doesn't take long to realize you cannot do it alone. Although it may appear that you are single-handedly working on a personal issue, you don't do so in an energetic bubble. You impact others around you, and you are impacted by a diverse set of people, including those you will never meet in person.

You are also affected by planetary energies, and when this impact feels negative, you will naturally seek the comfort that comes from knowing others are in the same boat. Sometimes you receive this reassurance directly from a friend or loved one. Other times you receive it indirectly by reading something or seeing a movie.

The more that you pay attention to the subtle messages of spirit in your life, the more you will receive validations from seemingly random sources. An example is when you are standing in line at the grocery store and overhear a conversation that speaks to what you have been feeling.

When you acknowledge your interconnections with the world and allow them to fuel your transformation, you place yourself on the fast track of personal growth. The paradigm shift begins inside of you, yet it requires your engagement with the world. When you interact with others, they can show you truths about yourself that you could not easily uncover on your own.

You can think of it as the world being your feedback system, giving you clues about how to move through challenges with more ease. By being observant, you can learn from others' mistakes and also gain an understanding of what triggers your issues. As an example, sometimes you will observe another person mired in a dilemma, and you can see a mistake he or she is about to make. This may remind you of a similar pattern you have and give you a helpful understanding about your own issues.

Sparking Beneficial Changes in Others

Another benefit of connecting with others is that when you do, you can spark beneficial changes in their lives. Oftentimes this happens without your conscious awareness. When you spark a beneficial change in someone else, there is a domino effect, with numerous people being positively impacted over time.

That includes yourself, of course, because beneficial energies you express in the world will return to you as a positive force at some future time. Therefore, regularly connecting with others is essential to your role as a divine changemaker.

The Challenge of Seeing Yourself Clearly

In general, regardless of how advanced you are, it can be challenging to see clearly into all aspects of your issues. You will benefit from working with a skilled and competent person outside your close circle of friends and family. It could be a healer or someone with another job description.

Why is this helpful? You are simply too close to the issues at hand, and you have a vested interest in the outcome. Therefore, being impartial is problematic. You may be a very skilled healer and able to work on yourself, yet your most troublesome issues can be difficult to access alone. For the same reason, it can be challenging to heal your own loved ones, even when you know them better than anyone else.

Changing yourself is a personal matter and is done from the inside out. It is not accomplished alone, however; you require assistance not because you are inherently lacking but because of your limiting human conditioning.

What is the limiting conditioning humans have had? Key elements include personal disempowerment, disconnection from spirit, and ideas of separation.

You have forgotten just how powerful you truly are! You are a natural creator, of course, but you have learned to place outside authorities in charge. You have learned to fear change and chaos, yet these elements are a natural part of creating anything new.

You have been conditioned to doubt yourself and to feel insufficient, resulting in a lowered self-esteem and general disempowerment. You lack a fusion of your physical reality with the force of spirit. Through countless experiences, you learned to separate physical reality from spirit. In doing so, you lost your home base that could naturally be with you everywhere, in any reality. That navigation tool became covered with dust and remained in the off mode for long periods of time.

You have forgotten the true interconnectedness of the world. Even though you hold within your DNA concepts of connectedness, you also carry polar-opposite concepts of separation. These false notions of disconnection have been continually challenged in the last century with the introduction of innovations like space travel, the Internet, real-time world media coverage, and increased routine movement of people and goods across international borders.

You have learned to think of yourself, once grown, as independent of your family. As part of this, you haven't learned to associate your challenges and dysfunctional patterns with your family's lineage going back numerous generations.

Transcending Your Conditioning

Once you acknowledge your conditioning, you have more power to transcend it. It's also helpful to remember that other people have had dysfunctional conditioning too. It is a part of being human. Remembering this can help you to feel less alone on your journey while also helping you to generate compassion for yourself and others. Being mindful of humanity's similar conditioning can also help you to become more accepting of your circumstances, including difficult situations involving other people.

The more that you can express compassion and acceptance for what is, the higher your energy vibration will be. When you stop going to war about what is and move into acceptance, you free up a tremendous force of creative and healing energy.

When you broadcast from your energy field the qualities of compassion and acceptance, you will draw to yourself an increasing number of positive experiences. As an example, when you express compassion, you are more likely to receive compassionate treatment in the world. Also, when you are compassionate, people are more likely to be magnetized to you.

When you learn to let go of feeling that you are either better than others or more handicapped than others, you can greatly accelerate your spiritual transformation. Why? First, you will be more open to receiving insights that come directly or indirectly from your interactions with others. Second, you will begin to see yourself more clearly once you drop the judgments and comparisons. Third, you will be more willing to reach out to others for assistance. Fourth, this willing and receptive attitude can connect you with more like-minded people. Fifth, you will be more receptive to the guidance and help that others can give you. Sixth, when you are counseled to consider a change in course, you will be more likely to give the suggestion serious thought and, if appropriate, take action on it.

Moving from Willfulness into Willingness

To be personally empowered, you must have the ability to move beyond your resistance, beyond your arrogance, and into a state of willingness. When you are willing, rather than willful, you have the openness required to catalyze true and lasting changes.

This openness will help you with your own transformation, and you will serve as a potent force for good in the world. Regardless of the type of work that you do, the consciousness that you personally bring to the work is a pivotal factor in how much beneficial impact you can have during the paradigm shift.

Identifying Arrogance

How do you identify arrogance? You can think of it as a mindset that says, "I am better than others." It is the opposite of being humble: the person expressing arrogance is prideful and self-important. When being arrogant, the person is ego-driven and often has a condescending manner.

At the root of arrogance is a lack of self-love. If you love yourself fully without condition, you have no need to show that you are important or better than other people. However, because few people have fully realized their potential for self-love, arrogance will show up in varying degrees from time to time.

Examples of things a person might say with arrogance:
"I'm only on the planet to help others."
"Isn't it amazing how messed up everyone is?"
"Notice how stupid he is."

A woman who says she is only on the planet to help others is discounting the help that she receives by being of service. Even an enlightened being continues to progress on his or her evolutionary path by being of service to others. There are levels of growth and levels of awareness at each stage along the path. No one is a finished product.

Discovering Your Unique Contribution

It is normal that you would want to know how you fit into the world and how you can be of the most service in birthing humanity's higher consciousness. Each person has a unique role to play.

To discover your distinctive contribution involves an ongoing process of becoming the most aware and awake human you can possibly be. It means regular inner work to clear personal issues that you might not have faced in more ordinary times. As you know, there is nothing typical about being alive today!

Each time you grow more spiritually and increase your vibration to hold more light, you avail yourself of new and expanded opportunities to serve. Being of service, regardless of what that service looks like, is how you can do your part in creating humanity's great shift.

Being of service relates to work you are paid for as well as helpful actions you take without payment. Your unique niche relates more to your personal energetic signature than to any job title. No one else has had the same life experiences that you have. No one else made these experiences mean what yours have meant to you, nor has anyone else responded to what happened in the same way.

Because of your own individual path and what you have witnessed and learned, you carry an energetic resonance all your own. If you could connect with this resonance from the higher dimensions, it would have a unique sound. Your distinctive signature involves key qualities and abilities you have developed over time. Some people, for example, were born into families talented in the arts. Perhaps they excelled as musicians, sculptors, painters, writers, or designers.

Even if you have no awareness of your past lineage, if you have worked in the arts, you likely have some abilities associated with success in that area. An artist often is called to develop and utilize qualities involving such things as imagination, curiosity, creativity, focus, observation, patience, tenacity, decisiveness, intuition, commitment, and good work habits.

The same qualities and abilities an artist hones on a personal level are also needed in the world. Someone out there can benefit from them. In fact, there is sure to be great demand for those who are skilled in using their intuitive right brain while also being able to observe and focus the mind to make intelligent decisions. These types of skills are an asset in countless types of work environments.

Making Your Life Count

Regardless of your age and circumstance, you can make your life count. What does this mean? You can make your life count by being present and awake to the many opportunities you are given to personally advance and help humanity evolve into higher consciousness. Be aware of these and act on them.

In order to notice more of these windows of opportunity as they arise, become mindful of just how precious your life really is. On some days when you are mired in mundane routines, it may be difficult to view life as precious. However, especially on those days, do your best to focus on the bigger picture of how auspicious it is to be alive today. Remind yourself of how living right now can greatly accelerate your enlightenment process. Enlightenment is not for a select few because it is your natural state.

Be grateful that you are on Earth now so you can be an integral part of humanity's great shift. If you can generate gratitude within you in sufficient amounts, you will find less to complain about. Your more positive mind-set will become a magnet to attract positive things into your life.

Your Place in the World

When you have questions of how to best contribute, start where you are. There are different ways that you can serve during each phase of life.

Young Adult

If you are a young adult, know that you don't have the rigid road map for life's success that your parents did. Be glad of that. Rigidity, in all of its forms, must fall away in the new world you and others are helping to create. There is no single way to contribute, no single path to career success, and no single worldly anchor to rely upon. To be sure, you most likely will have more than one type of job in your life, and sometimes it will be you who creates a brand-new type of position, company, or industry. Realize that you are not what you do for a living. Your job is like a coat you put on for a while: it may fit you very well, but it is not you. When you are working in a job that doesn't seem to fit, remember that you are always in a place for a reason. If you feel dissatisfied with the job, connect with your inner wisdom to determine why. For example, you could be there to work for a boss who triggers your pattern of perfectionism. If that is the main reason, and you clear your pattern with inner work, it may be easy for you to move on to another more suitable job. Keep in mind that any job, in any field, can be connected to your path of spirit. You can bring your light to any environment, and you can learn how to more fully express your light by being in a number of diverse situations over time.

Midlife

For people in midlife, to make this life count you will need to be willing to continually update your worldview and your skills. The pace of change on the planet is now more rapid than that seen by any previous generation. No one could have prepared you for this. You are required, much more than your parents were, to continually adjust to everything from new technologies to radically different methods of communicating and working. Almost as soon as you begin to figure out one novel device, something else very different takes its place, and you must adapt to that. If you work for a living, you must keep current with the market in your field of expertise, sometimes learning an entirely new set of skills. These skills include being up-to-date about how people in your field communicate and find work. You cannot afford to stick your head in the sand, refusing to learn these new ways. If you do, you may find yourself unemployed or underemployed. The other element in your adaptation process is the challenge of bridging your outer-world activities with your spiritual unfolding. Your DNA is changing as you rid yourself of old patterns, hold increasing amounts of light, and raise your frequency through higher-vibrational thoughts and actions. Staying grounded and focused is essential as you become more multidimensional and access the higher frequencies. After all, the whole purpose of becoming multidimensional while on Earth is to bring the higher spiritual energies into the human experience.

Retired or Elderly

If you have retired or are elderly, then in order to make your life count, you will need to stay interested in life, including your own personal growth, other people, and the outside world. Be as fully engaged with life as you can for as long as you can. Refuse to accept old-paradigm views of age and aging. Know that you have something to contribute, even if it's simply the wisdom you have gained from living life in the best way you could. People in your inner circle, and even strangers you see in public, can benefit from this wisdom if you will only share it. Trust that if you are still alive, there remains something for you to learn as well as something for you to share with the world. You can continue to evolve and grow spiritually until your very last breath. On the days when you feel you are finished with Earth's lessons, remind yourself of how beneficial even one more day is when you learn to love more deeply and less conditionally. Invite those opportunities into your life. Welcome them with gratitude and use the gift they provide for your advancement as a soul.

*

Tips: Connecting with Your Mission of Light

Here are some guidelines for approaching your spiritual path in ways that are more sane, more honoring of who you truly are, and more heart centered. Contemplate these to connect more fully with your mission of light.

1. Be willing to acknowledge the divine spark that exists within you. God—or the divine, or whatever name you use for it—exists within the DNA of all people on Earth. By exploring that DNA, which is like a record of who you are on every level, you can reveal elements of your divine heritage, past conditioning, ancestral lineage, present circumstances, and even future potential.

    Scientists are now discovering that there's a symbolic language that exists within your DNA that confirms your divine nature.

Your DNA even has a sound.[30] That sound is your divine light manifest in the physical. At your core, you *are* that divine spark with that divine light and divine sound!

Surrounding your divine self are layers of human conditioning that have caused you to have amnesia about who you truly are. You have developed self-sabotaging habits that obscure your true light. The same is true for everyone you meet. They, too, are divine and have the potential for enlightenment at some point in the future. Consider this the next time you are about to speak or act harshly with yourself or another person.

2. Begin to trust that you are ready and that regardless of your achievements to date, you can progress even further.

You don't need to wait for anything or anyone to shine your light. You can be that light and fulfill your mission one small moment at a time. Don't wait for big assignments; approach the small things with bigness. Don't let your age, health, worldly status, income, fame, or popularity prevent you from acting on your heart's wisdom.

Set your intention to trust this wisdom more in everyday situations. Trusting it and acting on it are the recipes for your success. Each time you let go of caring so much about whether you appear foolish or what others will think, and instead follow what your heart guides you to do, you move that much closer to manifesting what's in your highest good.

Your recipe for success, by its very nature, won't look exactly like anyone else's, so let go of comparisons when you find yourself making them.

---

30 See this book's recommended reading list for more information about the connection between DNA and sound.

If you are a senior citizen and feel you are complete with your contributions to this world, be willing to question this idea. Regardless of how much longer you have in this life, you can choose to continue learning and evolving until your last breath. In fact, don't be surprised if some of your most potent times are still to come.

3. Be open to changing your mind. As part of that, question more and more of the things you have long accepted as true.

Question even the intuitive guidance you may have received in the earlier days of your conscious spiritual journey. For example, you might have been told that your mission on Earth was to write a particular book or to help humanity in a very specific way. That guidance may have been appropriate for where you were on your path back then, but perhaps now it's no longer relevant or means something different.

Be willing to accept your greatness and your unlimited potential. Because of your conditioning, you have long accepted your false outer personality, believing it to be the real you. Consider that many of the concepts you have been taught, and much of what you have learned to see, are fabrications. A lot of what you think is real is accepted out of habit. Some of it seems true to you because your ancestors have passed to your generation belief systems that are based on lies. You inherited these in your DNA. You can change them, and in turn your experience of life, once you know that they reside in your subconscious. Therefore, as you are willing to explore this unknown territory within yourself and to change it at the DNA level, you greatly accelerate your journey into enlightenment.

4. Set your intention to replace criticism of self and others with curiosity about what really makes people tick. Dive deeper than surface appearances that won't give you the real picture.

   People are not all good or all bad. To believe that they are is a trick of the ego-mind that likes to categorize and see the world as a nicely wrapped box. Ask what's under the wrapping. Be curious about the dilemmas you and others face in the quest to become whole.

   If you are about to judge yourself or someone else, consider that we are always evolving. Allow your inquisitive nature to come forward and get into the space of wonderment. If you are willing to wonder how a person could act in the way that he or she does, you are one step closer to feeling wonder about the potentiality of the human spirit. This can open the door to miracles, unfolding one by one in your life.

   Be alert to subtle energies and learn to decipher them as you communicate with yourself and others. As part of that, learn to decode the messages your body communicates to you. Sometimes these messages alert you about potentially unwise choices. Other times they validate something you want to be true.

5. Let go of the desire to be rescued or saved. You don't need saving; that idea is part of the fabrication of traditional religions. According to this idea, you are not yet divine, and you must find someone or something outside of yourself to help you become divine. Certainly you can benefit from study with teachers who have experiential knowing of how to break free from human suffering. Keep in mind, though,

that the world's great teachers did not come to give you the divine spark, which is your essence.

The Buddha and other enlightened beings did not intend to establish religions or to be worshipped. They sought only to share what they had discovered about humanity's true nature and to open people to their natural state.

There are many great ones you can learn from today. Some of them are alive now, sharing universal truths in new ways that the modern person can more easily grasp. Other teachers are no longer in physical embodiment but are teaching humanity through their wisdom first presented long ago. The truths they came to teach are alive and real, even today.

These teachers are a gift to humanity, but do not set them up on a pedestal or think for one moment that they have something you can't also discover and embody. When you do this, knowingly or unknowingly, you are discounting your powerful ability to create change.

Don't forget that enlightenment is your true natural state and that it is actually encoded in your very DNA. As you recognize this and let go of false layers of energy that tell you otherwise, you will naturally discover and be able to harness your creative gifts. Begin to embrace this idea.

Allow the movement of spirit in your life to reveal to you what a part of you already knows: you have the answers to all of your own questions. In truth, you are here on Earth now to be a part of the greatest changes humanity has ever seen.

You and others like you are the creators of these changes.

Acknowledge yourself for this role and know that you would not have come at this pivotal point in Earth's history if you were not a divine changemaker!

Chapter 11

Rethinking Where and How You Live

You live on a planet undergoing the most amazing shift in consciousness ever witnessed by a generation. These pivotal years involve the greatest opportunity a person could have in any single lifetime to evolve into enlightened consciousness.

A couple of decades from now, you will not recognize the life you have on the Earth or your relationship to life itself. Meanwhile, you are blazing a path of transformation, because no previous generation has done what you are in the midst of doing. With each step, you are making a new trail for others to follow.

You Are the Architect of Your New Home

The planet's cultures are in the midst of a massive remodeling. You and others on the path of awakening are the architects. It is you who will decide what kind of Earth you want to inhabit and how you want to relate to the people and life here.

To make the wisest decisions, you will need to understand more about humanity's history. You will need to remember what you intrinsically know about the sacred and its connection to everything on Earth—from your body to the planet itself. You will need to discover a higher view of the unsettled feelings you often have. You will need to learn to feel more at home wherever you are. You will need to find a new fueling system for making changes—moving out of fear and allowing your inner wisdom to guide your choices.

Understanding Humanity's History on the Earth

From ancient times, humans have learned to migrate to other places, oftentimes very far from their homes and native lands. It was a common survival tool, put in motion to flee from invaders or to find food when it was scarce because of weather changes. Migration was also often born out of greed, with people seeking wealth or power by conquering a new land. Sometimes people simply left their familiar territory because of a passionate sense of adventure.

Your ancestors experienced the world as a vast place. Much of it was unexplored, and they enjoyed a feeling of open space. The native indigenous peoples remembered their connection with the natural world, passing on to their children a respect of the elements from which arise all forces of existence. These aboriginal people knew how to relate to the sacred because they saw the sacred in everything, including their own bodies. It was easy for them to find the sacred in everyday things and experiences.

Other groups of people took a different path. They forgot their relationship with the sacred. Over time, they looked increasingly outside of themselves for answers, and they sought external power. They forgot that their natural divine power was readily accessible inside themselves. Many were enticed by the possibility of reinventing themselves in faraway lands. The glamour of having something new was very appealing.

With each generation, a growing sense of separateness from the sacred was accompanied by an innate longing to be at one again.

People learned to define themselves as separate; they learned to view spirit as something outside of themselves.

People forgot their natural power within, and they learned to look to the external world when they were challenged in life. When people encountered obstacles and hardships, the learned tendency was to fight or flee. This set in motion an energetic cycle in which even more hardships were magnetized.

To succeed, it seemed, people had to struggle and work very hard. They were taught that they had to compete with and conquer one another in order to win. They learned to compare themselves with everyone with whom they came into contact, friend or foe. Aggression was taught to each generation until it became embedded in human DNA as a typical response. The aggressive, competitive approach was born out of ignorance and resulted from a false sense of separation and fears that there would never be enough to go around.

If your ancestors had known a better way, the world would be much different today. Your personal experience of life on Earth would be markedly different too. Why? You inherited in your DNA the belief systems and worldviews of your ancestors of long ago. You never met the members of your family's ancient lineage, but your DNA carries their energy. Held deep within your subconscious, away from ordinary view, the very old patterns of aggression continue to play out in your modern-day life.

At some point in this life, you woke up to the idea that you are here to shift the balance back to *light*. You are doing this for yourself and also for humanity. Your own life is a constant barometer of where the balance of light is within you, showing you the layers of falseness not yet cleared.

This may seem unsolvable at times. You may sometimes feel like a victim or be angry at the faceless sea of humanity that has lived in ignorance for so many generations. You may wonder how you can counter such a load of energetic negativity housed within your own DNA.

You may question whether you can change and whether there is *time*. You may doubt your own power and ability to help create the most amazing transition your Earth has ever seen. You may wonder whether you have what it takes to be an integral part of the shift in consciousness. You may seriously question whether it is possible to birth a new kind of world that is peaceful and cooperative.

Know That Everything Can Change—Trusting You Can Change

Be willing to trust, right now, that there are solutions for each of these dilemmas and that you have a key role to play. Know that everything can change—trust that *you* can change. You must believe this for the change to happen.

As you consider whether you can believe this, keep in mind the following. Your DNA is a kind of record keeper of who you are and what you believe on all levels. Like a personal akashic record, it stores energetic imprints of your past, present, and future.[31] These imprints include negative belief systems as well as encodements reminding you of your natural divine state. This means that once you clear the false beliefs and patterns that are not a part of your true essence, the core you are left with is divine!

To accelerate your enlightenment journey, it can be helpful to acknowledge daily that you are a divine being. Remind yourself that you are connected to the divine, universal flow of energy and that you can create *any* reality you choose. Remember that the limitations and separation you feel are a fabrication of limited human conditioning. Reflect at least once each day on the idea of the sacredness of your own body, of your life force, of all sentient beings inhabiting the Earth, and of the life experience itself.

When you face obstacles, avoid the temptation to resist them and to weave a story around them. These strategies are not only useless,

---

[31] Akashic record is a Sanskrit term for a library of mystical knowledge encoded in a nonphysical plane of existence. In some references, the records are described as a collection of all knowledge of human existence and the history of the cosmos.

but they waste precious time. Instead, face your obstacles head-on, doing the inner transformational work required to clear discordant energies. The more space you can clear within yourself in this way, the more light you will be able to house.

A Restructuring of Your DNA Is Under Way

As your physical body holds more light, the restructuring of your DNA will be accelerated, and you will be able to broadcast higher-frequency energies into the world. This is the catalyst for the bigger changes you seek on a planetary level. Each person making his or her own changes contributes to the whole.

Be willing to make a commitment to your own spiritual path and make regular recommitments to keep this energy alive within you. If you begin to lose interest in your journey, you will lose momentum.

To successfully navigate the uncertain times ahead, it is essential to develop and deepen your skills of intuitive awareness. Without these skills firmly integrated into all aspects of your life, fear can influence your decisions.

Fear colors your view, hindering your ability to choose wisely. When you are in fear, you can become immobilized just when you need to act. Your reality may seem to become fuzzy and chaotic, and if you move into panic mode, your higher guidance may seem out of reach.

Everyone around you is moving through transitions of one sort or another. This is true even for those who seem to be asleep. The more advanced spiritual practitioners often experience the energetic shifting at an accelerated pace.

One reason for this is that increased awareness tends to go hand in hand with an amplified ability to sense energy. Some people find that they become so sensitive to vibrational shifts that they feel Earth changes occurring halfway around the globe.

Likewise, as consciousness expands and a person's heart opens more fully, the emotions and cellular impact can be intense. Expansions in consciousness—sometimes referred to as ascension—will open you to feelings with which you are unfamiliar. You can become quite sensitive and sometimes have unexplainable aches and pains. Headaches and flulike symptoms are not uncommon.

If you can think of it as a massive restructuring on a deep cellular level, and if you appropriately take care of yourself, the energetic fallout will be lessened. Use common sense and your intuitively guided reason to indicate times you may need medical attention.

The Great Migration—Rethinking Where You Live

There is now a great migration of humanity. People in all corners of the world are moving from city to city and sometimes to different countries. You may not be one of the ones moving to another city, but you *are* impacted by those who have moved to where you live. You are also impacted by those who move away, such as family and other loved ones.

Sometimes the change in location is fueled by a natural disaster such as Hurricane Katrina or a tornado that wipes out most of a rural town. Migration also occurs in response to war and changes in political rule. In recent times, millions of refugees have fled oppression, often displaced by war or forced from their native lands by political tyranny.

If you think you are not personally impacted by the refugees of Africa or Iraq or Tibet, think again. It is now common knowledge that the planet and all of its inhabitants are intrinsically connected. Even at a DNA level, people are more alike than they are different.

Viewed from space, the Earth is a single planet in the sky, with a supply of interdependent resources and an intricate network of energy. What happens in one place has a ripple effect in many other places.

People today are much more aware of this natural interconnectedness. Because the planet is now in a cleansing mode as part of the birthing of a new consciousness, Earth changes occurring over the next several years will prompt many people to move from where they are now. This includes those who currently can't imagine they could live anywhere else.

If you begin to have a strong feeling that you should move to another city, state or country, how can you approach this sanely? How can you go about it in ways that support your soul's path?

※

Tips: Relocating to a New Home

If you feel that another location would be more suitable than your current home, and you think that you are clear about which specific location is best, check in with your heart and intuitively guided reason and ask questions such as these.

- How does this location better serve the path of my soul?

- What are the factors that I may have neglected to consider yet that are important?

- What role does fear play in the move to this place?

- What needs completing where I am before moving there?

- What do I need to research and take action on now, related to the new place?

- What is the best timing for the move?

- Is the move best approached in stages, and if so, what are they?

- How long before I will be ready to relocate, and what factors determine this?

- What can I do to speed up my readiness to move?

- Who are the people best suited to help me with the move?

- What people or factors in my current life could delay the move?

- What will I miss most when I leave my current town?

- Who (other people/pets) and what (belongings) do I take with me to the new place?

- Am I meant to maintain any base in the location where I live now? If so, what is it?

- Who do I know in the new place?

- How can I grow spiritually there, continuing my service in the world?

- What are my opportunities there to connect with like-minded people?

- What opportunities will I have there to continue learning?

- How can I continue my current interests and daily activities in the new place?

- Do current or future probable circumstances warrant a rethinking of my choice?

If you are unclear about the specific city of your relocation, refer to the questions above and ask them about locations that you would likely consider.

Remember to listen to your heart at all times. Consider factors such as lifestyle, weather, finances, work, health, and your spiritual path. If you are deciding between two cities, for example, you may want to ask questions about each one to determine which place may be more in alignment with where you want to be headed energetically.

One question to ask could be, "How would living in X city allow me to open up more to spirit than living in Y city?" Know that each town has a personality and an energy all its own. Look into what these are for each place to see how the location may be harmonious with your own energy. Research latest projections available about the place (including weather patterns, water supplies, energy costs, population growth, cost of living, demographics, traffic, accessibility, politics, freedoms, and sense of community).

Reconsidering How You Live

No matter where you live, it is essential to continue your spiritual growth and to make this a priority. To live in a spirit-connected way *is* the answer for living peacefully in the midst of chaos and uncertainty. This way of being is natural and available to anyone; it is your divine birthright. To access it, you must align your human personality with your soul.

Fears and fear-based thinking must be brought into your conscious awareness. Belief systems that keep you bound to cycles of pain must be cleared at a cellular level. The limiting patterns you hold within you are like yesterday's newspaper—old news. They are not relevant today, yet they influence your responses to people and life situations. These limiting energies cannot continue to be a part of your DNA, or else you will be blocked from your wholeness and full soul expression.

You will feel more free and whole with each layer of falseness that you clear.

To feel more peaceful about where you live, it can be helpful to make a point of feeling gratitude for something in your environment each day. How about the sunshine if you are blessed with pleasant weather? What about the brightly colored red rosebush you see each day you come in and out your front door? And don't forget the park where you love to walk your dog just before sunset.

Even if you plan to move to another city at some future time, you will want to fully utilize all of the gifts of your current location while you are there. There is a human tendency to discount the positive side of a situation when one is focused on the negative.

In the modern society of disposable products and short-lived relationships, people have learned to be dissatisfied with what they have as soon as they learn something better is available. This goes for places as well as products and relationships. You can always find people who are leaving your city and people who will tell you that other cities are safer or better in some other way. Use your discernment.

If you hate your city and can find nothing of redemption there, you will sabotage yourself with a downward spiral of energy. This negative energy will keep you locked into the hate, and it will draw more situations for you to hate. You will then take this negativity with you as you settle into a new city. No one in his or her right mind would want to pack a poison in their moving van and drink it when settled in a new locale. However, you take your conditioned mind with its limiting belief systems everywhere you travel. This means you take along any poison that you have not discarded before your move.

Therefore, if you realize you have feelings such as anger or blame when you think of where you live now, be willing to investigate the sources of those responses. Perhaps your unresolved dislike of your city has something to do with personal experiences you associate with that place. Examples could be divorce, unemployment, or another challenging crossroad. If you can separate the happenstance from the location where it happened, you can begin to see the big picture more clearly. No place is all bad or all good. These are judgments. Know that your experience of any place is a direct reflection of the inner state of your consciousness. When you change your consciousness, everything else around you changes.

※

Tips: Staying Centered When the Road Gets Rocky

For help in staying centered when the road gets rocky, consider the following.

1. **Surround yourself with things and people that remind you of the sacred**. This can include visual and auditory reminders of spirit in your life. Get creative with this and make it fun. Visual reminders can be a colorful altar, a candle, a flower, or a crystal that has meaning to you. Auditory reminders can include music that feels sacred to you and sounds that help you connect with a peaceful state. Diffuse an essential oil for a fragrance that uplifts your spirits and calms your mind. Spend time with people who are positive and who help you connect with your own goodness. If you feel that there are not now enough people like this in your life, focus your intent and prayers on manifesting additional companions. Then pay attention to who shows up in your life and make an effort to develop and sustain meaningful and reciprocal relationships.

2. **Become more mindful of what you take in with your senses**. What you see and hear is registered at very subtle levels. People have a tendency to believe they cannot be

harmed by the daily dose of TV and other media—this is a false idea. The world's messages are often panic-oriented and can trigger your own personal fears of doom and gloom. Set your intention to be as awake as possible when you take in such messages. Get into the habit of being your own censor of what you will and will not focus on. Avoid mainstream news, especially with visuals, just before sleep. At the end of the day before going to bed, learn to clear your mind of outside influences, worries, and thoughts. Invite your higher wisdom to guide you into a peaceful sleep, asking to awaken easily and with greater clarity and peace about the issues of your life.

3. **If you are impacted directly or indirectly by a disaster, remember that your role as a spiritual practitioner is to take the high road of spirit**. A direct impact could be a fire in your backyard or a hurricane destroying your home. An indirect impact could be anything from an earthquake in the city where your family lives to your intuitive sense that you may personally be affected by a disaster in the not-too-distant future. Either way, remember to take that high road. This is the road of spirit, and it is the only road that will get you to the other side of the crisis sanely. Know that you have an ability to do this, even if it appears to be a very grave situation. If you can step back from the situation frequently and go into your heart, you can reach a place of sanity. From that place, you can intuitively know what to do. You can be guided about what to say to others, and when to be silent. You can be shown the appropriate responses that come from love and compassion rather than fear and panic. You can be an example for others who in that moment do not have your wisdom and courage. When you access this kind of wisdom, you will find stability. The energy of this

stability will then automatically broadcast out from you in a way that helps others. This is how you can help.

Preparing to Reside in Your New Home

When you have reached the end of humanity's great shift process, a brand-new type of world will exist. This new Earth will be full of light, and you will have plenty of people with whom to share that light.

You want that place to exist right now, of course. Because you really are at the helm—being the divine changemaker that you are—know that your focusing on what you want to create keeps you in the driver's seat. Don't wait for your new-paradigm Earth to magically appear. Create it in your mind with your imagination right now. As you consider the next ideas, get creative about what you want to happen. If you like, you can write down your ideas in a specially designated notebook that you keep on your sacred altar. You can add to it as thoughts come to you and then refer back to it later for inspiration.

※

Process: Imagining Your New-Paradigm Earth

Imagine that the new-paradigm Earth is a location you can move to, leaving your old life behind to start fresh. Consider what it would look like, how it would feel, who would be there, and how you would be living your life's purpose.

As you read this, check in with your heart and intuitively guided reason, inviting a response to the following questions about this imagined place. Consciously intend that you will not censor your imagination or the visuals and feelings that come to you. Give yourself permission to acknowledge anything you visualize that matches your current experience. Why? Because you may already be residing in the new energies at least some of the time right now! Approach this with a sense of play and allow it to be fun!

What It Looks Like

First, consider the terrain and other outer-world elements of this new-paradigm home. How does this new place look different from the one you currently inhabit? When you imagine it, are you living in the same home, neighborhood, and general locale? What are the biggest changes you notice? What remains the same as you have now?

What kind of physical environment do you spend time in, and how does it look different? What sort of colors or other decorations are beautifying the space? What do the colors and style say about you? What are the main differences in your décor, furniture, type and amount of space, and things like the view and the level of quiet?

How is the space configured to support your connections with spirit? How is the place arranged to help you connect with nature? Does the place have fewer things than your current one, allowing you to quickly find objects when needed?

Where is your home located in relation to where you work or serve others? If it is not in the same place, how do you travel from home to the other location, and what do you do to maintain a peaceful and joyful inner experience as you travel? If you work or provide service from your residence, how do you balance your life and your life force? If you work outside the home, what does your work environment look like?

What It Feels Like

Now that you've considered what this new-paradigm home looks like, shift your focus to feeling. How does it feel to you to be there? When you imagine each element of your new location, notice any feelings, such as joy, empowerment, spaciousness, and relaxation. Look for passion, creativity, productiveness, and physical aliveness. Pick up clues to bonding with spirit and being at home in your own skin.

Who Is There

Now that you've gotten in touch with some feelings of the new place, consider who is there with you. Do you see some familiar faces, and if so, who are they? Who are the new people, and what makes them stand out as people you want around you? Get a sense of how you meet them, including any actions you take and the state of your inner life that magnetically draws the perfect people to you.

Who is missing from the picture? If you don't see them in your immediate vicinity, expand your view to discover whether they live nearby, perhaps no longer interacting with you in intimate ways.

As you visualize this place and with whom you are sharing life experiences, allow a knowing to come to you about how you interact with key people. Who are your close friends and companions for life's journey? Do you have a life partner, and if so, what is he or she like? How does sharing your life with this person enhance your life experience and help you to accelerate your enlightenment?

What types of groups of people are you interacting with? A group of people can be small or large, from two friends who share a common interest to an international group of like-minded people. How have you developed your ability to connect with these people? What specifically has helped you to make the connections? What common bonds or interests do you share with these people?

Focus on your work environment in the new place and get in touch with who is there with you. Notice any familiar faces? In general, who are you working with or serving?

Pay attention to how many people you see in your work sphere. Perhaps the number is different than in your current life. Where do they live? Has your ability to touch others with your gifts expanded to other locations? Imagine a map of the world and see where these people are. Also, notice what qualities these people have, and how these qualities are in harmony with you and your spiritual path. Visualize how interacting at work with a more enlightened group of people helps to feed you on a spiritual level.

How You Express Your Life's Purpose

As you visualize this new-paradigm home, allow your heart and intuitive right brain to connect you with specifics of how you express your purpose.

What is your approach to life that allows you to live fully and to express your gifts? See pictures within your mind as though on a movie screen, indicating what it means to live life as fully as you were intended to. See yourself living life to the fullest: no holding back, no waiting for approval, no seeking an outside source to tell you everything is okay, no being angry about the past, and no worrying about the future.

As part of that, imagine some of the gifts you alone can express in the world. Open your awareness to the really big picture here. "Big picture" doesn't mean your ego is running the show with lofty ideas of who you are; it simply means stepping back enough to realize the jewels that reside within you.

These are the qualities and abilities that, when fully expressed in the world, are distinctive to you. Most of these are quite simple. Some may seem to be related to what other people also express or can do. However, know that your gifts cannot be expressed exactly the same way by anyone else.

Keep in mind as you read the list that your real gifts are more about being than doing. If there is a doing element involved, what's important is how you do it. A few examples you may relate to are included here.

Consider Your Gifts

- Able to listen deeply with compassion and caring
- Capable of communicating clearly with the spoken or written word
- Skilled in expressing positive qualities (unconditional love, kindness, acceptance)
- Proficient in working with space (organizing it, clearing it, Feng Shui)
- Able to handle details and zero in on what's important
- Talented with numbers and the ordering of things
- Competent as a parent or a caregiver
- Skilled in understanding and working with the natural world (animals, plants, crystals)
- Good with color and style, intuitively knowing which complement each other
- Able to be resourceful, finding solutions and insights helpful to self or others
- Proficient in working with one's hands (crafts, building, sewing, massage, art)
- Capable of creating something brand new (music, words, art, dance, design)
- Able to create harmony, to organize, and to bring a cooperative spirit to endeavors
- Skilled in helping others with transformation (counselors, healers, intuitives)
- Capable of teaching others (teachers, spiritual leaders, writers)
- Able to help others in a unique way with a service or product
- Proficient in helping others to shift human dysfunctional patterns
- Talented in mass media expression that can help change the world (actors, writers)
- Able to lead others, generate cooperation and positive changes (politicians, executives)

- Capable of visionary approaches (inventors, entrepreneurs)
- Able to step back from challenges and see the big picture
- Skilled in whole-brain thinking and a spirit-directed approach that's heart centered
- Understanding of the keys to wellness, longevity, and a joyful life
- Able to be patient with others, self, and the world
- Skilled in bringing laughter and lightness of being into the lives of others
- Talented at accessing and utilizing intuitive abilities

Reflect for a few more moments on your gifts, this time inviting spirit to help you expand upon what you now understand. Ask for guidance about how to more fully utilize the gifts you have. Ask for spirit's view of your gifts—what they are, which ones are most vital to your path of light, what you can do to further develop them, and how you can best give them in the world.

Your gifts are meant to be given, and only you can give them. Let go of comparing your gifts with those of others. Challenge your doubting mind when it tells you that you aren't gifted or that your gifts aren't enough. This is nonsense.

Set your intention to make full use of your gifts, not simply to help your own spiritual advancement but to help others. When you are giving your gifts without reservation, your soul can express more fully in the world. There is a genuine joy that comes from this.

This joy of expressing your soul—giving your gift, whatever it is—serves as the fuel that energizes you, sparking your passion and helping you to maintain a steadiness when life gets rocky.

When you are complete with this process, imagine that the new Earth you have created in your mind is now anchored within your heart center. See it there in present time. Trust that this is what you have the ability to create.

A New State of Consciousness

The new-paradigm Earth you have just imagined is not an actual location. It's not a place you can pack your bags and move to, like you could move to London or Toronto. This place is a vibrational one, related to a state of elevated consciousness.

What you are contemplating here is a brand-new reality within which the new more enlightened human will be born and peacefully coexist with other sentient beings. You and others like you on the path of awakening are creating this place right now!

At times, even without consciously knowing it, you are able to elevate yourself enough so that you have glimpses of this new-paradigm energy. During your dream time, too, you have a taste of this as you connect with intuitive insights about your spiritual transformation. Knowing this can be an incentive to work more with your dreams and the richness they can provide you for personal growth.

In the truest sense, most changes involved in creating the new Earth are within you. They occur as you open to more of who you really are, drop your past, let go of future fixations, and move into being really awake, present and alive in the body you inhabit.

As you are learning to do this—becoming conscious of your thoughts, words, and actions—you get in touch with your real authentic power. You are remembering just how powerful you are and taking back your power a bit at a time. You are learning to take responsibility for your creations. You are remembering more about who you really are, what really matters, and why you are here now.

The more that you focus on these higher purposes, instead of worrying or complaining about what's wrong, the more quickly you will advance.

Chapter 12
Humanity's New Chapter

Your inner wisdom led you to read this book. That part of you has all of the answers about living in these unique times. Your wise self knows that this unique cycle of time is not the end of life but a transition into new beginnings.

Your everyday self, however, may be doubtful. That conditioned part of you remains immersed in linear illusions about what is possible. You have learned to doubt things that you could not prove with your eyes or by other physical means.

You see massive changes taking place and notice that much of your familiar world is falling away. However, you do not yet see the new world that you want to live in. You may sense that your new Earth is on a cosmic drawing board, being created in the background as you and your society struggle with a multitude of challenges. Your ego-self, however, wants proof that a more light-filled world is in the making. Your ego-self, which is impatient and afraid, gives you repetitive messages of doubt. Your inner wisdom, which does not need material evidence, trusts in the process of evolutionary change.

On some days, it may seem as though nothing is really changing.

It may even appear as though humanity is descending rather than ascending. In those times, it may appear as though there's no way out and that all of humankind is doomed.

It is common to feel weary, angry, and even hopeless when weeks of uncertainty and chaos turn into months and even years with no end in sight. The challenge in this cycle is to remain in balance in the midst of the enormous cleansings happening on a personal and planetary scale.

Everyone Is Impacted

It is very helpful to remember that the transformational cleansing is impacting *every* form of life on the Earth, from the plants and animals to children and adults of all evolutionary stages. Nothing is exempt, not even the Earth itself. Keeping this in mind will help when you feel hopeless, alone, or unable to take your next step. To acknowledge this helps you to have a larger perspective and assists you in generating compassion for yourself and others.

You can also have more compassion when you recognize that people are at different stages of awakening. Not everyone you meet will be ready for the great leaps in consciousness that you are seeking. Some may be ready in general but need a bit more time. Go gently with yourself and others. *Everyone is divine!*

It can be scary to wake up to the destructive effects of hate, ignorance, and greed. It can be disheartening to realize that the majority of humanity is still asleep and unaware of the paradigm shift. It can be disappointing to experience continual lengthy delays in manifesting your personal dreams. It can be frightening to investigate your own negativity. It can be overwhelming to realize how much effort is needed to reach enlightenment.

Deciding to Care

Oftentimes, it can feel like the world's negativity is disturbingly worse and overshadows the light. You may sometimes feel as if no one cares. At this moment, how about affirming for yourself: "I care." It is each of our caring—and our light—that makes the difference. Do not wait for others to care before you do; decide to care now.

Remember that we carry our own light. Do not wait for others to light your way. It is up to each of us to connect with and express our light. It is our responsibility to care and to discover how to be more compassionate so that our caring is done with kindness.

When you come from a place of caring and compassion, it is easier to be present and awake during chaos.

It is also easier to face truths as they are revealed. There will be much information, previously hidden from view, coming out of the closet over the coming years.

A Time of Transparency

In the coming years, it will become harder to hide truth. The walls that separate fact from fiction will weaken under the force of humanity's emerging light consciousness. Transparency is becoming the watchword of the times.

What does this mean? And how is this relevant for you, the divine changemaker? On a global level, it means that many of the disparities and dysfunctions of the world will come out of the shadows of ignorance. As this happens, longstanding out-of-balance situations will be seen and recognized as detriments, even more than at present.

Likewise, universal truths about energy and the interconnectedness of all life will emerge into the mainstream with increasing speed. There will be a growing sense of awareness across the planet that many things are not really as they have appeared to be for a long time.

Until fairly recently, mainstream thinking has been in a box wrapped tightly with string. The string is now loosening, and light is beginning to shine on the contents within the box. As this process of unveiling continues, things outside conventional thinking that you have long believed to be true will be receiving noteworthy mention from unlikely sources.

Do not be surprised when you see announcements of cures for devastating diseases. Some diseases may even be reclassified as researchers more fully understand how the body's interconnected energy systems work.

The planet's history will come under a microscope as policymakers and scientists grapple with solutions to the world's growing list of concerns. Examples are climate change, imbalances in resources, population growth, species extinction, and a troubled global economy.

People who were seemingly unawake before will begin to connect with a desire for a more heart-centered life. Underneath that desire will be a remembrance that there is a spiritual force that is at the core of each being. This is the divine spark that is within all life.

The early stages of this remembering typically manifest as a general discontent. When the dissatisfaction grows sufficiently, people begin to question more deeply and to ask for different things than they are used to receiving.

Understanding Others

People will have varying timetables and experiences during their awakening process. Some people you know who previously showed no interest in spirit may all of a sudden ask questions about the deeper meaning of life. Keep this in mind so that you will more easily connect the dots when your friends, colleagues, and loved ones begin to awaken and to act differently than before. You will delight in their waking up, yet their actions may seem bewildering.

Sometimes their questioning will be cloaked in nonsensical debating or complaining. It may appear that some of their irritation is because of something you did. Oftentimes what you did or did not do is only a catalyst for their discontent, so it's not personal. If you can remember this when you are thrown into the center of the other person's wake-up chaos, it will be easier for you to find your balance.

Honing Your Discernment

During this cycle of great change, you will have ample opportunities to hone your abilities of discernment. As the prevalence of transparency increases, you will have much to ponder and examine. Some of the truthful information coming to light will be packaged side by side with lies. This means that part of what you are shown is true but the overall picture may be misleading. Some who pretend to be transparent will present a mixture of true and not-so-true information.

To be sure though, the truth will come out on all things in time. The veils of deception can no longer be held in place as the planet moves into a higher consciousness. The hidden—whether it involves truths, lies, or a suppression of facts—will naturally become increasingly transparent.

You as a Divine Changemaker

Remember that, as a divine changemaker, you are alive now to be at the forefront of changes involved with shifting the planet into light. To be a divine changemaker means that you are moving into conscious creation and taking back your power.

You are acknowledging spirit and recognizing that you come from spirit. You are finding ways to return to the heart-centered way of being that is your true nature. You are seeing that most people have forgotten their divine heritage. You are observing how people have learned to be disconnected from each other and from the divine force that is meant to be the food of life.

As a divine changemaker, you are among those taking the lead during these times of planetary crisis. Keep in mind that being farther along on the path doesn't make you special or better than anyone else. However, your light and the ways that you express it can be of tremendous help to others who are in the earlier stages of waking up.

Your light can also be a pivotal beneficial force to others traveling shoulder to shoulder with you. Other people need to know that they aren't alone. You give each other the reminder that this is a group effort. You can help one another to move more easily through the chaos and to stay sane. You can be the rock of stability for each other.

The people in your energetic sphere of influence are facing challenges similar to those you face—great uncertainty, sweeping changes, economic reconfiguration, ongoing chaos, and strained relationships. They face these things regardless of whether they are as prepared as you are. In your past experiences, you have had preparation that some other people are only now initiating. Your advance preparation will help you greatly now.

One factor that's helping you even now, more than you likely recognize, is that you have been introduced to many useful tools for coping. And you have learned some basics about how to respond to life with intuitively guided reason. You have discovered that the key to peace is to find out how to create peace within yourself. You know without a doubt that your relationship with spirit is the glue that puts all of the disconnected pieces together.

Putting What You Know into Action

Now is the time to put all of what you have learned into action. It's important that you act on what you know. Do this even when you feel that you don't have all the answers. Start from where you are and more answers will come to you as needed. Trust that your light-infused actions will make a difference in what happens next—in your soul's progression and in the future of our beloved Earth.

Remember that people have a distorted idea of time. It may appear as though no one was preparing for the great shift of life on Earth. To the untrained eye, the current turmoil may feel like a recent phenomenon. This point of view runs counter to the way our universe really works. As you will understand more and more, it's really about cycles that are continually in motion.

The cycle of the Earth's current waking-up process has been gaining momentum for many years. However, now there is a magnification process involved. This means a much faster parting of the veils that long have kept people in ignorance. It means increasing amounts of transparency involving all aspects of your society. This is significant.

An Unprecedented Demystifying of Life

The trend toward greater transparency has nothing to do with politics, religion, or desires of special interest groups. Likewise, it has nothing to do with what's right or wrong. The movement into greater clarity goes hand in hand with the great shift of the ages. That shift involves a thinning of the veils that have long kept the masses in the dark.

Many of the world's problems have been building for a very long time, yet only recently has this started to become apparent to the general populace. Similarly, the life journey for people here on Earth today is a continuum—a cycle of energy put in motion over time.

People have a tendency to forget the past as well as lessons learned in key relationships. The awakening across the planet is changing this. When memories of the past are triggered, reality-shifting truths may be revealed. People then can identify and heal dysfunctional patterns. As this healing occurs, people can shift into their full potential.

The demystifying of life on the grand scale occurring now is unprecedented. As a result, you likely have ongoing questions about what is real, what to pay attention to, and how you fit in.

Even if you are a seasoned spiritual practitioner, you can become anxious when discovering that your early life training did not fully prepare you for the level of unfolding now under way. Go gently with yourself and others who also are finding their way out of the dark. It will be easier on some days, harder on others.

The Blinders Are Gone

In many cases it will be a bit like the racehorse that has its blinders removed after the race and before being turned loose into open pasture. Sometimes the horse will respond wildly, running as fast as it can in the direction of freedom yet having no specific destination in mind.

At other times, the horse will move smoothly and effortlessly into the open field, feeling confident and in good spirits. On occasion, the horse will stand in place, immobilized and in a daze. If feeling sufficiently aggravated, the horse may rear up and kick its handler out of defiance. If it is let loose with other horses, its herding instinct may come into play. The horse will then follow the lead of the dominant horse.

People often respond similarly to the racehorse when faced with the need to make radical changes. There's a learned tendency to bolt away from restrictions even if there's no clarity about to where one is bolting. There could be more clarity if people had more experience and confidence with accessing their heart's inner wisdom. With no intelligent plan, the person who bolts ahead is really no better off than before.

Similarly, people often let fear be an immobilizing force rather than the catalyst to do great things.

Pack mentality is a serious obstacle as well. This is especially true in times when people are feeling isolated and craving connection with others.

※

Questions: Knowing What to Ask Now

To avoid being like the wild racehorse, here is a list of key questions you can ask on a regular basis. Come back to these questions whenever you desire more clarity, more focus, more balance, and more inner confidence about your path of light.

1. As I consider an issue or situation, am I looking at both the relevant details and the big picture?

2. What is the key missing piece of information that will allow me to have clarity?

3. What is in the way of my seeing what I need to see?

4. How am I sabotaging my own progress?

5. In what ways am I giving away my power?

6. What is the one change I could make in my life to radically shift out of past rigid conditioning and into a more enlightened state?

7. As I consider the current outer-world news and prophecies, which things are really true, which are assumptions, which make me the most fearful, and which cause me to feel the most hope?

8. How comfortable do I feel in becoming more transparent with myself, my loved ones, and my outer world?

9. What am I afraid to know about myself?

10. Have I remembered today that I am a divine changemaker, contemplating what that means in action?

Power to Change the World

Some say humanity is now living in its eleventh hour, the last moment when change is thought possible. Examples are all around you of other species nearly or already extinct. Beneath the oceans and under modern-day cities are clues about ancient human civilizations that vanished relatively quickly due to either abrupt changes in weather patterns or human-caused misapplication of natural laws.

Science, more than at any other time in recorded history, is able to project outcomes based on current scenarios involving Earth changes. A projection is not the same as reality in the here and now, of course. Also, the projections relate mostly to external things, like climate change and planet resources. Scientists rarely factor into their projections the element of human consciousness and the true power that humans have to change the world.

The scientific experts who warn of catastrophes have focused extensively on the harm people can do rather than the good.

Still, the dire projections of where humanity may be headed have given the masses a large enough wake-up call to stir things up. The changes that are needed now will not come out of complacency or apathy. People must begin to care not just about themselves but about humanity as a collective and the planet as a sacred home.

The view will need to be broad, the vision big, and the dream expansive. To survive and thrive, humanity will need to embrace brand-new approaches, be willing to take risks, and let go of endless naming of wrongs.

At the core of your being, you know this to be true, and you know that it applies to you on a very personal level. You also know that the divine spark within you is able to access boundless inner resources. When you access your true authentic power, the old-paradigm rules no longer apply. Your view broadens, your vision enlarges, and your dream expands. Unlimited possibilities abound!

Your Life Has a Purpose

You are alive now to take part in the shift in consciousness occurring during these times. You may sometimes lose sight of this larger perspective. None of your life so far has been an accident or has been wasted. There was a purpose to all of it, which you will understand in time.

For right now, it is enough to know that you are here on purpose. You are not a victim of other people or circumstances. You are a very powerful divine changemaker, understanding more and more each day what this means in practice. You have played an instrumental role in helping to change humanity's mind-set from one of rigidity and fear to openness and love. You have done that each time you moved out of your rigidity and fear, and each time that you have questioned these responses in your outer world. You have done this as you focused increasingly on how to create more openness and love—not only within yourself but on the planet. You have done this when you have held the vision of a new Earth that is heart centered and loving.

Each time you have helped in these ways, you have become part of the solution your world needs, and has always needed, when fear and hate dominate the human experience. There is now a great acceleration in humanity's awakening.

The Heart of Humanity Speaks

The heart of humanity is speaking—asking for a return to love. This is the fuel for the current reconfiguration of society now in full swing.

As the economy and other structures get an overhaul, you are reexamining your values, your aspirations, your relationships, and more. With that assessment you may feel a whole range of emotions—from anxiousness and uncertainty to gratitude and joy.

With the expanded energies present now, it becomes easier to identify and work through issues that block your joy.

Although there is no shortcut to enlightenment, you do benefit from being alive now during our unusual quickening. Things previously hidden from view become obvious, and you can access great spiritual openings to other dimensions. This means an expanded view of what you normally see, an expanded perception of feelings, and an expanded ability to move into a higher-vibrational state of consciousness. This higher frequency helps you to connect with your multidimensional self. As part of that, you naturally connect more with your heart, your intuition, your courage, and your ability to forgive and let go.

Your multidimensional self already exists within the higher frequencies. Claim that self now.

Recognize You Are the Light of the World

You are the light of the world, and you are here now to shine that light. As you hold more light within you and radiate that light out from your heart center, you move out of your pain. This happens because you become more aware of patterns that have kept you frozen in fear. You are able to see these patterns more clearly, and you have less resistance to facing them head on. As you do that, you will catapult yourself into a life with more joy.

Your divine self, residing within your human form, is naturally joyful. It is inherently loving and fearless too. This is your timeless and natural self; it does not need any external thing or circumstance to feel joyful.

On those days when you feel unhappy and dissatisfied with how things are, remember who you are at your core. Remember that your energy field is regularly recalibrating. Your DNA is changing and adjusting so that you can hold increasing amounts of light. Those changes are happening even faster as you work consciously with your DNA.

New Levels of Energy Are Available

You are accessing levels of energy and information you could not even imagine before. Changes are happening very quickly, and it is often challenging for you to correctly perceive how much you are shifting. However, trust that you are accessing new levels of awareness as you progress. Your intuition is heightened, and your sensitivity level is expanded.

Physical Symptoms

On a physical level, this often means that you experience aches and pains that cannot be explained in the usual way. You will get used to these and will discover how to understand the difference between an occasional headache or flulike symptom and a serious medical condition requiring a doctor's care.

Sometimes you will experience physical distress that falls somewhere in between these two categories. An example could be a headache that comes from an imbalance in your nervous system or digestive tract. As your body regularly readjusts to the higher frequencies, you may need to make changes in your self-care, diet, or belief systems held within your DNA. The shift in consciousness involves energy and awareness. You cannot effectively hold the higher-vibrational energies if you are out of balance on any level—physical, emotional, mental, or spiritual.

What you will discover is that some of your headaches and flulike symptoms are a natural part of energy shifts. They can be a signal that your body is adjusting to a higher frequency. When this occurs, the discomfort you feel is not from an illness and will pass. Get into the habit of tuning into your body. When you discover how to interpret your symptoms, you will have less stress and more peace of mind.

The higher-vibrational energies are a frequency that relate to consciousness. As you raise your consciousness, you also raise your frequency. In tandem with this, you naturally become more multidimensional, and all of your senses—including physical and intuitive—are heightened.

This means that you are able to sense things you were not aware of before, and you have body sensations you cannot explain in conventional terms. In general, the more awake you become, the more sensitive you become. As an example, sometimes you can experience insomnia after eating a food you ate before without a problem. Another time you may wake up in the early hours of the morning due to an energetic response to a massive earthquake halfway around the world. Sometimes during a seemingly ordinary day, you may feel anxious without being able to explain why.

Your DNA Is Changing

These times are naturally going to bring up your old unfinished business. That means dysfunctional patterns from your past. A DNA-level pattern involving power issues, for example, could surface and set off a kind of red alert in your nervous system. Because many of these patterns are rooted in your past and your family's lineage, you might overlook what's really going on and think your symptoms are something else. You might even think you're having a panic attack or worse.

As you address your past patterns and regularly update your self-care and diet, you will become more comfortable with your own energetic shifting. As you select your food and self-care, a good question to ask is this: "Will this substance or health regimen support me in raising my energy frequency?" The answer to that question will help you to decide the best course of action.

Know that when your frequency is high enough, disease cannot thrive in your body. You will be more joyful too!

Remember each day that you live during historic moments on the Earth. The secrets of humanity's past—and your own past—are coming to light. It's also a time when you have access to significantly more energetic momentum to create the kind of world you have long sought to inhabit. These two transformational factors make this a very unique time to be alive.

Opportunities to Remember

When you look back on these times in the years to come, what do you want to remember? Will you think of these moments as having been a time of great opportunity?

Consider the kinds of opportunities that are present right now. Imagine how even one of them could help shift the Earth into a planet of light. Picture what your human experience would be like then.

※

Checklist: Tapping into Today's Unique Opportunities

1. **Hidden knowledge is being uncovered.** Ancient teachings about the nature of life, universal laws, and how to become free of suffering are moving out of secrecy and exclusion. Until recent times, this knowledge was limited to select groups of people. If you were not fortunate enough to be

born into the optimal conditions to receive the teachings, you could not benefit. Today, you as a spiritual seeker can discover and utilize these ancient mysteries. You can read books, learning from the great sages who lived long ago. You are able to participate in sacred spiritual teachings, receiving the wisdom of esteemed spiritual lineage holders and other adepts. You have the ability to access a wide range of views, deciding with the help of your heart's wisdom what is true for you. You can discover how to uncover your own secrets, becoming aware of and healing longstanding dysfunctional patterns that have kept you feeling small. Imagine how resolving even one of your major obstacles could help you to become more self-realized.

2. **Change is faster.** During most other phases of humanity's development, a person could not progress that rapidly during his or her lifetime. This slower momentum of change meant that people were much more limited. A person could plant seeds for enlightenment, but spiritual progression during his or her life span was minuscule compared with now. Your path of spiritual awakening is no longer measured by a third-dimensional yardstick.

3. **The old is quickly crumbling beneath your feet.** The old, outmoded structures and ways of being are rapidly falling away. Remember that these are the pieces of your society that do not function; they are not in alignment with where you want to be. The dysfunctional cannot remain if you are to create a more light-filled world. To be sure, the rapid disintegration of the old, nonworking order can be scary and disorienting. You haven't lived through this much shifting at one time before. However, you are now waking up to your true role as a divine changemaker. That means you are remembering that you are divine and are purposely

here now to make the needed changes. As you and others realize that, you help yourselves and the world to move into enlightened consciousness.

4. **You now have tangible evidence of connection.** Your ancestors did not have the benefit of living in such a small world. It hasn't really gotten smaller, of course; your awareness of yourself vis-à-vis others globally is what shifted. You can thank human technology and ingenuity for helping to close the gap. With global communications and speedy travel available to most locations across the planet, you now can tangibly feel your connection with others. It is these expanded levels of connection that can help foster the changes you and others seek. The more that people understand the intricate connected dance of life, the greater the likelihood of partnership. You have jumped into the deep end. It's okay, though, because you have plenty of company. You can join with others in community, finding innovative ways to solve the seemingly unsolvable.

5. **Humanity is at its crossroads of the great shift of all time**. There is nothing like a crisis—or better yet the current crossroads—to move people out of complacency. The kinds of progressive changes involved with the great shift will not happen when you are complacent. Different choices are made when you wake up to understanding that you want changes, and that you can choose a different path. You make these alternative choices when you begin to feel empowered and decide to act from a place of empowerment. The positive changes happen when you see the truth of what you and others have created, understanding that new choices must be made. The more that you can honestly face the truth of what is occurring, the more quickly you can discover solutions for roadblocks. As you do so, humanity's

crossroads take on a new meaning, and you can find a way to become optimistic. Embracing optimism rather than pessimism, you vibrate at a higher frequency, helping you to be a potent divine changemaker.

These are only a few examples of the countless opportunities you have at your fingertips because you are alive now. In order to fully appreciate them and benefit from them, you will want to regularly contemplate the big picture.

Seeing the Big Picture

It is normal when coexisting with such great opportunities to sometimes forget the larger view. If you are like most people, you have plenty of anxious moments about the amounts of change occurring. The sheer speed of it may make you dizzy.

You may sometimes feel smothered by the magnitude of input you regularly receive on numerous fronts. Perhaps you doubt your ability to get your own answers. You may question whether you can accurately access your heart's wisdom.

Go gently with yourself. This is what your heart would tell you to do. Your heart knows your deepest longings, even beyond those you consciously recognize. It knows what is in your highest good.

Your heart understands your challenges, your resistance to changes, and your potential to succeed with what you came to achieve.

When you listen to your heart, you can move out of your black-and-white thinking and into a place of clarity. From that place, you can remember what is truly important.

When you recognize what really matters, your next steps become easier to take. You can then connect with the opportunity at hand with a sense of empowerment.

Contemplating the Big Picture

Considering the big picture means looking beyond surface appearances and the minutiae of day-to-day life.

The changes that you are helping to create are massive. They touch upon every part of society. They impact how you and others relate to one another. They are connected with a brand-new paradigm of what it means to be human.

The shifts under way go to the core of who you thought you were. You are being asked to reconsider your false notions of reality and your role in them.

Creating a Life worth Remembering

If you could see yourself as spirit sees you, there would be no doubt about the importance of this life. You would understand why it's so vital that you wake up fully and walk the Earth like the divine being you truly are.

You would be inspired to make your best efforts to create a life worth remembering. You would realize that each moment counts. You would know the potency of using your present time to masterfully create a new way of being.

※

Tips: Taking Charge of Your Life

1. **Set your intention daily to be receptive to new ideas.** Ask for divine guidance to help you uncover and heal more of your dysfunctional past. Find out what the troublesome situations you see or face personally can show you about yourself. Be willing to look at and act upon what you see.

2. **Remember that change is a natural part of life**. More changes are happening now because you are living during the time of the greatest shift of the ages. Decide that you will make change your friend rather than your enemy. Give yourself permission to open your eyes to what is not working and to let it go without a grudge or fear.

3. **Avoid shutting down your senses**. Your physical and intuitive senses are integral to your ascension into the higher frequencies. You don't want to numb them with substances, overwork, or a nonstop diet of media input. Your body is the earthly temple for your soul. It will give you vital information about what's important, what and who to trust, and what's out of balance.

Your emotions can be your greatest helper or your worst enemy. Discover how to identify how you feel and when you feel it. Become intelligent about how you respond to what you feel. Decide that you will use your emotions as a beneficial tool for your growth, with harm to none, including yourself. If you realize you are anxious or depressed, address your feelings without judgment. Remember that anyone can feel these things. The key is to find solutions so you don't go into self-sabotage mode.

4. **Look deeper than surface appearances**. You need to find out how to look beyond what is presented, beyond what is announced as fact. These are times of increasing transparency, but it is consciousness that will determine how you see things. Not everyone will perceive events the same way; those who aren't ready or don't want to see the truth will have their own version. Do not feel you must convince them on your timetable. Do not give your energy away in senseless arguments. Stay in your center, in your

own truth. Remember that truth relates to the eternal realms. In those realms, no proof or manipulation is required. *Truth simply is.*

5. **Reach out to help at least one person daily.** This can be a stranger or someone you already know. Do this without desire for reward or acknowledgement.

6. **Take a few moments each day to connect with someone you know.** Invite a dialogue with this person, sharing as genuinely as you can. Remember to listen with single-pointed attention to this other person. You do this by being in present time and by tuning out the chatter of your inner and outer worlds.

7. **Set your intention that you will grow from your interactions with others.** Allow your relationships to be the catalyst for your embodying and expressing more love in the world. Keep in mind that it is through your relationships that you evolve. Relationships with others are the foundation of your process of change.

Your One Choice about Change

You really have one choice to make when it comes to change. Are you embracing your role as divine changemaker, or are you allowing yourself to be a victim of change?

There is much you want to change about the world that you see. The most productive way to initiate those changes is to focus on being as loving and kind as you can be. Include yourself in the equation!

Whatever challenges you face become the energetic fuel of your path of light. Your obstacles, when faced and transformed, become luminous gems you share with the world. Rather than complaining about how many problems you have, express gratitude for the luminous gems that you can create and share.

Keep future dates and other linear reference points in perspective. The great shift occurring now is more of a process than a single event. The evolutionary progression has been unfolding with increasing momentum during your lifetime.

Whenever something ends, something new can begin. That's what you want, after all—something brand new!

These historic moments represent an enormous potential for humanity to create a new, more light-filled world. You are here to participate, to cocreate needed changes, and to benefit personally and spiritually.

You came not for one date in time but to have a front-row seat as the Earth ascends into a higher consciousness. The seat you have taken is not stationary; it and you are moving constantly. You don't realize this as you sit there, but it's true!

Your movement into higher levels of being won't always feel comfortable. Sometimes you will feel dizzy or simply tired. Sometimes you will want to cover your eyes to avoid seeing what is there. Sometimes you will question whether you can go on, but do not worry. The eternal you has no doubt that you can take the leap that you came to take.

A Brand-New Start—For You and Humanity

From the point of view of linear time, you live during a chaotic transition from the old fear-based ways to a brand-new paradigm. Massive amounts of change are taking place, and yet it is common to feel like you are living in the gap between old and new. On some days you may feel uninspired or even hopeless, not grasping how you will move from the old to the new.

From the perspective of eternal time, today is a brand-new start. You and humanity are beginning a new chapter. This moment in time is when you are most able to change what happens next. What changes would you like to put in motion right now? What energetic signature would you, as a divine changemaker, like to leave behind for the generations to come?

Afterword

Awakening Process for Divine Changemakers

To accelerate your awakening, contemplate these questions on a regular basis. Allow your heart to speak to you about what is important and about what you can let go of in order to become freer and more joyful. Resist the temptation to censor yourself. Simply allow the questions to bring new insights into your awareness.

If you were on Earth for just one day ...

What would you want to see?
What sound would you want to hear?
What sweetness would you like to taste?
What aroma would you like to smell?
What sensation would you like to feel?

Who would you forgive?
Who would you thank?
Who would you laugh with?
Who would you share your real self with?

What would become important?
What would not matter any more?
What would you want to remember forever?

Glossary

1980s—A time of cultural waking up, this decade is often described as the dawn of a new age. In this period, people began caring more about the world and questioning their place in it. The information age began, with personal computers and cell phones introduced into homes and businesses. Fueled in part by computers and increased access to information, there was a growing understanding of the world's interconnectedness. A war or natural disaster in one place was immediately known to people thousands of miles away. An example was the famine in Ethiopia, which was televised globally. The media attention led to Live Aid benefit concerts featuring many popular stars, creating awareness and raising millions of dollars. During the 1980s, there was renewed interest in addressing the environment and the impact we are having on the planet. Noteworthy political events included the collapse of the Berlin Wall and other markers of traditional communism, and the end of the Cold War.

2012 window—The window of time connected with 2012 involves a cycle of great change. The changes are already happening and will continue for many years to come. The year 2012 is a date, but its true meaning cannot be found on a calendar. The date became popularized by those who interpreted numerous end-of-the-world prophecies. These include predictions made in 1555 by Nostradamus, a famous French astrologer and physician. Nostradamus, in fact, did not mention the year 2012, but his name somehow became associated with 2012. This false association, based on interpretations, set in motion a whole string of doomsday theories, many of which still persist.

The time period to focus on, when considering Earth's pivotal years, is not the year 2012, but our current years of major changes. The 2012 window refers to a pivotal cycle of time of human history, when energetic forces catalyze a revolutionary paradigm shift. This shift is about a radical change in consciousness. It relates to humans becoming awakened to a more light-filled way to exist.

The 2012 window of time is symbolic of a period during which humanity is facing its greatest tipping point, having the opportunity to choose a dramatically different path. Humanity is at a crossroads during this auspicious window of time. People can individually and collectively choose to create a new type of existence that is based on love.

Because the 2012 window relates to choice and humanity's future is not predestined, the actual span of time involved cannot be defined. The full process of creating a light-filled world will, in hindsight, be seen as one of stages. Those stages will be unfolding for many years after 2012.

akashic record—In this book, the term "akashic record" relates to the energetic record of personal history within our DNA. The DNA in our cells is a kind of record keeper of who we are and what we believe. The energetic imprints stored in our DNA are a record of our past, present, and future potentials. Akashic record is a Sanskrit term meaning sky or the heavens; in this context, the record refers to a vast universal storehouse of mystical knowledge encoded in a nonphysical plane of existence. Nostradamus and other prophets throughout history claimed to be able to access these records to understand humanity's past and to predict the future.

apocalypse—An ancient Greek word, apocalypse means a revelation or lifting of the veil. During our modern times and current paradigm shift, the term can be updated to apply to the great awakening of humanity. People are uncovering truths that were always there. Information that has been hidden from awareness is coming to light as people wake up and remember their true divine nature. This word is highly charged in many doom-and-gloom circles because of its association with Armageddon.

Armageddon—This is an ancient Greek term that comes from religion. In the Christian tradition, Armageddon is often used interchangeably with apocalypse, cited in the Book of Revelation, the last book of the Bible. This text describes prophetic visions indicating the end of the world. This is a viewpoint based on the idea that humanity's destiny is predetermined.

In fact, humanity does have a choice of how to respond to Earth's pivotal years. Because of this, the more appropriate way to view Armageddon is as a pivotal choice point. Humanity is at a tipping point, when its choices will determine the future of generations to come. Armageddon is symbolic of these moments of decisive conflict. Choices are being made over time and it is the cumulative effect of these choices that will determine humanity's future.

ascension—This is a natural process of energetic unfolding for the planet and its life forms. It is a progression of spiritual growth during which a person raises his or her frequency of thought and emotion. Lower levels of frequency involve fear; higher levels involve love. People today are in the process of raising their frequency out of a fear-based existence. When a person expresses thoughts and emotions that are based on fear, his or her growth is limited and existence is dominated by worry and stress.

As a person evolves into the higher frequencies of love and intuitively guided reason, life can become joyful and more fruitful. As a person holds higher-frequency energy, he or she is able to access a multidimensional state that allows for great spiritual openings. This means an expanded view of what a person normally sees, an enhanced perception of feelings, and an increased ability to connect with his or her higher wisdom. The shift from fear to love has a profound impact on each person and on the whole of society. This radical shift is paving the way for a brand-new type of world.

compassion—The light-filled world in which we want to live cannot exist without compassion. When we have compassion for ourselves and others, we have empathy and genuine caring. To feel compassion is to feel respect. The ability to feel compassion is natural, but we often cannot access it because of our fear-based conditioning. For thousands of years, we have learned patterns of self-hate and selfishness. This conditioning blocks our ability to cherish ourselves and others; we learn to be hard on ourselves and when we interact with others, it's often with a selfish attitude. A key to enlightened living is learning to develop compassion for ourselves and others. This learning happens in stages as part of our spiritual growth. We can discover how to move out of selfishness when we practice imagining ourselves in the shoes of others, feeling and experiencing what they are experiencing. To see the world as someone else sees it helps us to develop compassion.

divine changemaker—A divine changemaker is a person who is learning to connect with his or her divine nature, living life in ways that help support the creation of a more light-filled world. This person is actively making needed inner changes as part of progress on his or her spiritual path. During an ongoing growth process, the person learns to live in the present, to express power appropriately, and to become conscious of his or her thoughts, communications, feelings, and actions. In doing this, developing love and compassion for self and others, the person advances on the path of enlightenment.

The life of a divine changemaker is an example for others. The person discovers how to put enlightened principles into action; his or her ideas become tangible manifestations in the world. This is a person who becomes a guide to others on the path, helping them to understand how to live in enlightened ways. In this book, the term "divine changemaker" describes the role of those who are alive now to make the changes for a more loving world.

divine power—The energy of divine power is genuine and light-filled. This kind of power, although natural and accessible to everyone, is the opposite of ego-based power long prized in the world. When a person accesses his or her divine power, there is no fear and no need to control or manipulate. This kind of power is not self-serving and there are no games involved. The objective is not winning or proving superiority; the person expressing divine power is connected to his or her inner self and expresses that self in the world. The paradigm shift now occurring on Earth involves individuals, groups of people, and countries moving out of ego-based power and into this natural power fueled by love and light. When divine power becomes the new paradigm, enlightened living will be within the grasp of people everywhere.

DNA—The letters "DNA" first became big news in the 1950s, when American biologist James Watson and English physicist Francis Crick announced information about the structure and function of DNA. We always had DNA in our cells but its function was mostly a mystery. Today there is a vast, growing body of knowledge about the spiral-shaped DNA contained in our chromosomes. The DNA is constantly communicating instructions about life processes—from cell growth and longevity to inheritance and a host of other things. It is now understood that we can influence our own DNA through a number of means, including lifestyle choices, thoughts, and energetic healing processes.

DNA healing—This is a form of energy healing that addresses imbalances at a DNA level. One of a growing number of energy therapies practiced today, DNA healing is a holistic approach to wellness. It takes into account the whole person—body, mind, and spirit; it recognizes the influence our thoughts and emotions have on our body and our overall state of health. Clearing of DNA-level patterns is addressed through energetic healing. Patterns can stem from a person's life experiences or from inherited influences. Intuitive healers trained to see and work with subtle energy fields are able to identify and clear sabotaging patterns in the DNA. This modality is a complimentary method designed to integrate with other forms of health care. It is not intended to take the place of doctors or traditional medicine.

frequency—Everything in the universe, including the human energy field, has a frequency. It is believed that there is a connection between a person's frequency and his or her health. As an example, negative thoughts can lower a person's frequency; things like meditation and prayer can raise frequency. As people raise their consciousness to hold a higher frequency, they can begin to move outside of the limitations of society's third-dimensional norm.

A frequency is an energetic level that can be measured. In scientific terms it is the measurable rate of electrical energy flow; instruments like the SQUID magnetometer allow scientists to detect minute energy fields around the human body. Intuitive healers, rather than using machines to monitor energy fields, typically determine energy levels through the subtle senses. As an example, a trained intuitive may be able to sense energy changes within body systems and overall energetic shifts.

G8—The idea of a forum for the world's major superpowers emerged after the 1973 oil crisis. The G8 is a group of nations including Canada, France, Germany, Italy, Japan, Russia, the United Kingdom, and the United States. Representatives of key countries meet to discuss global issues including the economy and international trade, health, energy and the environment, climate, and terrorism.

Originally, the G8 was the Group of 7 and included finance ministers from the United States, the United Kingdom, France, Germany, Italy, Canada, and Japan. The Group of 7 became the G8 in 1998 for political reasons, when it became clear that Russia could no longer be excluded.

G20—The G20 is a political body also known as the Group of 20 Nations. Established in 1999 to expand upon the G8, the G20 is a global forum on international issues. The group was created in response to the financial crises of the late 1990s and in recognition of the need to include emerging-market countries in global discussions. Members include finance ministers and central bank governors from nineteen countries (Argentina, Australia, Brazil, Canada, China, France, Germany, India, Indonesia, Italy, Japan, Mexico, Russia, Saudi Arabia, South Africa, South Korea, Turkey, the United Kingdom, and the United States) and the European Union.

Although the larger G20 is more inclusive than the original Group of 7 and G8, it still excludes many of the 192 independent countries recognized by the United Nations as of May 2008.

Gregorian calendar—This calendar is the internationally accepted civil calendar. First decreed in 1582 by Roman Catholic Pope Gregory XIII, after whom it was named, this calendar was adopted by key world countries over the following centuries. Calendars such as this were adopted throughout history, often in response to the religious and political beliefs of the times.

Before more advanced agricultural societies, native peoples used the Earth's three natural timekeeping units. These include the day (time span of Earth's revolution on its axis), the month (time span of the moon's orbit around the Earth), and the year (time span of the Earth's orbit around the sun).

higher self—The higher self is the part of a person able to access higher wisdom and to be at one with the divine. Often described as higher consciousness, this is the part of a person able to access higher guidance and clarity. When a person receives intuitive insights from his or her higher self and applies them in life, there can be progress on the spiritual path. The higher self is a bridge between a person's conditioned personality and his or her eternal divine essence. Throughout history there have been numerous meanings of this term; likewise there have been diverse ideas of how and why a person connects with his or her higher self. In this book, the author refers to terms like "higher self," "spirit," and "soul" in generic ways. The idea is to allow the reader his or her own view of what these terms mean.

inner prophecy station— Everyone has a natural intuitive ability that can be developed and honed; intuition provides helpful inner guidance about life. When a person becomes skilled in going within to receive inner wisdom, he or she taps into an inner prophecy station. Being able to receive one's own answers helps a person to progress on the spiritual path.

Kali Yuga—According to Hindu teachings, the Kali Yuga, or age of vice and hate, follows the Satya Yuga, Treta Yuga, and Dvapara Yuga. The ancient Indian term "Kali Yuga" refers to the last of the four stages of human evolutionary cycles.

A majority of interpreters of Hindu scriptures thinks that humanity is now in the Kali Yuga. Believed by many experts to last 432,000 years, the Kali Yuga is associated with times when humankind degenerates spiritually.

The Yuga cycle is viewed quite differently by some religious scholars, who question the length of time that each period lasts and which stage actually exists now. Some of these experts believe that the Kali Yuga is about to come to a fiery end, allowing a new age, or Satya Yuga, to start.

linear—The conventional approach to life is linear. This viewpoint can be rigid and fixed. With a linear perspective, traveling forward in a straight line and progressing sequentially from one step to the next, a person may view things in black and white. Often relying heavily on logic and doing mainly what worked in the past, the man or woman with a linear view can miss seeing the larger picture and having in-depth understanding. This old-paradigm approach can prevent a person from experiencing life fully. The shift in paradigms under way during Earth's pivotal years means that people are opening to multidimensional approaches; there is an allowance for a wider range of ideas and options. The creativity that can come from this new approach will help humanity to create a more light-filled world.

Maya—The Maya is an ancient society that studied time and human cycles. They left behind sophisticated calendars, studied by modern scholars who seek to understand today's times of great change. According to some scholars, the Maya are the most advanced ancient civilization to inhabit Central America and Mexico. Known today for its advanced mathematics and mapping of the stars, the Mayan civilization reached its peak between AD 300 and 900. During Earth's pivotal years, many people are seeking ancient indigenous wisdom for answers to our seemingly irresolvable multitude of crises.

Mayan calendars can be interpreted in numerous ways, but many believe they indicate that we live during a long cycle of time about to end, paving the way for something brand new. Many scholars who have studied the Mayan traditions believe the Maya understood human cycles, including the one in which we live now.

middle path—The middle path is the one in the center; when a person travels this path, avoiding extremes, a sense of balance is found. The idea of a middle way or path was originated by the Buddha; he called it the path of wisdom, for it led to his enlightenment. People in modern times have the same challenges faced during Buddha's lifetime; the conditioned world is one of extreme highs and lows. Great joys are often followed by great sorrows. When a person becomes practiced in traveling the middle path, he or she discovers moderation and a way to put life into perspective. To travel the middle path is to discover enlightened living.

multidimensional—New-paradigm thinking has multidimensional approaches. This means an expanded view of possibilities. People are awakening to a bigger-picture view of reality. Society's conventional linear perspective is evolving into a multidimensional one that takes into account a wider spectrum of ideas and options. As part of the spiritual growth process, people can increase their ability to perceive reality through more subtle means. Intuitive skills allow a person to add depth to conventional-world perception by incorporating the spiritual dimensions.

opposites—Oppositional thinking is showing up in every sector of society these days. As is common during times of great change, differing viewpoints are seemingly miles apart. One group wants one thing; another group wants the opposite. To oppose something means to actively disapprove of that thing. Oppositional thinking is often accompanied by the energies of competition, conflict, judgment, resistance, and combativeness. Anger and fear are often present as people feel threatened by differing opinions. Extremes leave no room for a middle ground of reason. As people in society awaken, oppositional approaches will be replaced by those involving a cooperative spirit, allowing compromises and creative solutions.

paradigm—This term refers to a societal or personal method of doing things, one that is accepted as the norm. In the world in which we live, the paradigm within which we operate is a very powerful indicator of consciousness. That is because the paradigm relates to our values and what we decide is acceptable to do or not do.

As human beings, we tend to filter our experiences through the paradigm operable in our world. We learn to see our world through the current paradigm lens and to define ourselves and our potential by the prevailing paradigm model. Today, for example, we look at our planet as a more interconnected whole. Photographic images of

Earth from space have helped to create a global wave of caring for our planet.

A brand-new paradigm of enlightened consciousness is in the process of being born. It will replace the old paradigm involving a species so driven by technology and greed that it could destroy itself.

The new model, which has been evolving into existence over time, holds the promise of humans evolving more consciously, choosing to cooperate with one another, and coexisting without violence.

solstice—This is a period of time when the sun is at its greatest distance from the celestial equator. It happens twice a year, the winter and summer solstices. It is an astronomical event that has often been linked with celebrations of holidays and a change in seasons.

The solstice of December 21, 2012, is thought of by some Maya researchers and other wisdom keepers as a kind of marker that shows the end of a very long evolutionary pattern. When interpreting the meaning of such a date, keep in mind it is a linear reference point; the shift in cycles predicted by the Maya and others is happening in stages. The most important point to focus on is the present, when you have an opportunity to change what happens next.

soul—Sometimes used interchangeably with terms like "spirit," "mind," or "self," the soul is typically thought of as the spiritual part of a person. According to some traditions, it is linked with a person's essence or core. The word "soul" has been used in many ways throughout history, in part depicting the views of the tradition. Both Socrates and Plato, for example, defined the soul as the eternal essence of a person. For the purposes of this book, soul relates to a person's spiritual nature or true self.

spirit—Many people and teachings consider spirit to be the same as soul. The energy of spirit is an integral part of our being. In the conventional world, our spiritual nature is often discounted; our conditioning teaches us to focus on the outer world and on what manifests in the physical realm. People learn to seek physical things and physical validations. Success, for example, is often viewed in terms of how much money a person has or what position he or she holds within society. This is a limited view that does not include the element of spirit. The key to enlightened living is to incorporate spirit into every element of life; it must be fully integrated with the physical self. In order to skillfully navigate the shift into a new-paradigm consciousness, a person needs to put spirit first and then to include spirit in his or her thinking and actions.

synchronicity—A synchronicity occurs when two or more seemingly unrelated events occur together. An example of a synchronicity is when you have a dream about meeting a tall woman who offers you a job and the next day your friend introduces you to a tall woman who is expanding her business. To effectively work with synchronicities a person needs to develop an ability to look beyond the obvious. The subtleties of energy, which take a trained eye to notice, reveal hidden dimensions that most people don't see. As a person advances spiritually he or she becomes more skilled in connecting the dots between events.

third dimension—Humanity is in a process of evolving into a higher frequency that is above the octaves of fear. The fear-based existence associated with the third dimension involves limited thinking, feeling, and being. People have lived in this type of existence for thousands of years. It is not about a specific location. It relates to consciousness.

During Earth's pivotal years, a huge dimensional shift is under way; people are learning how to move out of fear and into love. It is this shift into love that will revolutionize how life is lived on our planet.

wisdom keepers—The wisdom keepers of our planet are those who understand and pass on universal wisdom. This includes timeless knowledge coming from the world's ancient societies. This wisdom helps us to understand humanity's past and reminds us of ancient solutions for healing and survival. The knowledge of these elders, passed on from generation to generation, can be a helpful guide of what to do and what to avoid doing. Ancient wise ones often told their stories, depicted in artwork, of how their societies were threatened by human conflicts or by climate change.

Wisdom can also be passed on within families. The wisdom keeper of a family is one who remembers and practices the family's traditions of wisdom; an example is a woman who today uses herbal recipes of her ancestors as therapeutic remedies.

A divine changemaker is a modern form of wisdom keeper. This is a person who is learning to hold and practice timeless knowledge about the path of enlightened living. He or she teaches this knowledge to others by example and through sharing.

Recommended Reading

The author has found the following resources helpful in her spiritual transformational journey.

Arguelles, Jose, *The Mayan Factor: Path Beyond Technology*, Santa Fe: Bear & Company, 1987.

Becker, Robert, Gary Selden, *The Body Electric: Electromagnetism and The Foundation of Life*, New York: Harper, 1998.

Benson, Herbert, Marg Stark, *Timeless Healing: The Power and Biology of Belief*, New York: Scribner, 1997.

Borysenko, Joan, Miroslav Borysenko, *The Power of the Mind to Heal*, Carlsbad, CA: Hay House, 1995.

Braden, Gregg, *Fractal Time: The Secret of 2012 and a New World Age*, Carlsbad, CA: Hay House, 2009.

———. *The Divine Matrix: Bridging Time, Space, Miracles, and Belief*, Carlsbad, CA: Hay House, 2008.

———. *The God Code: The Secret of Our Past, the Promise of Our Future*, Carlsbad, CA: Hay House, 2005.

Bruyere, Rosalyn, *Wheels of Light: Chakras, Auras, and the Healing Energy of the Body*, New York: Simon & Schuster, 1994.

Calleman, Carl Johan, *Solving the Greatest Mystery of Our Time: The Mayan Calendar*, London and Coral Springs, FL: Garev Publishing International, 2001.

———. *The Mayan Calendar and the Transformation of Consciousness,* Rochester, VT: Bear & Company, 2004.

Capra, Fritjof, *The Tao of Physics: An Exploration of the Parallels Between Modern Physics and Eastern Mysticism,* New York: Bantam, 1984.

———. *The Web of Life: A New Scientific Understanding of Living Systems,* New York: Random House, 1997.

Chopra, Deepak, *Quantum Healing: Exploring the Frontiers of Mind/Body Medicine,* New York: Bantam, 1990.

Dalai Lama, *The Art of Happiness: A Handbook for Living,* New York: Riverhead Books, 2009.

———. *Healing Anger: The Power of Patience from a Buddhist Perspective,* Ithaca, NY: Snow Lion Publications, 1997.

———. *How to See Yourself as You Really Are,* New York: Simon & Schuster, 2006.

———. *The Universe in a Single Atom: The Convergence of Science and Spirituality,* New York: Morgan Road Books, 2006.

Doidge, Norman, *The Brain That Changes Itself: Stories of Personal Triumph from the Frontiers of Brain Science,* New York: Penguin, 2007.

Dossey, Larry, *Healing Words: The Power of Prayer and the Practice of Medicine,* San Francisco: HarperOne, 1997.

Ferrini, Paul, *Love without Conditions: Reflections of the Christ Mind,* South Deerfield, MA: Heartways Press, 1995.

Garrison, Cal, *The Weiser Field Guide to Ascension: The Meaning of Miracles and Shifts in Consciousness Past and Present,* Newburyport, MA: Weiser, 2010.

Goleman, Daniel, *Destructive Emotions: A Scientific Dialogue with the Dalai Lama,* New York: Bantam, 2004.

Hanh, Thich Nhat, *The Art of Power*, San Francisco: HarperOne, 2008.

Hansard, Christopher, *The Tibetan Art of Positive Thinking: Skillful Thought for Successful Living*, New York: Atria Books, 2003.

Hartmann, Thom, *The Last Hours of Ancient Sunlight: The Fate of the World and What We Can Do Before It's Too Late*, New York: Three Rivers Press, 2004.

Harvey, Andrew, *The Direct Path: Creating a Journey to the Divine Using the World's Mystical Traditions*, London: Rider & Company, 2001.

Hawkins, David, *Power vs. Force: The Hidden Determinants of Human Behavior*, Carlsbad, CA: Hay House, 2002.

Hay, Louise, *You Can Heal Your Life*, Carlsbad, CA: Hay House, 1984.

Hunt, Valerie, *Infinite Mind: Science of the Human Vibrations of Consciousness*, Malibu, CA: Malibu Publishing, 1996.

Jenkins, John Major, *Maya Cosmogenesis 2012*, Santa Fe: Bear & Company, 1998.

Leahy, Robert, *The Worry Cure: Seven Steps to Stop Worry from Stopping You*, New York: Three Rivers Press, 2006.

Lipton, Bruce, *The Biology of Belief: Unleashing the Power of Consciousness, Matter and Miracles*, Carlsbad, CA: Hay House, 2008.

———. *Spontaneous Evolution: Our Positive Future and a Way to Get There from Here*, Carlsbad, CA: Hay House, 2009.

———. *The Wisdom of Your Cells: How Your Beliefs Control Your Biology*, Boulder, CO: Sounds True, 2006.

Melchizedek, Drunvalo, *Serpent of Light Beyond 2012: The Movement of the Earth's Kundalini and the Rise of the Female Light 1949 to 2013*, San Francisco: Weiser Books, 2008.

Mipham, Sakyong, *Ruling Your World: Ancient Strategies for Modern Life*, New York: Doubleday, 2006.

Moyers, Bill, *Healing and the Mind*, New York: Doubleday, 1993.

Murphy, Joseph, *The Power of Your Subconscious Mind*, Englewood Cliffs, NJ: Prentice-Hall, Inc., 1963.

Myss, Caroline, *Anatomy of the Spirit: The Seven Stages of Power and Healing*, New York: Random House, 1997.

Naparstek, Belleruth, *Your Sixth Sense: Unlocking the Power of Your Intuition*, San Francisco: HarperOne, 2009.

Orloff, Judith, *Emotional Freedom: Liberate Yourself from Negative Emotions and Transform Your Life*, New York: Harmony Books, 2009.

Peirce, Penney, *Frequency: The Power of Personal Vibration*, New York: Atria Books, 2009.

Pert, Candace, *Molecules of Emotion: The Science Behind Mind-Body Medicine*, New York: Simon & Schuster, 1999.

Ray, Paul, Sherry Anderson, *The Cultural Creatives: How 50 Million People Are Changing the World*, New York: Three Rivers Press, 2000.

Rinpoche, Tenzin Wangyal, *Awakening the Sacred Body: Tibetan Yogas of Breath and Movement*, Carlsbad, CA: Hay House, 2011.

———. *Healing with Form, Energy and Light: The Five Elements in Tibetan Shamanism, Tantra and Dzogchen*, Ithaca, NY: Snow Lion Publications, 2002.

———. *Tibetan Sound Healing*, Boulder, CO: Sounds True, 2007.

———. *The Tibetan Yogas of Dream and Sleep*, Ithaca, NY: Snow Lion Publications, 1998.

———. *Wonders of the Natural Mind: The Essence of Dzogchen*

in the Native Bon Tradition of Tibet, Ithaca, NY: Snow Lion Publications, 2000.

Rosenberg, Marshall, *Nonviolent Communication: A Language of Life; Create Your Life, Your Relationships and Your World in Harmony with Your Values,* Encinitas, CA: PuddleDancer Press, 2003.

Ruiz, Don Miguel, *The Four Agreements,* San Rafael, CA: Amber-Allen Publishing, 1997.

Salzberg, Sharon, *Faith: Trusting Your Own Deepest Experience,* New York: Riverhead Books, 2003.

———. *Loving Kindness: The Revolutionary Art of Happiness,* Boston: Shambhala Publications, 2002.

Schenker, Daniela, *Kuan Yin: Accessing the Power of the Divine Feminine,* Boulder, CO: Sounds True, 2007.

Seligman, Martin, *Learned Optimism: How to Change Your Mind and Your Life,* New York: Vintage, 2006.

Shimoff, Marci, *Happy for No Reason: 7 Steps for Being Happy from the Inside Out,* New York: Simon & Schuster, 2009.

Targ, Russell, *The End of Suffering: Fearless Living in Troubled Times,* Newburyport, MA: Hampton Roads Publishing, 2006.

Thurman, Robert, *Inner Revolution: Life, Liberty, and the Pursuit of Real Happiness,* New York: Riverhead Books, 1998.

Tipping, Colin, *Radical Forgiveness: A Revolutionary Five-Stage Process to Heal Relationships, Let Go of Anger and Blame, Find Peace in Any Situation,* Boulder, CO: Sounds True, 2009.

Tolle, Eckhart, *A New Earth: Awaken to Your Life's Purpose,* New York: Penguin, 2005.

———. *The Power of Now: A Guide to Spiritual Enlightenment,* Novato, CA: New World Library, 2004.

Trungpa, Chogyam, *Training the Mind: Cultivating Loving-Kindness,* Boston: Shambhala Publications, 2003.

Wallace, B. Alan, *Tibetan Buddhism from the Ground Up: A Practical Approach for Modern Life*, Boston: Wisdom Publications, 1993.

Weil, Andrew, *Spontaneous Healing: How to Discover and Enhance Your Body's Natural Ability to Maintain and Heal Itself*, New York: Ballantine Books, 2000.

Welwood, John, *Toward a Psychology of Awakening: Buddhism, Psychotherapy, and the Path of Personal and Spiritual Transformation*, Boston: Shambhala Publications, 2002.

Zukav, Gary, *The Seat of the Soul*, New York: Simon & Schuster, 1990.

About the Author

Selacia is an internationally known writer, intuitive healer, and guide to others on the path of spiritual awakening. She is also the author of *The Golden Edge* and has been a writer her entire life. She is a former foreign correspondent with *The Wall Street Journal*, *The New York Times*, and other media. As an international journalist, she has decades of experience in the areas of world politics and social change, healing and consciousness, and spiritual transformation.

In her professional journalism career, Selacia covered the White House, US Congress, G8 meetings, economic summits, key heads of state such as Margaret Thatcher, and world trade talks. During her time in Washington, focusing on politics and macroeconomics, she reported on the Federal Reserve, World Bank, International Monetary Fund, and Fannie Mae. This early background gave her an insider's view of today's global economic meltdown and the politics of global imbalances.

Selacia is a pioneer in DNA intuitive healing, serving people everywhere who desire wholeness and a heart-centered life. In her global healing work, she has addressed the United Nations (SEAT). Her writings are read in sixty-four countries.

This prolific writer has in her ancestral family tree the beloved writer Henry Wadsworth Longfellow (1807–1882). Best known for works including "The Song of Hiawatha," Longfellow had a gift for simple, romantic storytelling in verse and a sound lyrical sense. His works were rooted in literature rather than in life. On the other hand, Longfellow's descendent, Selacia, focuses her writing to reflect real life.

She has dedicated her life to spirit and to helping others connect with their true spiritual nature. Naturally intuitive from an early age, Selacia has a lifelong connection with her own inner wisdom. Her spiritual guides include a group of highly evolved nonphysical beings called "The Council of 12." The loving energy of these wise guides has become an integral part of Selacia's life and work.

Selacia is known on all continents for bringing the wisdom of The Council of 12 to others in global meditation events focused on personal and planetary healing.

Over the past two decades, Selacia has undertaken in-depth studies involving healing, consciousness, and ancient shamanic and spiritual paths. As part of that, she has studied with a number of great teachers, including those from the Tibetan Buddhist tradition as well as leading-edge visionaries and healers. She lives in Southern California.

For further information, please contact Selacia at:

Selacia
Communication for Transformation Group
Santa Monica, CA 90405
USA
www.selacia.com
www.earthspivotalyears.com

Facebook:
Selacia, The Council of 12
Explore Living Fragrances with Selacia

And keep up with Selacia on Twitter:
http://www.twitter.com/selacia

Printed in Great Britain
by Amazon